WORLDS APART

A JOURNEY TO THE GREAT LIVING
MONASTARIES OF EUROPE

by Tudor Edwards

COWARD-McCANN, Inc.

NEW YORK

40324

For
BARBARA ST. CLAIR

CONTENTS

PROEM   1

Chapter

  1 The Traveller in Search of Monasteries   3

PAST   13

  2 The Monastic Years   15

  3 Survivals and Revivals   30

PRESENT   51

  4 The Road to Lérins   53

  5 'Monasticon Gallicanum'   76

  6 'In Solitudine'   97

  7 The Baroque World   133

  8 Rococo   151

  9 Spanish Earth   176

10 Home Ground   205

INDEX   222

LIST OF ILLUSTRATIONS

following page 82

Subiaco, the cradle of Western monasticism

Mass being celebrated in an English abbey

Fruit-picking at Quarr Abbey, Isle of Wight

The Cistercian abbey of Poblet in Spain

A potter at work in an English monastery

A Carthusian in his cell; Valsainte, Switzerland

Working on scientific instruments at the Sacro Eremo, Camaldoli

Monks are read to during meals

The Benedictine abbey of Beuron, Germany

A Carthusian cutting wood in his cell; Valsainte, Switzerland

Silos, Spain. Old pharmacies are commonly found in European
monasteries

Scent distillery at Caldey Abbey, Wales

The Holy Mountain of Montserrat, Spain

Franciscan friars in procession at Assisi

A Carthusian reading; Miraflores, Spain

Guadalupe Abbey, Spain: The Cloister

Guadalupe Abbey, Spain

A Camaldolese monk at the Sacro Eremo, Camaldoli

The monastery on the site of St. Benedict's cave, Subiaco

Wood-carving in an English Benedictine monastery

Farm work on Caldey Island, Wales

The great baroque sanctuary of Einsiedelm, Switzerland

ACKNOWLEDGMENT

My thanks are due to the editors of *The Times*, *Art*, *The Tablet*, *The Month*, *Vogue* and *Heritage* for permission to reproduce material which first appeared in their pages.

I am so heavily indebted to so many people for their kindness by way of introductions and granting facilities to visit many of the places described in this book that I can only cite, collectively, the Abbots and Priors of all the monasteries concerned. A special measure of thanks must, however, be made to my friend the Rt. Rev. Dom Wilfrid Upson, O.S.B., Abbot of Prinknash Abbey, and his community.

T. E.

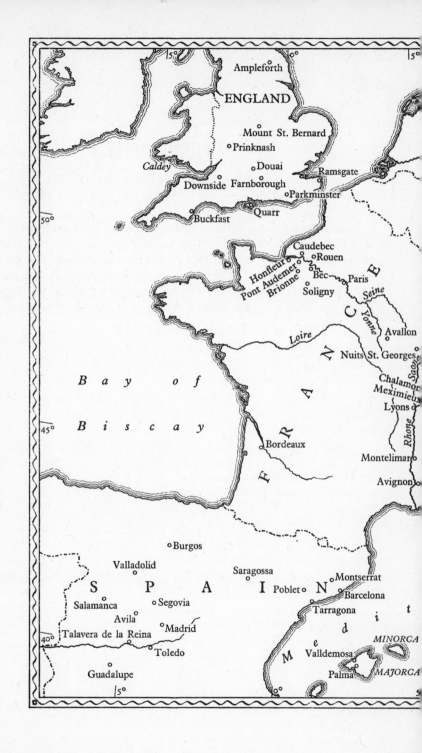

WESTERN EUROPE
Map illustrating the Author's travels

Scale of Miles
0   50   100   150   200   250

PROEM

1

THE TRAVELLER IN SEARCH OF MONASTERIES

WHEN you pass within monastery gates you are among men who have given up everything in order to possess everything. If their monastery is beautifully sited, lost in a forest or nestling in a valley or, as in Germany, set beside a lake, or, like so many in Italy, high upon a mountain peak—*Benedictus montes amabat*—let it not be matter for wonder. A monk is permitted to choose the battleground for his own soul, and he is permitted little else.

Your first encounter with a monk is a curious experience. You look upon him with something approaching awe and a deep curiosity. Your imagination vests him with supernatural qualities, with the power of sustained prayer and contemplation, with a mysticism that almost removes him from human kind. Or perhaps, like a certain school of novelists, you see him as an escapist or a refugee, a disillusioned lover, a discharged bankrupt or an ex-criminal who wishes to atone. It is most unlikely that he is any of these things. He is in fact mortal man, and like Shakespeare's Jew he will laugh if you tickle him, bleed if you prick him. Nor should you be deceived by his self-possessed air. Be sure he has many internal combats to wage —the Devil does not like monks. His ruddy countenance may not be the flush of health, and his fellows of waxen pallor probably suffer from lack of sleep. Few apart from his abbot will know his origin, and he may be an Oxford classical scholar or an ex-truck driver. The monastic habit, like khaki a great leveller, cloaks him in anonymity.

Eustathius in Armenia was probably the first to prescribe a monastic dress, while tradition attributes the skullcap to Anthony. Yet the monastic habit is in all probability almost the earliest dress common to man, or perhaps to the poor man, the dress of St.

3

Francis's *il poverello*. The various Orders have introduced their own characteristic features, but by and large the habit consists of an undergarment called the tunic, reaching down to the feet like the Greek *himation*, and a lighter garment with a hood attached thrown over it, like the Greek cloak or *chlamys*, and called a scapular. The shaven crown is a symbol of penance and humiliation, while the tonsure represents the crown of thorns.

The novice receives the habit at the clothing ceremony, when the community is assembled in the chapter house, and the abbot washes the novice's feet in imitation of Christ washing the feet of the disciples, after which each of the monks kneels down and kisses the novice's feet. He does not receive the cowl, the heavy outer garment with long sleeves and a pointed hood, until the ceremony of his final solemn profession. He then stands in the centre of the church choir reciting his vows, kneels at the feet of the abbot and each of the monks in turn, to receive the kiss of peace, and finally lies prostrate on the pavement of the sanctuary for the rest of the Mass. Thus is symbolized his renunciation of the world, his 'putting on Christ'.

As a guest in a monastery you will be privileged to share to a large extent in the life of the community. There is in the Luxembourg Museum of Paris a painting by Dauban showing a stranger being received by a convent, and it is a poignant interpretation of the fifty-third chapter of the Rule of St. Benedict. Your cell is little different from those of the monks, perhaps it *is* that of a monk, you dine with the community in the refectory, and the day, according to how you are disposed, may be bounded by the same canonical hours. There are few limitations, few exactments other than those dictated by your own conscience. At times you may even feel an intruder in this community of dedicated men. You know that their austerity is absolute, yours is softened by dispensations. Passing them in the cloisters you instinctively edge close to the wall, as do the novices in France. It is a world of intoned voices and Latin texts, of bells and plainsong, and of protracted silences, and there are the odours of incense, guttering candles, starched linen, wax polish, the dampness of ancient stone, stale food, feet, of men alone.

Resisting the night-office at an unearthly hour, one lies only half awake with the soft distant chanting like sea breakers pricking the conscience, and it is almost a relief when the brother rouses you.

How often has Brother Simeon or Brother Paul entered my cell with a lantern on a chill dark wintry morning, crying out *'Benedicamus Domino'*, to which, from beneath the sheets, I would mumble *'Deo Gratias'*. Or, in a Carthusian monastery, it is the *excitator* who thus rouses the community for the night-office.

After Matins and Lauds in one Benedictine monastery the monks attend to their toilets and clean out their cells, after which they assemble for Prime and private Masses. After this they have 'pittance' or a short breakfast, a modern innovation, which they take standing in the refectory, not all at the same time, since there is a coming and going from menial tasks. Guests may sit, drawing sustenance from libations of strong tea or coffee and helping themselves to excellent monastic bread and butter, all, of course, produced on the estate. Much of the morning is given over to study, though the work of the farm and ancillary crafts goes on. In the fields, blue-smocked lay brothers nod a silent greeting as they pass with pikel and muck-rake, bearing the smell and stain of the earth on which they labour to produce their food, and hooded cowherds look up with a quiet smile from their tasks. Otherwise one is alone, but it is companionship enough.

Dinner is at midday. Even meals have a sacred character, and the scene in the refectory is always impressive and moving. The monks file in, the abbot last. Often they stand in four long lines facing two enormous refectory tables; or there may be only two lines flanking a single table. The *Benedicite* is intoned and the monks, still cowled, bend low in several *Pater Nosters*. Some tuck their napkins into their collars, but the meal is not yet. The reader in the pulpit begins a text, and at a sign from the abbot the meal begins in silence, except for the lector reading edifying passages from a book or learned journal. The latter's monotonous high-pitched voice —for the reading is almost sung on one note—may seem a little inane until one is used to it. The meal ends spasmodically. Here and there the hoods are drawn over the heads. The servers kneel before the abbot's table. Then the abbot taps on the table with a small mallet, the signal for the reader to stop, and he does so, halting abruptly in the middle of a sentence, a word even. The reader descends from the pulpit, bows low and intones the words *Tu autem Domine miserere nobis*, and all rise singing the grace of thanksgiving, with more profound obeisances. Still solemnly singing, the abbot leads his monks into the church where the ceremony is concluded. Thus everything from manual labour to the necessity of eating is given a sacramental character, and the daily life has a distinct pattern and continuity by which all the various actions are related one to another.

The sparsity of monastic fare need be neither minimized nor exaggerated, but in most monasteries on one day a year the menu would do justice to a West End chef. It is the patronal feast day of the monastery, when there is general rejoicing and relaxation. I have lunched at the Benedictine abbey I know best on such a day, and sixteen fowl were slaughtered for the feast. The menu consisted of grapefruit, oxtail soup, roast fowl with sausages and vegetables, an iced sweet, local cider and coffee. It was on such a feast day that the celebrated gourmet Brillat-Savarin, author of the *Physiologie de gout*, was invited with the amateur orchestra of which he was leader to the Trappist monastery of Notre Dame des Dombes near Belley, to play in honour of St. Bernard. As Brillat-Savarin describes it, they found awaiting them a *paté* as big as a church, bounded on the north by a large joint of veal, on the east by a monumental pyramid of butter, on the south by an enormous ham, and on the west by a vast mound of globe artichokes. There was a great variety of fruit, and in one corner of the refectory a stack of more than a hundred bottles, which were kept cool by a fountain playing on them. They played at Mass next morning, and the dinner was served in medieval style, the second service comprising no less than fourteen roasts, while excellent coffee was served in deep bowls from which the reverend fathers drank 'with a noise of whales blowing before a storm'. There was more music at vespers, and the festival ended with a supper which in its delicate refinement belonged to a period even earlier than the dinner preceding it. Finally the cellarer was called upon to make his contribution, which turned out to be a veritable vat of burning sugared *eau-de-vie*. This was undoubtedly a princely celebration, but since it was held shortly after the fall of Napoleon it might also be regarded as an occasion of special joy marking the end of a period of great tribulation.

After lunch, or dinner as it is usually called, the monks are allowed an hour's rest, known as meridian. Though a stranger passing a brief space here can be intrigued and inspired by all about him, the early part of the afternoon can be a disturbing time. If he is without spiritual convictions he can be unutterably bored. In more severe monasteries, especially in winter, hunger and cold can become constant preoccupations. In Benedictine houses one does have some share of family life, but with the Cistercians and Carthusians one is quite alone, dining alone, sleeping in an isolated building. It can be a paralysing loneliness, unless you have the secret of being with God. If the craving for smoking must be satisfied it must be in the cell or in the grounds. Everywhere the crucifix reproaches any worldly thoughts, any sluggishness of mind or body. Everywhere is the atmosphere of prayer and denial, not only in the church but in chapels and oratories throughout the labyrinthine buildings, in corners of the cloisters even, where men are humbled and huddled on their knees. The entire monastery is inert. You move stealthily, on tiptoe. Read or smoke you will not, pray you cannot. You are assailed by a lethal boredom, depression, acedia, the medieval *accidie*.

The thirteenth-century Cistercian Caesarius of Heisterbach, in his *Dialogue*, gave Fourth place among the Seven Deadly Sins to *accidie*. Chaucer too condemned it, and for Cassian it was 'the demon of noontide'. There is a tendency among modern historians to regard *accidie* as a peculiar element in medieval casuistry not translatable into modern terms. But what is the catharsis of this twentieth century but the *accidie* of the medievals in a more potent and deadly form? T. S. Eliot indeed has written of it—the ennui of our time. Coleridge knew it well, and for Gray at Oxford it was a 'white melancholy'. Here it may be given a rather different concept from the theological one but its roots are fundamentally the same.

In English monasteries in the middle of the afternoon there is a welcome bowl of tea, known as *caritas*, and here again the monks drift in and out of the refectory, each standing in silence as he drinks with two hands firmly holding the bowl. After vespers a guest may well retire to the library, which has always an intriguing, sometimes celebrated, collection of books, for a monastery without a library is as a fortress without an arsenal. It is as a rule remarkably comprehensive, having not only its own highly-specialized subjects but even the entire philosophy of paganism, since one must be armed to defend Christian truths, while the most recent biographies, travel books, even novels may be available. The librarian may himself be a learned archivist or historian, and many monasteries have their own

men of letters. The Cistercians were originally forbidden literary
activity, and a clause in their *Carta Caritatis* decreeing that no Cistercian should write verse makes odd reading today when several of
their poets are known to the world.

Where there are guests they probably gather in a parlour during
the evening, when Father Guestmaster or friends in the community
and perhaps the abbot himself may be present. Tradition has it that
Dante knocked one night on the door of a remote convent in the
Apennines. On being asked what he wished, he replied simply *Pax*.
There are several reasons for this magnetism of the cloister. Visitors
still find there an anodyne for a jaded spirit, or they come to share
in the spiritual privileges, or they are toying with the idea of
ultimately entering such a community. There seem to be no valid
reasons, however, for the presence of others, of all beliefs, some
pagans, some introverts, some escapists, some decidedly in quest of
something or other and perhaps anxious to find out whether monks
have something to teach an atomic world.

Many of these people linger in the memory. There was the
neurasthenic whom we dubbed the Human Rocket, pulsating with
nervous energy and bearing the marks of a painful youth in which
the coming of death had been drummed into him. 'Listen to that
clock, Connolly', his parish priest used to say to him, 'it's ticking
away your life, you can't catch up with it; remember that your life
must end—keep death in front of you, Connolly.' His sister, who
appears to have been imbued with the same strain, made him as a
boy spend a night with the coffin of his younger brother. Later he
ran away to sea, but before joining his ship he had entered a dock-
land church to say four *Pater Nosters* and five *Ave Marias*. His ship
was torpedoed in mid-Atlantic. He was now subject to fits of cerebral
neurasthenia, and had been a voluntary patient in an asylum. Somehow he had found his way to the monastery to offer himself as a
lay brother.

Death is nothing in a monastery. It is indeed often almost
eagerly awaited in the spirit of the old martyrs, and when it comes
it is the easiest and most gradual of change-overs, the great day of
deliverance—the *janua caeli* or door of Eternal Life. And yet, as a
Scottish priest observed in the same monastic parlour, 'Death
is a terrible thing, ugly, painful and unnatural because the soul
is torn from the body.' In a sense, however, these monks have

already died, and their existence here is simply a purifying ablution-
ary process.

Then there was the Polish officer who had studied at Warsaw
University, where he was always quarrelling with his Left-wing
friends. Today those friends are the Minister of Production, the
Secretary of the Polish Communist Party and other formidable
people. There was the quiet unassuming district registrar from
India, with his stories of wanderings in the Himalayas, where he and
his wife had to abandon their mules and walk when the roads were
washed away, where villagers in remote hamlets prepared slices of
roast potato on fresh leaves for them, and where they encountered
nomadic shepherds from China. There was the pale ascetic boy who
stayed to work on the farm, studying Latin and philosophy in his
spare time prior to trying his vocation as a Carthusian. And there
was the handsome smiling young Canadian who, in the uniform of
the South Saskatchewan Regiment, spent a few days' leave in the
monastery. He knew instinctively that he was to die. Three months
later he was killed outside Caen.

At another time three Anglicans in search of an ideal gathered
around the parlour fire waiting for some miracle to resolve all their
doubts. One of them stayed longer than was good for him. He began
to mumble about monastic charity and the sound of the bells. 'Bells,
bells, bells—they drive me mad.' God rest his soul! What would a
medieval monastery not have done to him, for in addition to the
great bells in the tower calling for all the canonical hours and services, for Angelus and Ave, there were all manner of smaller bells.
There was the *signium* which aroused the brethren at daybreak, the
squilla announcing meals, the *campanella*, as above but for workers
in the garden and the fields, the *cordon* which summoned the
brethren to the abbot's side, the *petasius*, as above but for those at a
distance, the *tiniolum*, the call to retire to the dormitory, the *noctula*,
tolling at intervals throughout the night to call the 'watch' brethren
to prayer, the *corrigiumcula* or scourging bell, and still others.

In yet another monastery, many I once knew now lie in the plot
adjoining the monks' cemetery. One was a lover of music and a
minor dramatist who had been in charge of the BBC drama in the
old Savoy Hill days. He was a good talker and would recall his
Oxford days when he drank Imperial Tokay in the cloisters of
Magdalen, and not long before he died a portrait of him was hung in

the Royal Academy. Another was a Viennese Jewish artist, interned in France for the whole of the Great War. Afterwards he lived in the Cistercian monastery of Heiligenkreuz near Vienna, where he painted pictures for the refectory. In 1938 he was forbidden as a Jew to paint or to sell any of his work, and after unsuccessful attempts to live in monasteries in Italy and Belgium he came over here in 1939 and soon afterwards lived as a layman in the monastery. Others of a more fleeting acquaintance also lie there, their names, like those of the monks, beautifully and simply cut in Eric Gill-like lettering on plain wooden crosses.

Once a year, on the Vigil of All Souls, is held the ancient and moving ceremony common to much of Europe, the Jour des Morts of France, when the dead are remembered. Tiny lighted lanterns with red, blue, green and yellow reflectors are placed on the graves. Late in the evening the convent bearing lanterns file in procession along the dark hilly path to the cemetery. Here the monks, in their white habits and their heads cowled, move slowly among the graves of their former colleagues and friends, pausing here and there for prayer and recollection. There is always something of a Resurrection painting by William Blake in the scene, though an unknowing stranger passing along the high road would certainly be bewildered and possibly wonder if he had come upon a secret rendezvous of the Ku-Klux-Klan.

The last ceremony of the normal day, following shortly after supper, is Compline. In some monasteries this is immediately preceded by the *statio*, the station or assembling of the convent before entering the church. In the semi-darkness, the pale moonlight perhaps making filigree of the carved cloister arcades, the cowled figures stand like wraiths in the cloister walks. At a given signal the monks go, two by two, into the church, and on entering they sprinkle themselves with holy water for the last time that day (though Cistercians are offered holy water by their superior as they leave church). *Asperges me, Domine, hyssopo.* The choir is in semi-darkness. Two pale fat candles with dancing tongues of yellow flame burn on either side altar. Soon these too are extinguished and prayers are concluded in utter darkness. There is a moment's hush, and then there is only the swish of woollen habits as two by two the monks go to their cells. The great silence, *silentium*, has begun.

The stranger now creeps softly along corridors and staircase.

The entire place is as silent as the tomb. Those monks who have yet essential business to attend to make do with the minimum of speech. Perhaps if they are Cistercians they resort to sign language, a species of deaf-and-dumb show often said to derive from De Rancé's *La Trappe*, though it was known in the Middle Ages, and the medieval Syon Customary describes about one hundred such signs. This is now so comprehensive that in the Cistercian abbey of Chimay in Belgium during the last war one of the monks, in the face of tommy-guns pointed at him by storm-troopers, could convey to a brother monk the details of his 'interview' with their German captors.

Night in the world belongs, perhaps, to the Devil, but here one is safe in a spiritual powerhouse. This silence is after all so much more than the silence of emptiness and death. In the box of one's cell time and space, if they exist at all, are but accidents. You are buried in darkness, on the shores of infinity. You face the *noctium phantasmata* with confidence, though sleep may come delinquently.

PAST

2

THE MONASTIC YEARS

DESPITE Cassian's belief that some kind of semi-monastic community existed from the time of the Apostles, the fever of asceticism which drove the Nile dwellers into the deserts would seem to mark the beginning of Christian monachism. The colonies of Egyptian *therapeutae*, seen and reported by Philo the Jew in his *De Vita Contemplativa* before the year 50, maintained regular fasts and met once a week for some sort of communal worship, as did the first monastic bodies after them. The contributory causes of this ascetic tradition were many, but prominent among them were a dualistic conception of the universe, the decay of Graeco-Roman morality as shown in the sixth Satire of Juvenal, and a motive of personal salvation.

This stampede into the silence of the deserts, with its incredible alloy of savage self-mortification and an almost divine humanity, its marathon of whippings and hair shirts and exposure and fasting on lentils and figs, was brought under control by one man of genius, a man of uncompromising asceticism yet a man of profound humanity with a sympathetic understanding of the problems of his time—Anthony, the first of the Desert Fathers. It was Anthony who established, about the year 305, the *lauras* of northern Egypt, monasteries in which each anchorite curled up in his separate cell and met for common service only on Saturdays and Sundays. The Antonian rule thus represented a compromise between the solitary life of the anchorite and the closely-knit cenobitic systems of the later European monastic Orders, both roads to the same end.

A few years later St. Pachomius founded a *coenobium* or community of monks under the first known rule, at Tabennisi away to the south in the Thebaid, where he directed some fourteen hundred monks. Here the social principle was more fully organized, common services in church more frequent and labour placed on an organized basis. By the middle of the fourth century the sand-blown monasteries of the Wadi Natrum alone housed five thousand monks, while Serapion at Arsinoë ruled another ten thousand, though these numbers should be viewed with caution.

This form of corporate monastic life spread in every direction and set the original pattern for all later monasteries in east and west. Eastward it penetrated into Syria with Saints Basil and Hilarion, and Basil's rule became the basis of the monastic system in the Eastern Church, though there was no Order in the Western sense. Athanasius established the life in Rome. Martin of Tours carried it into Gaul, where Cassian founded the monastery of St. Victor at Marseilles and St. Honoratus that of Lérins. From the island of Lérins off the Mediterranean coast of France St. Patrick may have taken it to Ireland, where it is said that two thousand monks were living in community at Banchor. The success of Irish monasticism soon reacted upon Gaul and Italy, largely under the impetus of St. Columbanus, who founded Luxeuil in the Vosges and Bobbio in the Apennines. By the year 566 St. Columba had reached Iona.

The austere practices of such early British monks as Guthlac at Croyland and St. Cuthbert on the Farne Islands were western survivals of the ideals of St. Anthony and St. Simeon Stylites. This primitive pattern with its excessive austerity, so cardinal a maxim of Oriental monachism, was out of place in western Europe, and it was re-shaped by the sane realist Roman mind of St. Benedict. This young aristocrat had barely reached his majority when in the year 500 he turned his back on the seedy sycophants of the decaying capital and fled to the mountains of Subiaco, passing on his way Hadrian's villa and Tivoli, where Horace spent his leisure. Thus on his way into the waste lands he saw for perhaps the last time the symbols of what he was renouncing, the flesh and the will. The intellect he could still claim—and his soul.

Benedict retired to a cave high up beneath a beetling crag which looked over a precipitous valley, a cave today enclosed in the little monastery of the Sacro Speco, which, fastened to the mountainside, resembles one of the hanging convents on Mount Athos in the Aegean. Here he gathered about him men of a like sensibility of mind and spirit, until his reputation was such that the monks of a neighbouring monastery, ambitious to have for abbot one so famed for sanctity, begged him to accept the charge. His zeal for reform was so unwelcome, however, that in an attempt to get rid of him they presented to him a cup of poisoned drink. Benedict having, according to monastic usage, made the sign of the cross over it the vessel broke in pieces. The perfidy of his companions thus revealed, Benedict returned to his grotto *vultu placido et mente tranquilla*— with serene countenance and tranquil mind—as Gregory the Great put it. It is to Gregory, who was abbot of his own monastery in his ancestral palace on the Coelian in Rome before he was made pope in 590, and whose *Pastoral Rule* and *Dialogues* exercised a great influence on the Middle Ages, that we owe most of our knowledge of St. Benedict.

Over a period of some years Benedict, now habitually clad in the rough sheepskin cloak of the poor shepherd, founded a dozen monasteries in and about Subiaco, but dissensions among some of his all-too-human neighbours made it expedient for him to seek a new site. Wandering across the Campagna in the year 529 he came to a small mountain near the ruined fortress town of Cassinum. There the saint cut down the grove of Apollo, where the god was still worshipped two centuries after Constantine, and founded the great monastery of Monte Cassino. It was here that the Rule of St. Benedict was drawn up, most probably for his own communities, though it has recently been suggested that it was written at the command of Pope Hormisdas for the monks of the Empire.

This Rule provided the basis on which the monastic norm was established in the whole of northern and western Europe (with the exception, for a time, of the Celtic civilization) from the middle of the sixth century. It prevailed alone for some six hundred years, until the first reformers drew up their own rules. These later rules were, however, still based upon the original, which, *mutatis mutandis*, prevails even in the winter of this twentieth century. As a legislative document it owes more to Pachomius than to any other, though Benedict's conception of the cenobitic ideal, the family life, largely derives from Basil. In its wisdom and sincerity it is one of the masterpieces of the early Middle Ages, prescribing a common life of absolute regularity and strict discipline and catering for all its practical contingencies.

The Rule is a brief document divided into a prologue and seventy-three chapters of most unequal length. These are devoted not only to details of the psalms and prayers to be used in the Divine

Office, but also to the great monastic virtues and offices, of obedience, humility and silence, of the abbot and the procurator, of what kind of men the guestmaster and cellarer must be, of faults and their correction, of how guests should be received, of whether monks should receive letters and tokens, of obligations for those monks making a journey, and numerous other matters. Despite such necessary provisions for the running of what virtually became landed corporations, and despite the many external accomplishments for which the Benedictines became noted, the life which St. Benedict was prescribing was intended solely to develop supernatural motives and supernatural virtues. Liturgical prayer, spiritual reading and manual labour were the chief instruments necessary to accomplish this.

St. Benedict died about the year 547. Less than forty years after his death Monte Cassino underwent its first destruction at the hands of the barbarians. The monks survived and fled to Rome, taking with them, according to Paul the Deacon, 'the book of the holy rule, the weight for bread and the measure for wine'. Monte Cassino was to rise like the phoenix from its ashes, to become the most celebrated abbey in Christendom. Meanwhile the new Benedictine Order spread. Augustine, prior of the monastery on the Coelian, took it to England. Boniface took it to Germany, Ansgar to Scandinavia, Swithbert and Willibrord to the Netherlands, Rupert and Emmeran to Austria, Adalbert to Bohemia. It swept across the Pyrenees and into the Muslim territories of Spain. In Switzerland and eastern France the pioneer work of Gall and Columbanus was developed by their monasteries, now become Benedictine.

In England the new Roman Benedictinism quickly ousted the native Celtic monachism, which was largely centred in the north though it had penetrated southwards to such isolated outposts as Glastonbury. Now came Wilfrid to establish the Rule at Ripon and Hexham, and Benet Biscop to plant it at Wearmouth and Jarrow, the homes of the gentle monk Baeda whose *Ecclesiastical History of the English People* was unrivalled throughout the Middle Ages for its accuracy and candour. Beside the Tor rising steeply above Glastonbury, the Mount Tabor of the Somerset plain, Dunstan strove to mould his community on the new pattern. Aldhelm gave new life to Malmesbury, Ethelwold gave it to Abingdon and Oswald to Ramsey. A new rich vital stream of monastic life flowed through the Severn and Avon valleys, at Evesham, Worcester, Pershore and Winchcombe. Before the Conquest monastic life had blossomed in other centres which are now almost classical names—St. Albans (soon to produce Mathew Paris and his *Gesta Abbatum*), Westminster, Ely, Peterborough, Coventry, Bury St. Edmunds (its *Chronicle* to be written by Jocelyn, a native of the town before he took the black habit), Gloucester, Winchester and others.

The Norman Conquest marked the beginning of a new epoch in English monastic history, and soon monastic life all over Europe conformed to a single pattern and had the same regularity and rhythm. The day, based on the Roman reckoning, began at about two o'clock in the morning and ended at six in winter and eight in summer. The focal points were the six canonical hours and the night-office ('Seven times a day do I praise thee, O Lord', sang the Psalmist). The monks slept in their habits and made their toilets not on rising for the night-office but when they had changed into their day shoes before Terce. Shaving and bathing took place on fixed days about five times a year. The bloodletting or *minutio* which began in the interest of health became a regular relaxation (since it brought the privileges of the infirmary) which the monks underwent four or five times a year. Meals were confined to the *duo pulmentaria* (two portions) of St. Benedict—*prandium*, the chief meal, at midday and *cena* or supper, known as *collatio*, at about 5.30, though times of meals as of the offices changed with the seasons. Prior to the chapter mass the weak and infirm were given extra sustenance in the form of *mixtum*, bread soaked in wine.

Church and domestic buildings were grouped around a cloister, a well of light and fresh air with arcaded walks for exercise, and the prototype must have been one of the angular sheltering wall structures of the deserts, such a monastery perhaps as that of Qalaat Seman in Syria. Adjoining the abbey church, in the eastern range, were the chapter house and parlour, in the southern range was the refectory, and in the western range, below the common dormitory, was sometimes placed the calefactory, where the monastery's single fire burned from All Souls' Day until Easter. This was, more or less, the traditional plan, with deviations due either to the terrain or to some specialized feature of the community, while the later Orders introduced their own characteristic elements.

The business of the monastery was done in the chapter house, where there was also a daily Chapter which usually consisted of the *prétiosa*, martyrology, necrology, sermon and *clamationes* or complaints. The officials of a large monastery were numerous, but common to all were such officers as the cellarer, infirmarian, sacristan, treasurer, chamberlain, hosteller and librarian. The cellarer had to provide wine, bread, salt, honey and incense, numerous specified pittances and all seasonings, and he had to furnish the refectory with plates and napkins. The infirmarian had to keep the entire convent in infirmary time and obtained and prepared all meat. The sacristan provided oil, wax and candles, kept the lamps trimmed and burning, repaired bells and ropes, had the custody of altar ornaments and relics, kept the church clean and even in some places provided pittances during Lent. The treasurer was in charge of the binding of choir books and the repair of vestments and choir capes, and he had the custody of the plate and the treasury key, while he sometimes served a common pittance on feast days. All tools, books and indeed almost everything were drawn from a common store to which they were returned, for St. Benedict, well over a thousand years before Karl Marx, had cut out the pride of personal possession and had established his community on the lines of a naturally developed collectivism.

The first recall to a life more eremitical and austere than the Benedictine appeared in Italy in the institutes of Camaldoli and Vallombrosa. St. Romuald of Ravenna was the founder of Fonte Avellana, a congregation of hermits, and Camaldoli. Fonte Avellana early came under the influence of Peter Damian, but it was not until half a century after Romuald's death that, in 1072, the Camaldolesi were formally constituted and given a Rule, when the Order was made a double one by the addition of cenobitic houses following St. Benedict's Rule and interpreting it literally. A younger contemporary of Romuald and one influenced by him was John Gualbert of Florence, who like Romuald became a monk of San Miniato above Florence and left it for Camaldoli, only to leave there in order to found a cenobitic community at Vallombrosa not far distant. Both men consciously turned for inspiration to the earlier monachism of Syria, Palestine and Egypt. Both established precedents. At Camaldoli there existed all the elements which reappeared almost a century later north of the Alps at the Grande Chartreuse, while Vallombrosa established the system of lay brethren.

These Orders (the Camaldolesi still exist) had little direct in-

fluence beyond the Alps and none at all in England, but the movement towards a stricter, simpler life with varying interpretations of
the Rule of St. Benedict was felt and developed in France. The most
important and significant of the various institutes that came into
being about this time were the Carthusians and the Cistercians. The
Carthusians, the Poor Brothers of God, were founded by St. Bruno,
a canon of Cologne and a teacher at Rheims and Paris, who appears
to have entered the Benedictine abbey of Molesmes. St. Robert, the
future founder of Citeaux, was abbot at that time, so that the two
greatest reformers among Benedictines were then in the same
monastery. At Bruno's request Robert gave him a piece of land at
nearby Sèche-Fontane, to which he retired with a handful of men
of similar convictions. But Bruno wanted nothing less than to con-
template eternity, to return to the spirit of the Thebaid, and a site
was found for him in the mountains of Dauphiné, where the
little company was installed about midsummer of 1084. St. Bruno
was to die at La Torre in the mountains of Calabria, but the
hermits of the Chartreuse followed the precepts of their leader
even at that distance, and the hermitage became the Grande
Chartreuse.

The original tendency to be purely eremitical was soon coloured
by a compromise combining Benedict's Rule with the precepts of
the Desert Fathers. The Carthusians, however, remained solitaries,
or as near to being solitaries as any monks ever came. Each reform
initiated its own bye-laws or what might be regarded as a supplement
to the original Rule. Thus about 1127 Dom Guigo, fifth prior
of the Grande Chartreuse, compiled the *Consuetudines* or
Customs, a remarkable document, as too is his *Meditationes*, an
account of his own spiritual life which is almost unique in medieval
literature.

The Carthusians retained the traditional elements of liturgical
prayer, *lectio divina* and manual work, but just as the Benedictines
stressed study and the Cistercians manual labour so the Carthusian
emphasis was placed on the purely contemplative life. Thus the
brethren met in church only for the night-office and vespers, the
rest of the canonical hours and devotions being recited privately in
the cell. Meals were also eaten in the solitude of the cell, passed
through the *guichet* or hatch by a laybrother, as they do today (and
as do the Camaldolese hermits), save on Sundays and feast days

when meals were, and are, served in a common refectory. Diet was
rigorous and flesh meat wholly excluded. Discipline included the
wearing of a hair shirt, held in position by *lumbaria*, bands resembling
loincloths around the waist. Reading and work was also done in the
cell or its little garden. Later, to soften the rigours of such a life and
in the interests of bodily and mental health, there was the weekly
spatiamentum or fraternal gathering and walk outside the monastery
enclosure. At the beginning there was no 'Carthusian rite', but the
Mass remains the shortest of the Latin Masses, barely altered since
the eleventh century. Nor was there an organ, since instrumental
music, along with monstrances and copes, was prohibited.

The distinctive architectural features of the *chartreuse* (Italian
certosa, Spanish *cartuja*, Portuguese *cartuxa*, German *karthaus*,
English charterhouse) were the ranges of cells or individual three-
roomed houses opening out from three sides of the great cloister,
with another cloister for the laybrothers' quarters, while the church
was divided in two by a screen separating the choirs of priests and
laybrothers, resembling the *iconostasis* of the Byzantine and Eastern
Churches, though there is no documentary evidence to support the
theory that there was a distant connection. The Carthusian monastery thus resembled the *laura* of the desert hermits, and its plan is
little altered even today.

The Order spread across Europe, and the Carthusians made
another forty-four foundations in that same fifteenth century, a time
when the primitive spirit and fervour of other Orders had declined.
By 1521 there were some two hundred and six charterhouses spreadeagled across the Continent. New foundations were made even after
that. The first *cartuxa* in Portugal, Scala Dei at Evora, with its
immense cloisters lined with delicate tiles, was established in 1587.
There were Carthusian monasteries from Gripsholm in Sweden,
founded by the Regent and under royal protection, to Valldemosa on
the island of Majorca (later occupied by the Chopin-George Sand
ménage), from Mount Grace in Yorkshire to Pletterje in Yugoslavia.
Most of them are silent now, and deserted.

Despite some later ostentatious architecture the Carthusians
remained true to their first principles. They had no external accomplishments, and their writings have always been largely confined to
ascetical and mystical theology. The spirit of their medieval dis-
cursions and exercises still fires the soul and the imagination. Such

are the written works of Dom Lanspergius and Nicholas Love, Prior
of Mount Grace, of Denys de Ryckel, known as Dionysius Cartusiensis and also as *Doctor Ecstaticus*, and of that anonymous
writer at the Grande Chartreuse, in some mysterious way the
'ghostly son' of the monk Bovo, who wrote for the monks of Witham
A Book of the Fourfold Discipline of the Cell. This last is as valid for
Carthusians today as it was then. There is about it the essence of the
solitude in which it was engendered, and it makes the solitary cell
seem as delectable as the Hesperides. It is a world of 'ghostly
reading' and 'ghostly livers'. It is still, and there is the same note of
inconsequential unreality as these white-habited monks, bearing
their little talc-windowed lanterns, issue from their cells and make
their way through the vast chilly cloisters to the darkened church
for the night-office.

The Carthusian of today holds the position of a *ne plus ultra* in
the monastic life. The Carthusian vocation is the mystic peak, the
Everest to which all aspire but few attain. The original way of life,
in form and in spirit, remains unchanged, and fears that the Carthusians must adapt themselves to the modern world if they are to
survive have proved groundless in post-war years, which have seen
a resurgence which has made itself felt even across the Atlantic.

The Orders of Tiron, Savigny and Citeaux came into existence
about the same time, all following immediately after the Grande
Chartreuse. Tiron and Savigny sent colonies to England before
Citeaux, but since their characteristics were similar to those of
Citeaux, and since, moreover, they were shortly absorbed by the
greater Cistercian Order, they may be summarily dismissed. It was
on Palm Sunday in 1098 that a group of Benedictines led by St.
Robert left Molesmes to make a foundation in the swamps and
thickets of Burgundy. This attempt to follow a more literal observance of the Rule was not immediately associated with the birth of a
new Order, but further dissensions at Molesmes, to which St.
Robert was recalled, created a wider rift, and an isolated experiment
soon developed into the new and powerful Cistercian Order. The
initiation was largely due to St. Robert's successors at Citeaux, St.
Alberic and the English St. Stephen Harding. Soon the *Carta Caritatis* and other documents were compiled to uphold the principles
of the new foundation.

The man virtually responsible for its survival was St. Bernard of Clairvaux, who at the head of thirty companions arrived at Citeaux in 1112. Bernard soon wielded a decisive influence in the politics of Church and State. He helped to overcome the anti-pope Anacletus, he preached the Second Crusade, and he led the attack against Abelard and Gilbert de la Porrée, as he did against Arnold of Brescia. His writings, filled with personal mysticism, were to influence the later development of Franciscan literature, and his true doctrine is largely to be found in his remarkable sermons on the Song of Songs. It is only in recent years that his literary genius and his humanism have been fully assessed.

Bernard abhorred the Order of Cluny and its champions Peter the Venerable and Abelard (not a monk, though he died under the wing of Cluny), and he delivered a fierce tirade against Cluniac luxury. He referred scornfully to candelabra like 'veritable trees of bronze', and concerning Cluniac sculpture he asked, 'Of what use are these ridiculous monsters, these ferocious lions, centaurs, tigers and soldiers, in places where monks devote themselves to study?' This summed up his ideas on architecture and decoration, and the logical extension was the prohibition of stained glass, painting and richly carved capitals. This austerity was now extended even to the choir. Altar cloths were to be of linen, crucifixes of wood, and all ornaments of base metals. Certain vestments were completely abolished. Church services were simplified, not only to avoid ostentation but possibly also in order to place more emphasis on manual labour, which included a great deal of manuscript illumination but which later came to be interpreted as agricultural work. A habit of undyed wool, which later became as white, was adopted in contradistinction to the 'black' Benedictine and as a symbol of a new life. The monks slept in their habits on hard pallettes, rose at one or two o'clock in the morning, and lived for the greater part of the year on one meal a day, renouncing the pleasures of flesh meat, fish, eggs, milk and white bread. They observed an almost perpetual silence and spent many hours in prayer. They hoed and planted and reaped and garnered in the fields, in harvest time keeping their rakes and pitchforks by their bedside instead of returning them to the common store. Finally, the most revolutionary changes were in the constitutional framework and the introduction of *conversi* or laybrothers, who by performing the greater share of menial work safeguarded the seclusion of the monks (already established, however, a little earlier at Vallombrosa, and possibly, according to some authorities, even from the beginning).

The sudden arrival of St. Bernard and his companions at Citeaux so swelled the community there that daughter-houses were quickly founded at La Ferté, Pontigny, Morimond and Clairvaux. Each colony, as was customary, consisted of the superior and twelve religious, representing Christ and His Apostles. Thus did the thirteen set out for Clairvaux, in processional order, the abbot walking first, crucifix in hand, the others following, two by two, in silence, laden with all the requisites for celebrating the Divine Office, sleeping on the bare ground when night overtook them. Thus did Bernard, as elected abbot, bring his monks to Clairvaux, which grew to have as many as seven hundred brethren, including a hundred novices, and which today is one of the chief prisons of France (while Citeaux itself has been restored to the Cistercians).

Ultimately the Cistercians came to have about seven hundred and fifty monasteries scattered over Europe, and convents so numerous, especially in Germany, that the later annalists of the Order had no adequate records. Famine, plague and war and a changing society, combined with attacks both from within and without, all but damped that fine contemplative spirit fired in the dismal swamps of Citeaux. There were yet to be distinguished ecclesiastics but there were not again a Bernard of Clairvaux, an Aelred of Rievaulx and a William of St. Thierry, though a later Renaissance brought some remarkable Cistercian figures.

There were other new growths in France during this early period, notably the Orders of Grandmont and Fontrevault which appeared about the year 1100. Grandmont made a compromise between the Benedictine and Augustinian rules, though its members were strictly regular canons and not monks. Communities of canons had, of course, existed almost from the beginning. As early as the year 391 St. Augustine had established communities of regular clergy in Africa, but it was not until the latter years of the eighth century that a rule of life was introduced by Chrodegang, Bishop of Metz, for the clergy of his cathedral, which was adopted by similar congregations. The later bodies of canons regular lived a quasi-monastic life based on a rule modelled on an instruction of St. Augustine of Hippo. They had neither the limitations nor the rigours of the purely monastic Orders. For all their vows they were in close touch with the outside world and were virtually administrators of a parish. They retained the right of private property and did not have to resort to a common library or store. They were thus highly successful in England and on the Continent, where the traveller may be familiar with such historic Augustinian houses as those of St. Maurice and St. Bernard on the high pass over Canton Valais, and, in Austria, St. Florian and Klosterneuberg with their Baroque splendours.

In many ways the most attractive body of canons, since it compromised between the Augustinians and the strictly monastic Orders, was that known as Premonstratensians or Norbertines. This was created *c.* 1120 by St. Norbert, a native of the Rhineland and a friend of St. Bernard, at Prémontré near Laon. These canons wore white habits, and while they largely followed the Augustinian rule their constitutions showed a tendency to follow Cistercian models. Their architecture too was influenced by the Cistercians, and for a short time indeed they authorized the latter to make visitations on their houses, an arrangement which soon terminated because of differences of opinion. To liturgical prayer and manual work they added apostolic activity, and though the active apostolate almost disappeared in the later cloistered life recent years have restored it to pre-eminence. The Order was slow to reach England, where it ultimately had thirty-one houses, mostly colonized from Newhouse and Welbeck, but it came to have over six hundred houses in Europe. Prémontré has lost its church, and its elegant Louis XV buildings now house a lunatic asylum. It is especially in Belgium that the Order now flourishes, in the ancient houses about the moody Campine, and also in Central Europe, at Strahov in Prague, where St. Norbert himself is enshrined, at Tepl in Bohemia, the fortress-like Lelesz in Hungary, and Csorna, with the façade of a palace, on the same wide plains.

In the later Middle Ages many congregations of hermits or solitaries came into being, particularly in Spain and Italy. Meanwhile the changing needs of later medieval society had been met by entirely new forms of religious bodies having a more flexible policy and indeed a more flexible organization and framework. The 'ordres foure' of Chaucer refer to the most important of these bodies—the Franciscans or Friars Minor, the Dominicans or Friars Preachers, the Carmelites, and the Hermits of St. Augustine or Austin Friars. The first two indirectly owed their inception to the powerful sects of heretics of the period, the Cathari or Albigenses and the Waldensians, for among the measures adopted by Pope Innocent III to restore unity to the Church were ecclesiastical reforms which aimed, among other things, to restore the lost art of preaching. In response to his appeal there came forward two men of marked ability and equally marked differences in character. Both founded mendicant Orders of friars which later became noted for their scholastic attainments, having in each case circuits bounded by special provinces, while the members were not confined to the limits of a single house. In each case too there was intentional direct contact with society in preaching and missionary work.

Francesco, a layman of Assisi in Italy, was the founder of the brotherhood dedicated to the Lady Poverty and the purely apostolic life. It might also be said that he was the founder of that charmed bright Umbrian landscape of poetry and legend. A forsaken travellers' shelter near the leper hospital at Rivo Torto, so small and mean that Francis had to chalk the name of each friar over his narrow sleeping-place, was the first Franciscan settlement. Fifteen years later, in 1224, they came to Canterbury. Presently they went to the ends of the earth, and they are still there—at San Luis Rey and Santa Barbara in California, beside the Mount of Olives in Jerusalem, on the belfried island of Badia off Yugoslavia, at the Madonna del Sasso terraced high above Locarno, at Pantasaph in the hills of Flintshire, in Assisi itself, and in the mission fields of the world.

The Spanish Dominic Guzman, a canon of Osma, seems to have been as fiery as Francis was gentle, and he was essentially a realist. His Dominicans were a fully centralized and mobile religious Order occupying a position more akin to that of the Jesuits of the later counter-reformation, and later still they were to become an essentially liturgical Order, as they are today. They reached England three years before the Franciscans, and, significantly, they went straight to Oxford. Dominican theology and philosophy rapidly attained its peak in the *Summa Theologica* of Thomas Aquinas, but after that it was outclassed by the brilliance of the English province of the Franciscans—in William of Ockham, Roger Bacon and Duns Scotus, not to mention the Italian Bonaventure. Yet the Dominicans had other human riches, men and women like Fra Angelico and

Catherine of Siena. Like the Franciscans too they began with
austerity enough, but their houses later achieved the magnificence
of Batalha in Portugal, San Estaban in Salamanca in Spain, and San
Domenico in Bologna, where lies the holy Dominic. Their ancient
church of San Marco in Florence is still served by Dominicans, but
the adjoining convent is now a secularized museum-piece, a perfect
example of a small medieval convent, the uniform box-like cells
ranged on the upper floor about the cloister, empty and forlorn and
rather like a doll's house; each cell is frescoed by Fra Angelico of
this house, and his pupils, and his innocent heavens and hells give
a unique vision of the world of Dante. In Florence too the Dominicans still hold the greater church of Santa Maria Novella, as they
still hold the convent of St. Maximin in Provence, where they are
the guardians of the reputed tomb of St. Mary Magdalene. They are,
like the Franciscans, once again in Oxford, and they are to be found
in such Victorian Gothic Revival friaries as Woodchester on the edge
of the Cotswolds.

A third mendicant Order, the Carmelites, had more affinity with
the Carthusians and in origin was purely contemplative and indeed
eremitical. Even its foundation is obscure, but it traditionally derives
descent from Elias himself on Mount Carmel, the Hebrew 'place
planted with trees'. Certainly the first recorded settlement was on
Mount Carmel in the twelfth century. Dislodged from Palestine by
the Saracens, groups of these hermits settled in remote parts of
Europe, and in the thirteenth century they reached England, where
the reforms of St. Simon Stock established them as a mendicant
Order. The later reforms of St. Teresa of Avila and the influence of
St. John of the Cross restored a great deal of the purely contemplative life, and in the sixteenth century a Spanish reform divided
the Order into two distinct congregations, 'Calced' and 'Discalced',
which exist today, while Carmelite nunneries are strictly enclosed.

There are other essential differences between monks and friars
and between monks and other religious bodies. There is no Benedictine or Cistercian 'Order' in the sense that the Dominicans and
the Jesuits are Orders, with Provinces, Provincials and a General.
The individual monasteries are autonomous. It was found desirable,
however, in order to maintain religious discipline and to facilitate
communications, to form groups of monasteries into congregations,
with an Abbot-President or Abbot-General who had, as he still has,

certain powers of visitation and definition, while annual General Chapters were held, and continue to be held, at the mother-house. These congregations are sometimes national and sometimes, as the result of a particular reform, international. The earliest of them was the English Congregation founded in 1215, in accordance with a decree of the Fourth Lateran Council of that year. Early in the fifteenth century was established the Congregation of St. Justina of Padua, which later took the name of Monte Cassino when that monastery adopted the usages of St. Justina. In 1418 in Austria Abbot Nicholas de Mazen reformed the great Danube abbey of Melk, and other Austrian monasteries associated themselves with it, though they were grouped into two congregations. Abbot John of Minden then grouped together the German abbeys to form the Congregation of Bursfield after the reforms originating in that house. In France two Benedictine congregations were formed in the sixteenth century, and in 1581, also in France, some Cistercians were grouped together under the reform of the Feuillants. In Spain there was the Benedictine Congregation of Valladolid, which was to give birth to the Congregation of Portugal, which in turn had as an offshoot the Brazilian Congregation. The Swiss and Bavarian Congregations were formed in the seventeenth century, and there were later to be other congregations, both Benedictine and Cistercian.

Meanwhile the monastic state in Europe showed a marked decline, obeying the law of mortality formulated long ago by Plato. Such congregations as that of Bursfield, established in good faith and with the best intentions, were too late to be effective. The closing of monastic houses by the Hussites in Bohemia in the sixteenth century heralded the full impact of the Reformation, which under the Protestant aegis brought the wholesale suppression of monasteries in Britain, Scandinavia and parts of Germany.

3

SURVIVALS AND REVIVALS

THE storm that withered the ancient growth created an unprecedented position in England, compelling those who wished to be priests of the old régime to pursue their studies in seminaries on the Continent. The plight of the monk who wished to continue under his vows was even more precarious, and flight to monasteries in France and the Lowlands, Italy and Spain was the only possible choice. This course was adopted both by individuals and groups, though they were few. Thus it was that the continuity of the English Benedictine Congregation was preserved, remaining intact to the present time.

The last of the long line of Westminster Abbey monks, and, so far as we know, the last survivor of the venerable English Congregation, was Dom Sigebert Buckley, who, infirm, blind and about ninety years of age, clothed with the habit of his Order two young priests on 21 November 1607. There is a tradition, it is no more, that this act of affiliation was performed within the very precincts of the secularized Westminster Abbey, in the gatehouse where he was imprisoned. Dom Buckley survived to sign the formal ratification of his act, not in his prison cell at Westminster (from where he had been released on the accession of James I) but in a friend's house in Hampshire, where he died early in 1610.

It is recorded that Dom Augustine Baker, antiquary, author of *Sancta Sophia*, and himself one of the first monks of the revived Congregation, 'mightily sought from the venerable old man' the way of living in the old monasteries. Unfortunately he could tell little, but he remembered that at Westminster they rose at midnight, and at supper had first a dish of cold sliced powdered beef, and after that a roasted shoulder of mutton. Hardly the austerity of St. Benedict, but then this was early in the sixteenth century.

Meanwhile the two young monks, Robert Sadler and Edward

Mayhew, now invested with all the rights and privileges of the old English Benedictines, served their novitiate abroad, and in 1608 an English monastery was founded at Dieulouard in Lorraine. Another group of English Benedictines, who seem to have been professed in Spain, had, however, established the abbey of St. Gregory at Douai in Flanders in the previous year. Yet another group, representing the old abbey of Bury St. Edmunds, established the abbey of St. Edmund near Paris in 1615. These centres became distinguished nurseries for the counter-reformation, and their communities established a splendid tradition of contemplation, education and even martyrdom. Many risked their lives, finding their way to England to work in a precarious mission-field, serving mass like other recusant priests but also fulfilling their monastic observance as well as they might, as they flitted from one country house to another, constantly living in the shadows. They were a *gens lucifuga*, a people who shunned the light. Some of them paid the extreme penalty, as did John Roberts, the first superior of Douai, Mark Barkworth, George Gervase, Maurus Scot, Thomas Tunstall, Ambrose Barlow, Alban Roe, Philip Power and Brother Thomas Pickering.

St. Edmund's outside Paris was a celebrated house. The exiled James II was a patron and was buried in the abbey church, as were his daughter Princess Louisa Mary and the Duke of Berwick. One of the last of the community to take his degree at the Sorbonne before the Revolution was Dom Charles Walmesley, a brilliant mathematician and at twenty-eight a Fellow of the Royal Society; he was later consultant to the British Government on the reform of the calendar, and when he became a bishop he consecrated the first bishop of the United States, thus fathering the entire American hierarchy.

In 1643 the abbey of Lamspring in Hanover, belonging to the Congregation of Bursfield, was lent and ultimately given to other English Benedictines. All these communities, among others, remained in France until the Revolution, after which they are to be encountered on English soil.

Nor did the English white company of St. Bruno entirely withdraw from their silent cells. During the Marian restoration of 1555-59 the former priors of Witham and Mount Grace with thirteen other Carthusians entered the charterhouse of Sheen, the royal foundation near London. Expelled from England on the death of Mary they took refuge with the Carthusians of Val de Grace in Bruges, and in 1578 they established the monastery of Sheen Anglorum in Bruges. Subsequently the community moved to Louvain and finally, in 1626, to Nieuport. Their house was suppressed with others in the Austrian Netherlands under Joseph II. The last prior of Sheen Anglorum, Dom Thomas Williams, died at Little Malvern Court in 1797, and the English Carthusian line was finally extinguished with the death of Dom Bruno Finch in Lincolnshire in 1810.

In Europe many Cistercians, though by no means all, had by now grown magnificent and lax, save for the reforms of the Feuillants, of the Congregation of Castile and a few others, chief of which was the Strict Observance or Congregation of Clairvaux, thus styled in contradistinction to the Common Observance of Citeaux. By the middle of the seventeenth century the Strict Observance prevailed in some six hundred Cistercian monasteries. To one of the monasteries held *in commendam*, the pernicious practice whereby an outsider held the office of superior in name only and pocketed all the revenues, came another Bernard to raise it from its sloth and to make its name such that a shiver would ripple through those who heard it. The monastery was La Trappe near Mortagne in France, a dilapidated establishment which had become practically a cesspool. The man was Armand-Jean le Bouthillier de Rancé, son of the secretary of Marie de Medici and godson of Cardinal Richelieu, then virtually the ruler of France.

de Rancé was obviously marked out for preferment and privilege, and his natural precocity was aided and abetted by three private tutors. At the age of eleven he was already (following another pernicious practice of the period) a canon of Notre Dame in Paris and commendatory abbot of no less than four monasteries. The only mitigating feature of all this was the boy's brilliance. Barely had he reached his twelfth year when he published a translation of Anacreon, with critical annotations. Louis XIII said that 'this lad knew more Greek and Latin than all the abbés in France'. Master of Arts at sixteen, he won first place in theological examination at the Sorbonne (thus surpassing the great Bossuet, who came second), but despite all this he kicked over the traces like all the French gallants of his age, waiting until such time as he could wear the mitre of his uncle as Archbishop of Tours.

Then something happened, a change of heart, a swerve of intellectual conviction, a parallel with Benedict's disgust at the hedonism around him. Renouncing all his riches, he retired to a monastery of the Strict Observance where he made his profession in 1664, and in the same year he was blessed abbot of La Trappe, which he already held *in commendam*. He now determined, in the face of bitter opposition from the entire Order, to make of La Trappe a model of the primitive observance, and in his ardour he went even further, attributing to the original Rule an almost magic power and giving it something of a metaphysical importance.

If Benedict had prepared his monks for life, de Rancé now prepared them for death. He imposed the most rigid order that had ever been laid on men. The community resisted his reforms and, rumour has it, made several attempts upon his life. Some monks left the monastery, others were won over, including one said to have shot at de Rancé and who was afterwards made sub-prior. The pattern that was to awe not only France but all Europe was now established—the hair shirts, the mortification of the body, the self-imposed discipline, the fasting and the perpetual silence and the manual labour, while the rules of the infirmary made the spectator shudder. There was in all this a pathological element more suited to the psychoanalyst's clinic. Even the situation of the monastery was said to have some Dantesque quality, for it was hemmed in with hills, forests and lakes from the stagnant waters of which thick exhalations rose in curling vapours which hid all but the dark grey towers. Within the monastery there were *mementos mori* in the medieval form of painted cadavers and souls writhing in the flames of Hell. Yet if La Trappe were a kind of penitentiary—de Rancé in a startling statement had intimated as much—the spirit informing it was perhaps at bottom one of love. This was suggested in some of the moralities inscribed throughout the monastery. Above the entrance to the refectory, for example, ran the legend: *Melius est, ad olera, cum charitate vocari, quam ad vitulum saginatum, cum odio*. (Better is a dinner of herbs, where love is, than a stalled ox and hatred therewith.)

The morbid fascination exercised by La Trappe was probably something akin to that of the French Foreign Legion earlier this century, since, for once, this was a period when the popular novelists' romantic themes of escapism in a monastery as the last resort of the disillusioned may have held good. Thus at La Trappe there were gathered together in the anonymity of the rough white woollen habit such men as the Count Rosemburg (who refused to see his own mother), the Chevalier Albergotti, the former Grand Provost of Touraine, repenting of a long political career in which integrity had not been conspicuous, the Honourable Robert Graham, and one of James II's bravest officers (both of whom James, a frequent visitor, to his great surprise encountered there).

As to de Rancé himself, the man of vision, the idealist, the saint and the fanatic of the *grand siècle*, perhaps no one has more squarely taken his measure than the Abbé Henri Brémond in his *L'Abbé Tempête*. 'Etna is a peak, like Mont Blanc, but a peak from which torrents of lava sometimes flow; we may admire it for its altitude, but scarcely for its lava.' de Rancé's favourite books were, significantly, Cardinal Bellarmin's *Art of Dying Well*, *The Imitation of Christ* and the *Vitae Patrum*. He was himself a prolific writer, producing some eight or nine volumes, of which the most reasonable (except for its attacks on other Orders) is *De la Sainteté et des Devoirs de la Vie Monastique*, while the most curious is *Relations de la Vie et de la Mort de Quelques Religieux de la Trappe*. Yet he rejected learning, it had no place in the perfection of a monk's soul, and he bitterly opposed what he regarded as the bookishness of the Benedictines and the Jesuits, a difference of opinion which culminated in his classic controversy with Mabillon. If learning was rejected, however, it cannot be said that La Trappe substituted contemplation, there was too much of the desert for that, too much of St. Simeon Stylites and the athletic marathon of competitive self-destruction. Yet when de Rancé died in 1700 he left a group of monasteries which were a credit to the spirit of St. Bernard.

The brilliant Dom Jean Mabillon, who all but vanquished de Rancé with his *Défense des études monastiques*, in which he ably refuted the exaggerated views of his opponent, was a member of the celebrated French Congregation of St. Maur. He was the annalist and hagiographer of his Order, author of the monumental *Acta Sanctorum* and of the *De Re Diplomatica*, which inaugurated the scientific study of medieval documents. The Maurists, who flourished for some two hundred years from 1618, had their chief seat in the abbey of St. Germain-des-Pres in Paris, and they were not altogether free from the heresy of Jansenism. They produced many such scholars, among them Dom Edmond Martène and Dom Ursin Durand.

Dom Martène studied under Mabillon at St. Germain-des-Pres and wrote a number of learned works on monastic history and liturgy. Dom Durand studied diplomatics at the abbey of Marmoutiers, and in 1709 the two joined forces to make a literary tour of France and the adjoining provinces to collect material for the monumental *Gallia Christiana*. The archives of some eight hundred abbeys and a hundred cathedrals were searched on this occasion. In 1718 another literary tour was made through Germany and the Netherlands, and the result of all these journeys was the fascinating *Voyage Littéraire des deux Bénédictins*. As a portrait of monasteries in western Europe in the early eighteenth century it stands almost alone. Dom Durand's theology ultimately having too strong a Jansenist colouring, he was banished from St. Germain-des-Pres and ended his days, still in literary pursuits, in the monastery of Blancs-manteaux.

French letters of the late seventeenth and early eighteenth centuries reflect that religious and philosophic current which was the Gallican reply to the Reformation. In the more puritan stream there was the beautiful seventeenth-century French of the celebrated convent of Port Royal, from which radiated that Jansenist heresy which held that the human race was corrupt and doomed to damnation, excepting those who were destined to be saved by divine grace, a heresy which became one of the great spiritual forces of the age, inspiring not only men like Dom Durand but also the Pascal of the *Lettres Provinciales* and Racine, who was educated at Port Royal but ultimately disappointed his teachers. It was an age of intriguing monastic literature. Besides de Rancé, Mabillon, Montfaucon, Durand and Martène, there is the *Voyages Liturgiques de France* by Sieur de Moléon, while Helyot's *Histoire des ordres monastiques, religieux et militaires* has a haunting gallery of drawings of monks, hermits and anchorites. Many such books are to be encountered in the monasteries of Europe. France and Italy are particularly rich, and in Belgium there are such musty leather-bound volumes as the *Presbyteri Chorographia Sacra Brabantiae* of Antoni Sanderi (1725), its stained engravings of lost monasteries and Baroque churches evoking an unreal world.

For this was the century of the Baroque and the Rococo. The greatest patrons of architecture and the arts were often bishops and abbots, and as they had spread the Gothic in the Middle Ages so they now adopted the new styles. It was a century of monastic rebuilding. Monte Cassino, Citeaux, even Cluny were largely rebuilt, the last to designs by that Robert de Cotte who was responsible for the Archbishop's Palace at Strasbourg and the dome of the Invalides in Paris. Prémontré was rebuilt to designs by Claude Honoré de Muin. In Austria Jakob Prandtauer designed the abbeys of St. Florian, Kremsmunster and, in part, Melk. In Germany there were the Zimmermans, the Asam brothers, whose masterpiece is the abbey church of Weltenburg upon the Danube, and Johann Michael Fischer, architect of no less than twenty-two Baroque abbeys, among them the incomparable Zwiefalten and Ottobeuren. In Switzerland there was Caspar Moosbrugger who designed Einsiedeln, as he designed Weingarten in Bavaria. In Italy the Neapolitan Vanvitelli designed the *certosa* of Padula and the Loreto of Monte Vergine. In Spain there was Hurtado, who was responsible for the fantastic sacristies of the Carthusians at Granada and Paular. And in Belgium there was Benoit de Wez, architect of a score of abbeys.

In collaboration with these there worked a host of brilliant painters, sculptors and *stuccatori*. Thus the greatest craftsmen of the age were associated with the monasteries, and many of them, as we shall see, were themselves monks. It is a far different century from that of the Reformation. The Gothic lingers in the north, but elsewhere its lament and despair and chilly adagio moods have given way to hope and joy and triumph expressed in dancing cupolas and opera-box balconies, in flying cherubs and coral-reef altars, in efflorescences of gold and silver and cream. The life of the monk, where it was truly lived with integrity, had not changed. He lived still by the seasons in a supernatural world, following the Rule of Benedict or that of some reformer, but his environment had in many places changed beyond all recognition.

So too had his external accomplishments. Where Anthony's monks had woven mats from palm fibre and crushed oil from sesame so later monastic ingenuity had begun the production of liqueurs and sweets. In Italy some monks, but more especially nuns, were noted for their sweets and ices. In Palermo the nuns of Santa Catarina made candied pumpkins and blancmange, while a neighbouring convent produced imitation fruits of almond paste. One Order of nuns, the Gesuati, was said to have been suppressed in the seventeenth century because their enthusiasm in the distilling of liqueurs and perfumes knew no bounds. In Spain and Portugal many sweets were and continue to be made by nuns. The *ovos moles* of Aveiro, for example, a sweetmeat largely made of eggs and now sold in little wooden barrels in the shops, were originally made in a convent in that town, while the Hieronymites of Seville still sell their *yemas de San Isidro*, an almost Arabian sweet of eggs and oranges, at the convent door, as the Carmelites of Avila sell their *yemas de Santa Teresa*. In France the nuns of Beaumes-les-Dames in Franche-Comte introduced several sweets which are still sold locally—the *pets-de-nonne* of fried lemon-flavoured doughnuts, *gaufrettes de Clairval* or waffles made with lemons and fresh cream, and cracknels shaped like the letter S. The nuns of Château-Chalon, also in Franche-Comte, used to make a sweet of eggs and milk whipped with castor sugar and vanilla, moulded with caramel and cooked in a *bain-marie*. This is still served, on demand, in local restaurants. Many of the sweets on sale today in Montargis were first made by the Benedictine nuns there—the honey bonbons, the candied cherries coated with chocolate, the burnt almonds coated with flavoured sugar, and the *rochers de Montargis* or coloured pebbles of sugar and aniseed.

We have yet to explore the remarkable range of liqueurs and tonics, largely of seventeenth- or eighteenth-century origin, still produced in Italy and France, together with the monastic wines and beers of Germany and Austria. Brewing privileges were granted to many German monasteries, and many of the great breweries in Bavaria and the Rhineland have a monastic origin, as has many a Ratskeller, the popular beer-hall-cum-restaurant in the cities. Today the traveller can still call for beer in the taproom of such monasteries as Andechs, which has a celebrated brewery, on the shores of the Ammersee, as he can at the Cistercian monasteries of Westmalle and Chimay in Belgium.

The Maurists were not the only Benedictines taking part in literary and intellectual movements. There were signs elsewhere in Europe of a return to the zeal and fervour of the primitive observance and of an intense intellectual activity. New congregations came into being. In Austria, Germany, Switzerland and Italy were to be found such scholars as Bernard Pez, Ziegelbauer, Gerbert, Schenck, Bacchini and Mechitar, who founded an Armenian Congregation in

Venice which was largely dedicated to intellectual pursuits. A note-worthy Benedictine achievement was the direction of the University of Salzburg, founded in 1617 by the prince-archbishop Marcus Sitticus, by the Benedictines of Bavaria, Suabia and Austria until its suppression in 1810. Among its professors was Dom Celestin Sfondratti, later abbot of St. Gall and subsequently a cardinal. The teachings of the Salisburgenses form a continuation of that of the Thomists and of the Salamanca school.

Now, however, the mounting forces of insurrection and agnosticism in France were about to culminate in the Revolution. In November of 1789 the apostate Bishop of Autun, Talleyrand, proposed in the National Assembly that the property of the religious Orders be confiscated, and early in the following year the Decree of Secularization was passed by the Assembly. The libraries of all religious houses were declared public property, and the books were collected in the main towns of the departments in so-called *dépôts littéraires*. Thus it is, to mention a single example, that the Municipal Library of Troyes now has 50,000 volumes from Clairvaux.

The Revolution and the Napoleonic wars swept bare the monasteries of Europe. For English monks and nuns in France the storm broke in 1793 with the decree against aliens. The Benedictines of St. Gregory's at Douai were imprisoned but were eventually able, in 1795, to reach England, where they were given hospitality by the squire of Acton Burnell in Shropshire, later moving to Downside Abbey in Somerset where they are today. The monks of Dieulouard ultimately found a home at Ampleforth in Yorkshire, where today the lineal descendant of Westminster Abbey stands.

The fortunes of St. Edmund's outside Paris were more chequered. The monastery became a prison at the Revolution but was restored to the monks until 1801, when they were compelled by another law to disperse and seek separate lodgings in Paris, supporting themselves by teaching and such work. In 1817 the prior, the last of the English monks in Paris, died. In the following year Dom March, to whom the late prior had willed the interests of his monastery, left for Douai with a few students and rebuilt the monastery. This survived until 1903, when, the last English community of Benedictine monks to return from exile, they were compelled by the Laws of Association to settle in England, at what is now called Douai in Berkshire.

In 1828 an English monk of Lamspring in Germany, which had been closed by the Napoleonic wars, established a small monastery at Broadway in Worcestershire which was then regarded as the successor to Lamspring. Ultimately this was removed to Fort Augustus in Scotland, where the sole survivor of the ancient Scots monastery of St. James at Ratisbon had a hand in the foundation.

Thus the English Benedictine abbeys of today are all fruits of the counter-reformation. So it is with the nunneries, though one of these, the Bridgettine abbey of Syon in Devon, is the sole pre-Reformation community, among monks or nuns, still existing in this country, having moved at the Dissolution to the Netherlands, to France and finally to Portugal, whence they returned to England in 1861. At the Revolution some fifteen long-established convents, all foundations of the counter-reformation, were to be found in Flanders, from Liège to Bruges, from Gravelines to Cambrai, while five more were situated within France. All these communities fled to England in 1794-95, not, however, without undergoing severe privation.

The Benedictine nuns of Cambrai were herded in tumbril-like waggons about the country and their chaplain, the aged President-General of the English Benedictine Congregation, Dom Augustine Walker, died of ill-treatment, as did four of his nuns. Only the sudden fall of Robespierre saved them all from the scaffold. Ultimately they were allowed to sail for England in a Danish ship, and in London the Duke of Buckingham placed his town house at their disposal. The community was eventually settled, in 1838, at Stanbrook in Worcestershire, where today it is the premier English Benedictine nunnery. The Benedictine nuns of Paris were imprisoned in the château of Vincennes, but they reached England in 1795, finally settling at Colwich in Staffordshire. The French Benedictine nuns of Montargis (whose sweets we have already noticed) also fled to England, where the Prince Regent and Mrs. Fitzherbert took a personal interest in them, the Regent sending his own coaches to convey them from Shoreham to Brighton, and today their descendants are at Princethorpe in Warwickshire. Another English community of Benedictine nuns, now at Oulton in Staffordshire, left Ghent as the town was being bombarded, when one young nun went mad from the sights and terrors and had to be left in a mental home in Belgium where she died.

It was the same story of flight and ordeal with many other communities, with the Carmelites of Antwerp, Lièrre and Hoogstraeten, who came respectively to Lanherne in Cornwall, Darlington and Chichester, with the Augustinian Canonesses of Louvain, who ultimately found a home at Newton Abbot, and with the Poor Clares of Dunkirk who came at length to Darlington and Dublin. The Augustinian Canonesses of Paris survived the Revolution, and they received the Duke of Wellington on his triumphant entry into Paris after Waterloo, while, at about the same time, the pupils of their celebrated school included the young George Sand, soon to turn her back on the nuns' teaching and to defy contemptuously all middle-class conventions. In 1860 the laying of a new road drove them to another convent in the suburb of Neuilly, where in the fighting of the *Commune* of 1871, the convent, filled with dead and dying, was sacked. When Clemenceau closed their school in 1909 the end was in sight, and three years later the nuns moved to Ealing.

The last community of nuns to leave France was the Irish Benedictines of Ypres, who held out until their convent was destroyed in the prolonged bombardment of Ypres in 1914. Aided by British troops, they reached St. Omer, where they were compelled to leave their bedridden abbess, and then England, finally settling in the granite neo-Gothic palace of a cotton merchant at Kylemore in the mountains of Connemara. One English community of nuns has remained in Belgium. The convent of the Augustinian Canonesses of Bruges has stood behind the brackish waters of the Quai Long since 1629, and though the nuns fled to England at the Revolution they returned in 1802.

Meanwhile other heroic and far more terrible journeys were being undertaken on the Continent, notably by those Cistercians of La Trappe whose wanderings were described by a later French historian as an *Odyssée monastique*. The Cistercian monasteries of France and the Low Countries were now lost, but the novicemaster of La Trappe, Augustine Lestrange, foreseeing the suppression of his Order, had successfully negotiated for an asylum in Switzerland. To his devotion and single-mindedness of purpose was due the second Spring.

Louis-Henri de Lestrange, the fourteenth in a family of twenty, was the son of a French officer who had served at Fontenoy and of an Irish mother. He abandoned a naval career for the priesthood, and in order to escape ecclesiastical honours he fled to La Trappe, where after more than a century de Rancé's reforms were still maintained with unflagging zeal. It was here that Dom Augustine, for so he had become, sought and received permission to negotiate with the Government of the Canton of Fribourg in Switzerland, who agreed to admit the Trappists and place at their disposal the unoccupied former Carthusian monastery of Valsainte. Immediately before the storm broke, Dom Augustine with twenty-three religious and several novices, leaving the remainder of the community at La Trappe, set out for the deserted mountain-set Valsainte. Here they lived on roots, leaves, black bread, and water from the mountain streams, they had no change of clothing, and they slept on bare stone floors until they could construct rough plank beds. They worked from ten to fourteen hours a day and rose with aching limbs at 1.30 a.m. on ordinary days.

This example soon attracted both proselytes and other Trappists who had escaped the fate of those put to work in chain gangs on the old hulks moored in the harbour of Rochefort. Such became the congestion that between 1793 and 1796 Valsainte sent out five colonies—to Piedmont, the Bas-Valais in Switzerland, Aragon in Spain, Lulworth in Dorset and the fifth in Brabant. In the following year a papal decree declared these houses to form the Congregation of La Trappe, with Dom Augustine as abbot of the mother-house. Several of the dispersed Cistercian nuns now hurried to Valsainte to put themselves under the direction of Dom Augustine, who promptly established a convent for them in the Bas-Valais. Homeless nuns of other Orders also flocked to this house of refuge, among them the Princess Louise-Adélaide de Bourbon-Condé and the Countess de Chabannes, a Cistercian nun of St. Antoine outside Paris, who became superior and later founded the nunnery of Stapehill in Dorset where she now lies.

It would seem then that all these exiles were now firmly re-established. But in 1798 the French Republican soldiery burst into Switzerland, and Dom Augustine's communities, as both religious and *emigrés*, were compelled quickly to leave. Here there was a dilemma. Neither the Low Countries, Germany nor Italy could offer them a safe asylum, while Spain was both difficult of access and hardly less insecure. Only Russia or Austria offered any hope. Dom Augustine decided to approach the Czar Paul III, but scarcely had the letter been despatched when the approaching enemy made a precipitate flight necessary. Fearing an unfavourable reply from Russia, the abbot decided to head for Vienna. The two communities of monks on Swiss soil together with the nuns were divided for safety and discretion into four contingents, and with the monks went some sixty oblates, boys whose education was in their charge and who wore the Trappist habit.

Detours stretched the journey into some three hundred and fifty painful miles, sometimes on foot, sometimes on mules, passing along precipitous bridle paths and over snow-covered peaks, while all were frozen and half-starved. The route lay through Constance, Augsburg, Munich and Linz, and the party continued to travel in several contingents, having a total strength of over two hundred and fifty, the nuns always having a couple of days' start. The Rule and the Office were maintained throughout the march, and each day's observance concluded with that haunting song *Salve Regina*, which is still chanted at the end of the day in every Cistercian monastery in the world. Hospitality was received at a number of religious houses, and near Munich the nuns stayed with the Archduke Carl of Bavaria in his palace of Furstenried. It was here that a message was received from the Czar, offering to settle two communities, one of monks and one of nuns, at Orcha in Russian Poland.

At Linz the entire colony embarked on the Danube in two flat-bottomed boats without cover or any kind of superstructure, so that all were crowded in standing position, the nuns on one boat and the monks and oblates on the other. Thus nearly a fortnight later they reached Vienna, where they sheltered at the Visitation Convent. The Austrian Emperor, Francis II, was willing to give the Trappists asylum but his hands were tied by the Government, who imposed such conditions that acceptance was impossible. Dom Augustine therefore sent half of his band to Prague, there to await further orders, the others remaining in Vienna, while he himself with two small communities of monks and nuns set out for Russia. At Orcha he installed the two communities in two abandoned monasteries and then continued alone to the capital to obtain an audience with the Czar, who received him kindly and acceded to his requests. The relieved abbot, marshalling his resources with military decisiveness, then sent instructions to his religious in Vienna and Prague to follow him into Russia, and since his community in Piedmont had now been dispossessed by the invading French he sent them the same instructions, appointing Cracow as the common rendezvous.

The Vienna contingent began the long journey in November of 1798, travelling in midwinter, their white habits an effective camouflage against the deep snow, often overtaken by storms and lost in a trackless waste, sleeping where they could when night overtook them. Two nuns and two oblates died and were buried by the wayside, and by the time the weary cavalcade reached Cracow several were crippled. Beyond Cracow the reassembled parties, crossing the River Bug, travelled in two caravans across the forests, tundras and morasses of the Russian Steppes. Roving packs of wolves were a continual menace, and at night the baggage waggons were ranged in a circle, the religious sleeping in blankets around a fire lighted in the centre, while a cord or wire was stretched around the bivouac some two or three feet above the ground.

In addition to the two houses at Orcha the Czar had now assigned them five other houses—two monasteries in Volhynia, one in Podolia, and a monastery and a convent in the Palatinate of Brzesc. All the communities reached their respective settlements in October of 1799, almost twelve months since setting out from Vienna. In the winter which followed, the temperature rarely rose higher than 32 degrees below zero, and at Mass every morning a chafing dish had to be kept on the altar to prevent the contents of chalice and cruets from freezing.

If the Trappists now felt that at long last they were settled in their cloisters they were quickly to be disillusioned. In March of the following year, 1800, the Czar issued a decree ordering all French citizens out of his dominions, and that Dom Augustine's communities were included was soon made clear by a special messenger who gave them three weeks to quit. Napoleon's decisive victory over the allied armies of Russia and Austria at Zurich was probably responsible for this action. Outcasts and wanderers once more, the exiled communities met at Terespol on the Russian bank of the River Bug, where they were faced with yet another dilemma. In order to leave Russia they had to cross the river into Austria or sail downstream into Prussia. Without passports they would be imprisoned in both those countries, and Francis II of Austria had in fact already issued an order for the arrest of persons wearing the Trappist habit on Austrian soil. Yet stay in Terespol they could not. They could neither stay in the town nor obtain permission to leave it.

The problem was solved by a sympathetic French officer serving in the Czar's army. He provided a large boat by which the exiles reached a small island in the river which was then neutral territory. The monks landed on the island. The nuns remained in the boat which was anchored close by, a floating convent. How intrigued the townspeople of Terespol must have been by the nightly sung Office, the snatches of plainsong drifting on the wind. A few weeks more and the passports for Prussia were obtained, and sailing down the Bug and Vistula, with yet more incidents *en passage*, the white companies reached Danzig where they were given medical assistance, for many now suffered from fever and paralysis. They finally reached Hamburg, where they spent most of the following two years, while Dom Augustine made further attempts to put his house in order.

With a subsequent lessening of tension in Europe many of the monks returned to their old houses, while others made new foundations in Italy and elsewhere. In 1811 further disputes arose, and Napoleon again suppressed all Cistercian houses in his dominions, largely because the monks could not agree to his declaration that the French Emperor was the legitimate sovereign of the Papal States. Dom Augustine as the chief antagonist was now outlawed throughout Europe and was compelled to flee to the United States, but he returned, bringing even more Cistercians with him, on the fall of Napoleon. La Trappe came out of the catacombs and the monks returned to all their old houses.

Meanwhile the colony that had been established at Lulworth in Dorset in 1795 (originally destined for Canada) was settling in. Dedicated to St. Susan, this was the first monastery to be built in England since the Reformation, situated near Flowers Barrow on the scented downs with sea winds blowing in from Arish Mell Gap. From the beginning there was a certain amount of local antagonism and the monks were inevitably referred to as 'French spies'. The most fantastic calumnies were trumped up, the magistrates of Dorchester had the monastery searched, and the Prime Minister requested an interview in London with the abbot. There appears indeed to have been a breath of minor scandal which, however, was not entirely the fault of the monks. One of the postulants, a James Power, who seems to have had all the qualities of a renegade and was constantly giving the abbot trouble, had his eye on pretty young Julia Woodforde, of the *Woodforde Diaries*.

The stories in this latter connection are so sensational as to be undoubtedly fictitious. It is said that Julia, who lived at West Lulworth, entered the monastery disguised as a soldier and accompanied by her father and brother officers. James Power recognized her and made an assignment on the shore a few days later. With promises of honourable intentions he persuaded Captain Woodforde and the latter's friends to 'rescue' him, which by some facile trick they did. Once away at Blandford, Power's invective and abuse of the monks were unrestrained. His subsequent conduct, however, proved him to be a rogue, and he died of fever in the tropics whither he had sailed in search of a fortune.

Whatever the truth of this unlikely tale, the community was certainly involved in conflict with both the local people and the Government. The abbot, Dom Antoine de Beauregard, a nobleman of some talent, decided in view of the restoration of order in France to return to their own country, and in 1817 they moved to the ancient abbey of Melleraie in Brittany, which was later to found Mount Melleray in Ireland, Mount St. Bernard in Leicestershire, Gethsemani in Kentucky and, indirectly, many others. Some of the monastic buildings of St. Susan's, derelict or used for agricultural purposes, still stand beneath Rings Hill.

Further suppressions of Cistercian houses occurred in Germany in 1810, Spain and Portugal in 1834-36, Switzerland in 1841-49, and in Poland by several decrees emanating from the rulers of Russia and Prussia. Later many monasteries in these countries were re-opened, and the numerous temporary resting-places and asylums of the Cistercians all over Europe became so many flourishing centres. The Congregation of La Trappe has become the Congregation of the Strict Observance, conforming to the primitive usages of Cîteaux (re-opened in 1898) and new Constitutions of 1925. It has continued into our own time to make new foundations all over the world. All Cistercian monasteries in the British Isles follow the Strict Observance. In addition there is the Congregation of the Common Observance, consisting of houses which adopted the reforms of neither Clairvaux nor La Trappe, and in this have recently been merged the small Congregation of Sénanque and the Congregation of Casamari in Italy. All have in common dormitories divided into cubicles (there are no cells), perpetual abstinence from flesh meat, strict silence and manual work.

With the Revolution many Benedictines similarly sought refuge in other countries or established short-lived houses about the frontiers. The French Congregation was the first of the Benedictine Congregations properly so-called to be restored after the Revolution, and it was the creation of a single man. Prosper Guéranger was born in 1805 at Sablé-sur-Sarthe near Le Mans. Ordained in 1827, he was for a time administrator of the Missions Etrangères in Paris, but he returned to Sablé in 1830, where he devoted himself to historical studies. Among the monuments in the vicinity was the medieval but abandoned abbey of Solesmes. He purchased the property and with the approval of the Bishop of Le Mans he re-established it, in 1836, as a priory under Benedictine rule. Other candidates came forward, and a few years later Dom Guéranger's institution was given papal recognition, was elevated to the status of an abbey and made the head of the newly-restored Congregation of France. Soon daughter-houses were established at the ancient monastery of Ligu89 and at Marseilles, while near Solesmes itself was erected the nunnery of St. Cecilia.

Dom Guéranger was responsible for the restoration of liturgical unity in France (and by his vigorous polemics he revealed the snares of the naturalism of his time). Solesmes became the centre not only of the study of the liturgy but also of its practice, and the plainchant of its monks was what drew Huysmans there, as it continues to draw others today. Its monks were prominent in the field of patristic and historical works, notably Dom (later Cardinal) Pitra, Dom Pothier and Dom Cabrol, while Guéranger himself wrote the monumental *L'Année liturgique*.

In England the seeds of the Oxford Movement were taking root in the obdurate soil of Anglicanism, Manning sat reading St. Chrysostom by the lamp of his phaeton as he sped along the country lanes of Sussex by night, Newman was about to leave for Santa Croce, Victoria had joined hands with Albert, the young Trollope was dreaming of *Barchester Towers*, and Pugin was building his stark neo-Early English monasteries, convents and chapels. Against this background the English Benedictines were expanding and flourishing, and two notable monks were already about to be elected bishops

—Dom Ullathorne and Dom Hedley. The first had been a seaman and was something of an authority on ship construction, and soon his denunciation of the penal settlements in Australia, which he knew at first hand, was to strike the national conscience. Before long there was an influx of monks from other countries, mostly refugees, whose temporary settlements were to become permanent growths.

Despite continued suppressions in Europe—to those already mentioned were now added the closures of the Risorgimento in Italy and Bismarck's *Kulturkampf* in Germany—the nineteenth century was a period of intense activity. It saw the birth of the Benedictine Congregations of Beuron, Subiaco and St. Ottilien, not to mention the Swiss-American and American-Cassinese bodies. It was the closing by a radical government of the Einsiedeln Benedictine school at Bellinzona that gave rise to the flourishing Swiss-American Congregation, since it enforced an exodus of monks from Bellinzona to St. Meinrad in the United States. Similarly the closure of many Spanish monasteries in 1835 had brought about the foundation of New Norcia in Australia. The *Kulturkampf* drove the monks of Beuron to Belgium, England and Austria. The French political unrest of 1880 caused the monks of Pierre-qui-vire to settle in the ancient English abbey of Buckfast, as the later Waldeck-Rousseau Laws of Association, in 1901, which expelled all French Benedictines, drove Solesmes to Quarr on the Isle of Wight. In this latter movement the expelled monks established a girdle of abbeys all over Europe, and when they returned to France in 1922 they were stronger than ever.

The acute anti-clericalism of the Waldeck-Rousseau period left the Cistercians, who had probably suffered enough, on their native soil, but it drove the few Carthusians into the longest of recent exiles. At the Grande Chartreuse (to which, after the Revolution, the monks had returned in 1816) some of the community hurriedly left for Farneta in Italy. The rest stood one day in their choir, silent and still, like marble statues in their white habits, facing a detachment of soldiers who had broken open the door of the monastery. As the name of each monk was read out, two soldiers stepped forward and seizing him by the arm forcibly removed him from the monastery precincts. In view of threatened resistance by the Dauphinois peasants, who had surrounded the monastery, the Government had found it necessary to remove the twenty-three monks with one company of infantry, two squadrons of cavalry, a detachment of sappers and reinforcements of mounted police.

The Government charge of political intrigue was so palpably false that not a single lawyer in Grenoble could be induced to take up the legal defence of the Government's action, and the Mayors of thirty Communes in the Dauphiné drafted a memorandum pointing out the inevitable ruin of many local families, while many men of letters, notably Francois Coppée, voiced the indignation of his fellow countrymen. All to no avail. The military were equally disgusted with the task of carrying out their orders, at the end of which one of the officers in charge broke his sword in two and resigned his commission. Most of those monks who had not gone to Farneta ultimately went to Tarragona in Spain, until Republican Spain drove them too to Italy. They returned to the Grande Chartreuse in 1940.

There has been development and change in most Orders, but the Carthusians alone, save for a few bodies of hermits, adhere to their original letter and have never needed reform. Until recently it appeared that their rigid unchanging way of life would have to be adapted to modern conditions if they were to survive. Recent developments have shown these premises to be false. Since the last war the Carthusians have made their first foundations in the United States and in Holland, and though there is a significant loss of ground in Italy the recent growth in Spain may augur well for the future.

So far during this century two world wars have disrupted the monastic life, but, as Lacordaire remarked, 'Monks and oaks are immortal.' Yet though the monk is still dominated by the ancient cycle of times and seasons, traditions and beliefs, it cannot be said that he inhabits a medieval world. He has not retired to an Ivory Tower. Indeed he probably works twice as many hours as the average man. Nor is the sanctity of the monk altogether a fugitive and cloistered virtue. If his primary object is his own self-sanctification he is almost equally concerned with the souls of his fellow men. He has, in fact, abandoned the world only to make a strategic retreat to a fortress from which he can attempt to direct mankind and perhaps preserve it from materialism, violence and possible decay.

The community of which the monk is a member follows the

pattern of the primitive Christian community, and the abbot is truly *abba* or father. Such a community is a living force and not an anachronism, and in many places it continues to make substantial contributions to education and social welfare, to agriculture and the arts. It concedes little, however, to the passing of time, and its ancient patriarchal way of life remains unchanged. It was in search of this way of life that the journeys which follow were made.

PRESENT

4

THE ROAD TO LÉRINS

THE train from Paris had put me down, in the early hours of a spring morning, at Montélimar on a bank of the Roubion and quite close to the Rhône. The little town was not yet fully awake, though some of the shops were already open and displaying the celebrated local sweetmeat made from syrup mixed with honey and whipped white of eggs and almonds and pistachio nuts and rose praline. Almost every shop front had a giant model of a nougat, which by night was illuminated. Here it was necessary to cut straight along one of the narrow streets into the heart of the town in order to avoid following the outer ring road in a continuous circle. It is an elusive place, wilfully mischievous in the Gallic manner, but when one has penetrated it there is little enough to detain the traveller. I sought out the Hôtel des Princes, formerly the fifteenth-century Griffon d'Or, where the surprised *patron* attended to my exacting requirements, providing a room for my shave and then an early breakfast in a flowered courtyard.

My objective lay seventeen kilometres away in the Tricastin of Dauphiné, close to the north-west border of Provence. There was no organized transport and I was faced with a forced march. Soon I was on the road to Aiguebelle. A taciturn farmer gave me a lift in a waggon which accounted for about six of the seventeen kilometres. After this there were a few somnolent hamlets until I came to the Cistercian nunnery of Maubec, standing in a grim neo-Gothic dress beside the road. There was not the slightest sign of life. Westward the plain of Montélimar was a hazy sage-green sea on which rode billowing pygmy ranges of chalk. Here and there were deserted cottages and farms, and this suggestion of desolation became finally tangible and absolute in the derelict hill village of Arllan, the first of a long chain of *villages abandonnées* strung out from the western edge of Dauphiné to the Italian frontier.

53

The landscape became ribbed with silvery rocks, standing out of a velvety ground like bones out of a once fat carcass. The tarmac shot up and curved through well wooded and obviously cultivated ground, and on the other side, in the valley below, lay an oasis, There was the Trappist abbey of Aiguebelle, girdled with spring woodlands and meadows and gardens which enhanced the ivory of its walls and the red pantiles of its roofs. In the sunlight it looked serene, almost Arcadian. The road dipped down and, levelling out, carried me right up to the gatehouse.

I pulled hard on the bell, and a little window opened to reveal the bearded head and massive frame of a brown-habited lay brother. I explained my business and produced credentials. He smiled broadly.

'*Oui, oui*, Père Jean de la Croix is expecting you, but he regrets he is detained in his parish and cannot see you until this evening. But your room is prepared.'

I followed the brother's instructions and passed along the white precinct wall of the abbey to climb a stone staircase to a terraced garden, where stood the hostelry. The ground lay deep in blood-red poppy petals, and chestnut trees spread their filigreed canopies. In the vestibule of the hostelry was a notice stating that visitors should ring once for the Père Hôtelier, twice for the Frère Hôtelier and thrice for the Aide Hôtelier. Knowing that the father in charge would normally be in the abbey and that the aide would probably be little more than a secular labourer, I rang twice for the brother who would virtually run the little establishment.

'*Qui est là?*'

The words floated up from the end of one of the long white-washed corridors, and while I was wondering how to reply a brown apparition glided towards me. Brother Paul was an elderly man with twinkling eyes deep-set in a tanned face, of which, however, one could see little for it was camouflaged by a flowing white beard and rusted moustaches, more in the Franciscan tradition. He was curious to know about the expected traveller from the heretic island.

'You come from London, perhaps?' he asked eagerly, almost insistently, and he seemed quite pained to hear that I did not. London he knew by repute; the Midlands he could not understand at all, though his eyes glimmered at the mention of Stratford-on-

Avon. Yes, he knew all about Shakespeare. He showed me to my room on the first floor, and he closed the door softly, almost apologetically, as he left. The room was spacious, and the primness of the narrow bed and rickety wash-stand was atoned for by a couple of eighteenth-century armchairs embroidered in *petit-point*, and a well-carved cabinet. There were in addition a prie-dieu, some disturbing religious pictures, a plaster statue of the Place St. Sulpice variety and other pieces of *bondieuserie*. The window looked over a red gossamer of fallen poppy petals, across to the tall chestnuts. There was a twittering of birds, and beyond that no other sound.

Aiguebelle was founded in 1137 by the Cistercians of Morimond, the daughter-house of Citeaux, and it was ultimately re-colonized, in 1815, by the Trappists of Valsainte. By the middle of the last century there were over two hundred monks here. Among those who entered were the Vicomte de Meaux and the Baron du Laurens. Père Jean-Baptiste Muard, founder of the celebrated Benedictine abbey of Pierre-qui-vire, entered upon his canonical novitiate here, and among the distinguished visitors was the Curé d'Ars. Inevitably colonies were made, and today Aiguebelle has six daughter-houses, including Notre Dame des Neiges in the Cevennes (R. L. Stevenson's *Our Lady of the Snows*, and an early testing-ground of the hermit-explorer, Charles de Foucauld).

I had timed my arrival nicely, for lunch was already about to be served. Brother Paul installed me in a parlour-cum-dining-room and I sat down to a solitary meal. There was no more than a hint of the austere fare of the monks. A dish of maize or millet, rather like gruel, was somewhat unpalatable, but soup, dessert, *vin rouge*, coffee and liqueur were wholly adequate, the liqueur being made by the monks and resembling Chartreuse in colour, bouquet and taste. It was a long drawn-out meal, with Brother Paul shuffling in and out and looking somewhat harassed.

Late in the afternoon Père Jean de la Croix called upon me. He was short and bespectacled, his weak nervous eyes riveted into a pale face that declared the contemplative and the scholar. He was the secretary of the Cistercian History Commission, and he was then bringing to completion, with his collaborators, important studies marking the eighth centenary of the death of St. Bernard (these were published in Paris in 1954). He spoke excellent English, but courtesy demanded that conversation fluctuate between both languages.

Père Jean was my mentor for the rest of the day, and indeed the day after that, though he was a busy man. We spent much time in the library, which is rather oddly dominated by a pagan sculptured figure of a naked male, a work of the late-nineteenth-century sculptor Fabishe, highly stylized and recalling Rodin's *Le Penseur*, a ponderous piece which seems to have found its way here from Lyons. This is one of the most perfect of all medieval Cistercian monasteries, its original ground plan and buildings intact, and apart from some later additions it is wholly of the Romanesque. True, the cloister arcades with their coupled stalks of stone bursting into leaf around the capitals are restored, all but one which remains in pristine condition, but overhead are the original rude barrel vaults. The chapter house and the scriptorium have massive pillars like monoliths from which spring these pirouetting vaults. No such arcades disturb the spatial concept of the enormous refectory, where springers of stone fastened to the walls alone support the great coved ceiling.

In the refectory the series of long narrow tables was laid for supper. When it came each would have a bowl of soup, some fruit, bread (a pound per day), and a tankard of beer. Year in year out no meat, no fish, no eggs, no butter, no oil, no seasoning. Permission to take butter was granted to laybrothers by Louis XIII. Few accept the privilege. A black crucifix painted with white skull and cross-bones, *memento mori*, stood on a table before a place which would be vacant. The monk had recently died, but for one month his share of food would be placed before the crucifix marking his absence. There are, however, some dispensations which may seem to be peculiar and even unnecessary. Thus monks who prefer not to sleep in the common dormitory are allowed to retire to tiny cells, almost cubby-holes or cubicles with striped curtains drawn across the entrances.

In the kitchens a brother was washing dishes in a great wooden trough. We passed along the cloister, hugging the walls (only the abbot and the prior are allowed to walk through the centre). We entered the church. There was sunlight streaming on to dazzling white walls, and there was the heady aroma of burning gums. Little ornament mars the Romanesque austerity of the building, which is as pure and simple, and as beautiful, as it was intended to be. There is a vista of arches and soaring vaults, with colour concentrated in the high altar, in the deep-set chapels of the transepts and in an occasional brilliantly coloured hanging or arras. In one transept a graceful night-staircase ascends to the dormitory, in the other is a little gallery for the sick, leading off the infirmary. The rich brown choir stalls are laden with the heavy antiphonals and psalters, magnificently bound and clasped, with metal crucifixes shining from the covers.

Two coloured Colonial monks made deep obeisances as they glided across the paving. They were tall and elegant, and when they pulled their white hoods like burnouses over their heads I fancied I was in a mosque in Barbary.

Time passed quickly at Aiguebelle. The days were punctuated by the ringing of the carillon, by the deeper more solemn bells, and by all the canonical hours. The brothers in their sombre brown kirtles would file into the fields or bend low among the vines. Others were at work in the distillery and in the locksmith's shop. The estate pulsated with life, and now to add to the animated scene there came a taxicab loaded with pilgrims, who lunched alfresco amid the gardens and grottoes, made their devotions at the miniature Lourdes and filled bottles with water from the spring. Among them was a mother who had come to see her son. He was barely out of his 'teens, and with fresh white habit, pink cheeks and shaven crown he might have stepped out of a painting by Zurbaran. The mother could not go into the monastery, so the son had to come out of his enclosure. Now they stood in an embrace beside the road. I recalled the early Cistercian attitude towards women and how St. Bernard and many another had all but rejected his own mother. This meeting filled me with a warm glow.

It was time to leave Aiguebelle, and it was arranged that a monk should drive me to Montélimar. The monk-chauffeur was a jolly bearded fellow who had been in Canada and had served with the French army in the Great War. He left me at the station and I boarded a train for Avignon.

When I reached Avignon it should have been dark, but the Rue de la République was ablaze, lined with restaurants and shops, caverns of light and luxury. I sought out a hotel which I had known before the war, but we live in an age of transition and there is no guarantee of finding today what existed yesterday. Consequently I was compelled to settle in the Hôtel de l'Europe off the Place Crillon with its memories of Lady Blessington and Count d'Orsay, of the Brownings and the Stuart Mills. After my experience of the past few days I needed a tonic, and I went, later in the evening, to a *dansant* where I could eat reasonably and watch lots of people. The tiny floor was packed with a surging mass of bodies. Rumba and *Moyen Âge*. There was the drumming of tomtoms and the cacophony of negro music. In this jungle the white man aped the black man. Yet less than a hundred miles away, at Aiguebelle, the black man was a cultured dignified being serving Mass—he had left the jungle for the ways of the white man. Though it was stimulating to see this zest for life, this Gallic capacity for pleasure, it was all rather bewildering. There seemed to be neither order nor form. The noise mounted to a crescendo, and I slipped out. Nor could I regain a proper sense of values and an internal peace until I had walked on to the dark and deserted Place du Palais, where the towering mass of the Palais du Papes was faintly gleaming and rather like an apparition. The encounter was quite startling, rather as though one were to walk out of Piccadilly Circus to come up against the beetling walls of Caernarvon Castle, if that were possible.

The mistral was scudding about my unprotected head, deafening me and chilling me to the bone, and I returned to the hotel, which seemed to be deserted.

A few days later I left for Sénanque.

Before me stretched the Plateau de Vaucluse, a rolling-stone country which, in the distance, dissolved into the softer country of the Comtat and the Midi. The sky was overcast, and a crisp wind which seemed to be a not-distant cousin of the mistral was blowing. The narrow sinuous road, somewhere between Cavaillon and Gordes, was deserted save for a woodcutter trudging homeward. I hailed him, and asked the way to Sénanque.

His long massive arm slowly went up and he pointed vaguely to the north.

'It's over there, monsieur,' he said, 'beyond Gordes.' He was obviously curious. 'Sénanque,' he went on, '*pourquoi Sénanque?*'

'To sleep,' I replied. 'I shall pass the night there.'

'Must you crawl into Heaven that way, monsieur? It is very severe. Nobody goes there, monsieur. You will find the beds hard —and you had best eat in Gordes.'

I shrugged my shoulders. I had arranged to go to Sénanque and there I would go. After I had gone a few yards he shouted '*Bonne chance*', and I returned his wave of the hand.

The *village perché* of Gordes was now well in sight, rising in spectacular solitude out of the plain, but what caught my eye were the ancient dwellings, long deserted and now resembling pictur-esque swineries, which were thickly clustered about the area, grouped together like a primitive settlement. All were built of rough stone slabs, with domed roofs like those of the Celtic beehive dwellings to be seen in the west of Ireland. This *maisonette des champs* as it is generally called is known in Provence as a *borie* (from the Latin *boris*) or sometimes simply as a *cabane*, but in other parts of France where it is to be found it has a variety of names.

The road climbed up to Gordes, winding across the northern end of the precipitous slope which, like a medieval military en-trenchment, flanked the hill town on its western side. From without, Gordes was a Walt Disneyish huddle of old stone houses dominated by a château, the whole fringed with olive and fig trees. But the vision was greater than the reality, and once within (or on top of) this peculiar place much of the charm was dissipated. The narrow *ruelles* tumbled down the steep slopes, and most of the houses were ruinous and abandoned. The plain tasteless eighteenth-century church was somehow wedged on to a tiny piece of level ground, and almost elbowing its façade was a bakery jettied over an arched passageway. There was a suggestion of dire poverty and a hint that Gordes might soon become another of those *villages abandonnées* so common in Provence. There were several miserable-looking curs huddled up in the Renaissance stone doorways of ruined houses, but there was little other sign of life. From this bleak belvedere there were some startling views of the now smoke-coloured Montagnes du Lubéron, rising out of the green sea of the plain.

Rain was falling. I entered the inn in the square and had a drink with the proprietor, who told me something of the fortunes of war in Gordes, where the Maquis had been active and the Nazis in reprisal had destroyed some twenty houses. Inquiries about Sénanque suggested that the innkeeper and the woodcutter were in league against me.

'You'll come back here, of course,' he said. 'We can put you up.'

No, I wasn't coming back. Monsieur Nouveau looked horrified.

'Well, surely you'll eat here—it's the last square meal you'll get.'

I smiled apologetically. No, I must push on. He shook hands as though neither he nor anyone else would see me again. I took the road to Sénanque.

Presently I was in the savage Sénancole valley. There was little but wild scrub to relieve the greyness of the ubiquitous stone, and though it was spring there was no sun to gladden the heart. In the bed of the valley below me lay the Cistercian Abbey of Sénanque (*Sana aqua* or healthy water), but the sinuous road went on and on before it redoubled its tracks on the lower level. It ran up to the abbey—and it went no further. I might have reached the end of the world. The monastery was small and compact, a primitive huddle of buildings raised in that first flush of twelfth-century austerity. But for this lonely settlement the landscape was devoid of anything connoting human existence. It was now pouring with rain, and the tempestuous de Rancé himself could hardly have devised a more penitential arrival. The abbey was securely gated against the world I was temporarily to leave, and it was with some misgiving that I pulled on the bell of the gatehouse.

The heavy bolt on the far side was drawn, and I was confronted with the tanned lined face of a postulant in a black gown. Yes, I was expected. He was smiling, eager and talkative, obviously pleased by this human contact. There were few guests, perhaps less than a score in a year, and most of these were secular clergy. At the moment there was no one. We passed through the outer court, along a corridor and up a staircase. The corridor on the upper floor was flanked by cells, the doors of which bore the names of patron saints.

'Here is your cell,' said my mentor, 'I shall see you downstairs presently for lunch.'

I was now quite alone and there was a Trappist silence. The walls of my cell were of white plaster. Beside the bed, with a crucifix above it, there was a washstand, a *prie-dieu*, a chair and a writing table. On the table stood a plaster statue of the Madonna, and on the wall above it was a large photograph of Dom Marie Bernard, Abbot of Lérins and founder of the reconstituted Abbey of Sénanque in 1854; the latter, like the crucifix, was garlanded with palm leaves which had lost their freshness. Dom Marie Bernard must have had a powerful presence, and though his eyes were those of a mystic they were so penetrating that they seemed to transfix me, and they were accentuated by the shaggy overhanging eyebrows and the skullcap.

There was something about him that recalled portraits of Cardinal Newman in old age. The privy was at the end of the corridor, on an open arcaded balcony which was exposed to the full blast of the icy wind. This was *confort moderne* with a difference.

When there was a gentle knock upon the door I thought that the postulant had returned, but the pectoral cross upon the breast of the patrician figure who entered revealed the abbot. He was reputed to be a firm disciplinarian, but the tolerance of his conversation and the courtesy of his manner did not suggest this. He was a busy man, however, and since we had little common ground he soon withdrew.

It was something of a relief when the postulant fetched me for lunch. His name, he told me, was Roger. That of course was his name in the world, for he had not yet taken his first vows and assumed a religious name. He was a man of about my own age, in his thirties, and came from Marseilles, where he had been a brush-maker. He seemed worldly enough, for he was fairly typical of the expansive and voluble Marseillais, and there was something of a mischievous sprite about him, the way his eyes shone out of his lined face when he smiled, and he was always smiling. Yet he had chosen self-abnegation in this wilderness. There was little to reveal the deep well of spirituality which one instinctively felt must exist beneath the flippancy. I gathered, however, that as a youth he had spent so much time in his parish church that when he went to a cinema in Marseilles he would unwittingly genuflect before taking his seat.

At the moment he seemed to be doing all the odd jobs; he was porter, messenger, labourer and dish-washer; his duties were exacting, his obligations numerous, his responsibilities infinite and his vocation sorely tried. But his spirit seemed to be unquenchable, and he was eager to serve, to inform and generally to talk, while there was a pleasant naïvety about his hopes for the future. He expected to be transferred to Lérins, the celebrated island monastery off the Côte d'Azur. His praise of Lérins was lyrical. '*Lérins c'est belle, c'est très belle, c'est l'abbaye la plus belle du monde—les palmes, les oranges, les citrons, les fleur . . .*' And he blew a kiss from his finger tips to give emphasis. This savoured of the point of view of the aesthete, an attitude of mind which is somewhat irregular and which certainly Maritain, not to mention the monastic authorities, would condemn. But one may suppose that a monk should be permitted to choose the battleground for his own soul.

Roger left me to lunch alone in the tiny parlour, also plastered, but containing one or two religious pictures and a monumental biography of Dom Marie Bernard. In Benedictine houses one takes meals with the community in the monastic refectory, but Cistercian houses maintain a strict enclosure, and guests, even secular clergy, are segregated. The meal was generous in proportions but was largely unpalatable, soup, hard-boiled eggs with a kind of cooked millet or maize, jam, a stale giant loaf which needed a stonecutter to break it, and *vin rouge*. I shuddered to think of the perpetually Lenten fare in the refectory, where the monks were now eating and drinking from bowls, their napkins tucked into their collars. I toyed with the food and looked casually at the life of Dom Marie Bernard until Roger returned. I envied his apparent warmth, for I was frozen with cold and there was absolutely no form of heating. We paced the outer court with its border of orchids and white hawthorn, and then Roger decided to show me over the remainder of the monastery.

The windows of the barn-like Romanesque church were nearly all broken, and externally the place seemed as grim and as poverty-stricken as La Grande Trappe in the seventeenth century. Once inside and it slowly dawned upon me that the church was not in use and probably had not been for almost a century. Obviously the cost of restoration could not be entertained or was deemed unnecessary for so small a community. The structure was not even paved, and the humidity of the earthen floor and stone walls beggared description. The church, however, was one of the finest Romanesque churches in France, and with the claustral buildings it presented one of the best examples of the early Cistercian plan in the south, comparable to its sister foundations at Silvacane and Le Thoronet. The two latter are dead and derelict, while Sénanque lives (though only just). On the north one range of buildings had been adapted for the small community of eight monks, and here the medieval refectory had been converted into the conventual chapel. This was the heart, the spiritual power-house, of this lonely settlement which found a meagre sustenance in the midst of the wind-swept and sun-seared limestone.

All this time I had not seen a single monk apart from the abbot and Roger, and the place had a dream-like quality; it was like a

wraith. I said as much to Roger. He assented. Yes, Sénanque was
perhaps too small. Did I know Aiguebelle? I did. The contrast
between Sénanque and Aiguebelle, with its community of eighty
monks, its comparative opulence and its full-scale operations, made
of the former something resembling a desert hermitage. I asked
Roger about the negro monks at Aiguebelle.

'Africans, Colonial monks,' he corrected me, 'we don't call them
negroes. They are to form the nucleus of a new foundation in
Morocco.'

What of the Abbey of Staoueli in Algeria, which had been closed
for some time, I asked. (This was probably the abbey which had
inspired *The Garden of Allah*, that piece of literary escapism which
so falsifies the spirit of the monastic life.)

'Staoueli failed', said Roger, 'because the valleys and plains were
too hot for Europeans. The new foundation will be high on a peak
of the Atlas Mountains.' [1]

We talked of the little Congregation of Sénanque, of which
Lérins is now the chief house, and which has a daughter-house in
Indo-China and another in Canada. It has its own particular cus-
toms, for meat is eaten twice a week and deceased monks are buried
in coffins instead of being put straight into the earth as in other
Cistercian monasteries.

Roger was presently recalled to his various duties, and until
supper I occupied myself as best I could. The rain persisted and
I was kept indoors, and since supper was largely a reproduction of
the previous meal I did not loiter in the parlour but retired to my
room. Chilled to the bone, I sat by my window, looking across to the
sodden brown morass of ploughed land and the vista of hill and
forest which flowed away beyond. The incessant rain seemed, if
anything, to make the silence more intense. Somehow I thought of
Chopin at Valldemosa. There were no other sounds. The community would already be in their hard narrow beds. I wanted desperately
to get away, for the place had now acquired the character of an
Etruscan tomb, but to leave on the following morning meant rising
at about four-thirty and leaving shortly afterwards, walking to
Gordes to catch the six o'clock 'bus to Cavaillon, the only 'bus that
day. The prospect, in the rain which showed no signs of abating, was
not to be relished, and I decided to stay on until the following day.

[1] Actually the foundation was made at Tibharine in Algeria.

I was alone with my soul, and had I been made of the stuff of which Roger was made I would now be examining my conscience and meeting my sins face to face. But chilled limbs and bodily unrest routed all attempts to do anything at all. I could only toy with pen and paper, and my mind vacillated between my present surroundings and a *dansant* in Avignon.

After an interminable night of insomnia I awoke to find rain glistening on the window. The sky was grey and restless, and the light had an opalescent quality. The day was long, and except for occasional encounters with Roger there was no one to talk to and certainly little to do. Nor were there any events to mark a division of time, and all the Offices of the day, the feasts and seasons of the liturgical year and the various operations of husbandry here seemed to be non-existent (an illusion, of course). I was stricken with overwhelming depression and gloom.

Between the showers I managed to walk down the valley, where the great upthrusts of stone running beneath hill and wood had ousted the verdure. I seemed to be the sole occupant of this mountain wilderness and was glad to get back to the monastery, where, even though there was no sign of human activity, the pikels and rakes and other tools propped against the farmyard walls at least hinted at the presence of human beings. Where and by whom the Sénancole liqueur was made was a mystery I never solved, and I began to suspect that the community possessed such another character as Daudet's Père Gaucher, dancing and crooning over his precious elixir.

As I was taking my solitary supper Roger poked his head round the parlour door. He had news. He was to go to Vaucluse on the following day on business for the abbey, taking sacks of grain to a flour mill and performing other errands. Consequently the abbey car would be available, and I could go with him as far as Vaucluse, from where I could get a 'bus to Avignon. I slept a little more soundly that night.

Next morning I breakfasted quickly for I was leaving Sénanque and, somehow, I wanted to absorb all I could in the short time at my disposal. I took a last look at Dom Marie Bernard, and I wandered backwards and forwards about the deserted buildings. Somehow Roger's life and those of the unseen monks now seemed tremendously sane and full. They lived by the sun and the feasts of the

Church in a world which was changeless and free from folly. They had made their pacts with life and death, and death when it came would be easy enough, a mere gradual transition.

Now that I had undergone the painful process of acclimatization I was in no hurry to go. The elements and the lack of transport, however, threatened to keep me here for ever if I did not grasp this opportunity. Moreover, Roger said that we could make a day of it, making a *circuit touristique* before I returned to the comparative noctambulism of Avignon. When Roger cranked up the all but obsolete car it seemed that in spite of everything I was destined to stay here, for half an hour elapsed before he could coax the vehicle out of the converted barn. But at last we were on the high road to Gordes, and Sénanque and its stony valley dwindled into the hills.

The business of the flour bags was obscure, for Roger called at a tiny bakery in the hamlet of Les Aubins and then halted at a farm-house where he had to manhandle the heavy sacks, exchanging our two bags for two others under the surveillance of the woman of the house, who stood there arms akimbo, saying nothing. Finally Roger disposed of these at a mill in Fontaine de Vaucluse. We parked the car in the square and walked beyond the paper mills and then along the wooded moss-grown banks of the River Sorgue, now in full spate for it was still raining, to the celebrated spring. This is a natural phenomenon, the Sorgue springing to full maturity from an opening beneath the towering walls of rock. All about are white stone bastions honeycombed with grottoes, and on the face of the rock is a Provençal inscription by Mistral and inscriptions from Petrarch. Near the bridge is the house in which Petrarch lived, quite different from his Italian houses in Arezzo and Arqua. Here he is reputed to have written some of those sonnets to Laura de Noves, a virtuous married woman (so far as we know) of Avignon. There is little else in the small town but an Empire column to Petrarch, a primitive church, and a clan of hotels and restaurants, and no place of pilgrimage can leave one so bitterly disappointed as this. We were now half-frozen and we warmed up with coffee. We spoke but little. For Roger silence too was conversation.

We took the road to L'Isle-sur-la-Sorgue, and here Roger remembered some urgent reason why he should not linger but should return immediately to Sénanque. I was quite sorry to see him go, and his eyes were still shining out of his lined face when he said goodbye.

'Write to me—and pray for me,' he said.

Well, I would certainly write to him. . . .

L'Isle-sur-la-Sorgue was once completely walled and is even now surrounded by water, or it appears to be since it is trenched by streams and canals. It is a melancholy little town with a maze of narrow streets, some of them filled with decrepit sixteenth-century houses and others containing factories which produce the carpets known as *tapis d'Avignon*. In the square is the large church which is partly Baroque and which was entirely refurnished in the eighteenth century. The spandrels of the arches are filled with gilded angels, and the west wall is almost Rococo in its exuberance, with sculptured gilt cherubim riding on soap-like clouds against a pastel-blue background. I wanted here to see the interior of the eighteenth-century hospital, through which a cheerful and stocky nun conducted me. We passed through the main hall, with a good wrought-iron staircase around which hovered some elderly rheumy-eyed patients, and entered the pharmacy, an elegant apartment, no more than a chamber, with a semicircular end containing rows of original jars, all of pale blue Moustiers porcelain. These beautiful pharmacies are to be found elsewhere in this area at Avignon and Carpentras, but the nun was emphatic in stating that the finest old pharmacy in France is that of Baugé in the Maine et Loire district.

Since it was yet early in the afternoon I decided to take a 'bus to Cavaillon before going on to Avignon. The town lies on the edge of the Lubéron mountains in a fertile area notable for asparagus and other *primeurs*. Some of these first fruits were exhibited in the market, but the most fascinating things were the raisins, which had a *marché des raisins* to themselves. These were heaped up in baskets laid closely one to another over a large area, ranging in colour from slate-blue to the golden brown of a rarebit, and since each basket had a crinkled white paper containing and surrounding the raisins they looked from a distance like a mass of giant dressed crabs on their shells. Until recent years these streets were also piled with melons, like pyramids of canary-coloured cannon balls.

There was little that I wanted to see in Cavaillon but the Louis XV synagogue in the Rue Hëbraique, which the *concierge* had to open up. The rich Jews of the Comtat enjoyed much liberty during this period, and they built synagogues which though externally plain were elegantly fitted up within. They are also to be seen in this area at Avignon, L'Isle-sur-la-Sorgue and Carpentras, but this is perhaps the best of them. It is filled with panelling and Rococo woodwork, the gallery supported on fluted columns and having a wrought-iron perron and balcony. All the fittings are contemporary, even to the *hechal* or cupboard housing the Rolls of the Law, the chandeliers, ornaments and cabbalistic texts. The building is incredibly tiny and intimate, sharply contrasting with the monumental synagogues of the Portuguese Jews in Holland or even that of St. Bevis Marks in London.

Almost as far as Cannes the Estérel falls to the sea, its cliffs rose-red, its valleys flooded with mimosa and oleanders and balsamic pines. The headlands are crowned with white, maroon and blood-red villas, so bright that even this fiery sun cannot suck the colour from them, and the hot choppy Mediterranean flashes into the innumerable bays and fjord-like *calanques*. There is a string of resorts, but though some of the smaller and more remote villages are delightful enough, there is little to stay for. It is possible to travel by 'bus along the winding road that clings to the coast as far as Cannes, and this journey, with its vistas of masses of red porphyry, exotic plants and the wide stippled sea, is at once spectacular and weird, a journey into the three-dimensional.

This is indeed the best way to approach Cannes, if one must approach Cannes at all. For me it was a necessary evil, since I was bound for the Iles des Lérins. Yet the experience is worth while. The 'bus staggers around a bend of the mountainous road, and there below is spread the glittering panoply of Cannes. Its composition is quite remarkable, and its Allées de la Liberté pranked with gardens facing the harbour is among the most animated and delightful marine thoroughfares in Europe. Here, mixed up with the palms and the masts of yachts is the statue of Lord Brougham, who invented the carriage bearing his name and who, about 1830, 'discovered' Cannes for the fashionable world. That he thought Cannes a place in which to die at leisure is indicated by the inscription he had placed over the door of his villa:

> *Inveni portum, spes et fortuna valete ;*
> *Lusisti ne sat-ludite nunc alios.*

He had set a fashion for dying at leisure in Cannes, and he was soon to be followed by the actress Rachel, who died in the Villa Sardou at Le Cannet, Prosper Merimée and William Bonaparte-Wyse. But it is becoming a little expensive to die in Cannes, and celebrities now move out to primitive villages when they see the sand running low in the hour-glass.

Today there is a sense of futility in the half-empty, mammoth (and often preposterous) hotels of this area, a sense of unreality in the lavish opulence remaining from the past, a suggestion of make-believe in the ducal proportions and fantastic styles of villas and public buildings. The long curving Croisette has the most glittering sea front in Europe, and the air of fabulous wealth remains. It is plumed with gallants, and desirable women, their sequined dresses flashing and scintillating in the sun, move elegantly in a perfumed wake of Molyneux, Chanel, Worth and Lenthéric. It may be that all this opulence is oppressive only to the impecunious, though there are declaimers enough among those blessed with both capital and intelligence. Chekhov, for instance, in a letter to his brother wrote:

'Good Lord! how contemptible and loathsome this life is, with its artichokes, its palms and its smell of orange-blossoms! I love wealth and luxury, but the luxury here, the luxury of the gambling saloon, reminds one of a luxurious water-closet. There is something in the atmosphere that offends one's sense of decency and vulgarises the scenery, the sound of the sea, the moon.'

Not all of Cannes, however, is thus cosseted. Behind the cosmopolitan façade lies a French provincial town, just another *ville de province*, with its flower market and its cafés of the *petit peuple*, while near the harbour is what remains of Smollett's 'little fishing town'. Here extreme poverty stinks in the nostrils equally with extreme wealth. In the light engineering factories of La Bocca the people work for the equivalent of £15 a month, among them a number of exiles from Tzarist Russia, who go to the little church on the Avenue Alexandre III, a study in oriental imagery, with onion-shaped dome and frontal bell tower, all in yellow and cream. For the architecture of the Côte d'Azur runs the entire gamut and is rich in such exotics as the summer casino, a miniature palace, it might be, of some rajah.

The short sea passage to the Ile Saint-Honorat cannot be measured in terms of time or distance, which are purely relative.

For Cannes and Lérins are as far apart as Cathay and Caterham.
This short voyage changes the current of the blood, and rational
analysis gives way to the faculty of wonder. The trim little boat
pushed off. Gradually the low-lying islands assumed form and perspective. First that of Sainte-Marguerite, with an attractive hamlet
clustered about the quay, where the few passengers dropped off.
Then Saint-Honorat, screened by Aleppo pines, silent and apparently quite deserted. The boat soon nosed back, and I was alone.
I had more or less to sense my way to the monastery, walking
through beds of aromatic pine needles. Presently the forest was broken by a short drive, and at the end of it rose the Romanesque walls
and turrets, gleaming white in the sun, of Notre-Dame de Lérins.

The gatehouse seemed to crouch beneath the shaggy umbrella
of a great palm tree. It was inevitably locked and gated, and I looked
in vain for such a notice as was posted on the guesthouse of Aiguebelle. Since there was no guidance I rang once.

A voice floated unnaturally from the depths, but before I had
time to reply the gate opened and a laybrother appeared. He was
pink-cheeked and ruby-lipped, but it may not have been the flush of
health. I was admitted into a small single cloister filled with sunlight
and the song of birds, where red, pink and white roses overflowed
the arcades and strewed the paving. The brother seemed loth to
to make conversation, not, I thought, because of his dedication to
silence, but because I had caught him at the wrong moment when
he was extremely busy. Indeed he appeared to be quite harassed, but
he smiled gently, assured me that I was expected, and then hurried
me along the cloister and into a cell on the first floor of the guesthouse. Pére hotelier would call upon me shortly.

My room was larger and more comfortable than that at Sénanque
and more resembled that at Aiguebelle. I could not complain, and
there was room enough to swing several monastic cats. Through
the open window a pale strip of the Mediterranean rose above a ridge
of pines and the rows of beans and lines of washing which filled the
immediate foreground. It was difficult to believe that I was actually
staying in the celebrated abbey of Lérins, which, *mutatis mutandis*,
had known the monastic observance for over fifteen hundred years
except for some short intervals.

About the beginning of the fifth century the monk Honoratus
and the hermit Caprais, having studied the monastic life in Greece,

Syria and Egypt, retired to this snake-infested island, where they were joined by others to form a religious community based upon the practices of the Antonian solitaries of the Thebaid. Ultimately it assumed the Benedictine model, and it became one of the most influential centres of theology and what was then regarded as science, a focus of intellectual movement, in Europe. The origins of monachism in Ireland may be traced to St. Patrick's reputed sojourn here, and from here the English St. Benedict Biscop returned to Northumbria to found the monastery which Bede entered as a child. From here went forth the sainted Bishops Hilary, Lupus of Troyes (in whom the barbarian Attila met his match), Maxime, Caesarius and Eucharius. Honorat himself in many ways recalls our own St. Iltud, and he was a great educationist. Later monks who spread the fame of Lérins included Raymond Féraud, the monastery librarian and poet, who, so Nostradamus records in his *History of Provence*, 'wrote divinely well in all manner of letters, and was, as to painting and illumination, sovereign and exquisite', Gregory Cortèse, the theologian who became a cardinal, Denis Faucher, philosopher and scholar, author of *Annals of Provence*, and Isidore of Cremona, the savant.

Such was the new Age of Reason in eighteenth-century France that in 1788 there were but four monks at Lérins. The Revolution brought its closure, and for some twenty years afterwards the derelict buildings were occupied by Mademoiselle Sainval, an actress of the Comédie Française, who made an Ivory Tower of the old fortified building, embellishing it as a rustic-cum-marine retreat and adding frescoes of lively shepherds and shepherdesses above the doorways. On her death the island became the property of an Anglican clergyman, but in 1857 it passed to a citizen of Draguignan, who took steps towards the restoration of the monastery. This was finally achieved in 1870, when the ancient site was colonized by the Cistercian Congregation of Sénanque, of which Lérins is now the chief house.

I was not to see the Père hôtelier until supper, and it was the Prior who called upon me. He was a tall slim man, friendly and smiling, and anxious to put me at ease. He took away my torn rucksack to be mended by a brother, and after taking me into the dim church he gave me *carte blanche* to wander where I would, literally letting me loose in the monastery. Most of the monastery is less than a century old, and the gleaming white walls with springing arches and soaring turrets look quite eastern. The cloister, filled with lovely roses and clusters of oriental flowers and plants, has two tiers of arcades, a double-decker arrangement normally found in Italy and comparatively rare west of the Alps. Swallowed up by this glittering caravanserai are the dwarfed archaic remnants of the medieval, the refectory, the chapter house and a small rude barrel-vaulted cloister in which were interlaced palms growing against the walls, not exactly cordoned but having that effect. Here in these scented acres was the sanctity of silence. So this was where Roger hoped to end his days, this was his abbey of Lérins. 'C'est belle, c'est très belle, c'est l'abbaye la plus belle du monde—les palmes, les oranges, les citrons, les fleurs. . . .'

The day, or at least the monastic day, soon waned. Presently a brother smelling of garlic fetched me from my cell for supper. In the refectory I met the other guests, a young curé from the north and a student from Grenoble. Oil paintings of former abbots in massive gilt frames adorned the walls, among them my old friend of Sénanque, Dom Marie Bernard, looking more like Cardinal Newman than ever. Earlier I had noticed his tomb in the church. We seemed lost around the immense table, and we grouped ourselves in the centre.

There was little conversation. The curé, by commonly accepted right, presided, looking after our wants and pressing us to this and that. Second helpings were few, for this early supper was hardly a milestone in Provençal gastronomy, though we were mercifully absolved from the almost perpetual Lenten fare of the monks. It consisted of a thin soup, a ragoût of cabbage and spinach and celery, with rice cooked in butter and tomato juice, followed by cherries, the whole washed down with rough red wine. The curé was a stocky man in his late thirties, his hair already falling away to a natural tonsure, and his cold eyes staring fish-like through his spectacles and appraising each of us in turn. But his manners were perfect. When he opened a bottle of wine he poured a little into his own glass before filling the others, in case of ullage. I felt sure that he had studied an eighteenth-century book which yet circulated among the French seminaries, Politesse et Convenances Ecclesiastiques, a guide to sacerdotal behaviour. But disillusionment was to come.

The student had now retired, and the curé joined me in a walk outside the monastic enclosure. We walked among the pines, and here and there, where the woodcutters had blasted the boles of trees and burned the residue, there was a warm lingering smell. There was a stirring in the bracken and high grass, and along the shore limpid water lapped over ivory rocks. We talked of many things, then of music, French music. Yes, I liked them all—Berlioz, Saint-Saëns, Bizet, Debussy. . . . The *curé* began to hum. Ah, Gounod, he murmured. I dislike Gounod and said so.

'What, you don't like Gounod—stupid boy!'

I dislike being called stupid and said so. The *curé* warmed up.

'England has no music, no architecture, no literature, no painting—nothing, nothing!'

I protested. Had he been to England? No? Then what did he know of English architecture? Ah, he had read all about it. And poetry, did he know no English poetry? Names ran like quicksilver off my tongue—Shelley, Keats, Wordsworth. . . .

'Ah, yes, lyrics,' he murmured with a patronizing smile, 'no epics.'

It was quite useless. Any observation I made only caused him to caper and gesticulate in exasperation. Then his arms made an all-embracing sweep.

'The English are all merchants and Labour politicians.'

'And soldiers,' I mocked, 'fortunately for you.'

Now he literally danced, and there was an angry knot of wrinkles on his forehead. He reminded me of Voltaire's *prêtre enragé*. We continued to mock each other until we had returned to the guest-house, where we fell into a respectful silence as the porter let us through the gates. The southern dusk turned palms and roses into filigree, and the neo-Romanesque buildings were a dull gold. On the staircase the argument broke out again. Then he gave me a stiff little bow and entered his cell.

Rather overwhelmed, I sat in my own cell, looking through the still open window and reproaching myself for creating this *mésentente cordiale*. Yet surely I was not entirely to blame, and I salved my conscience with all the stratagems of casuistry that I could muster. I remained, however, overcome by resentment, by the remoteness of this place and by the silence. It was barely nine o'clock, and in Cannes things would be warming up; there would be lights and music and women's laughter. Thus do hypocrites sigh for the fleshpots. I slept fitfully until the early bells put an end to the night.

I went down to breakfast much later than usual, in the hope of avoiding the *curé*. But he was there, alone, waiting for me. He was smiling. He produced a tortoise-shell case from a hidden fold of his soutane and offered me a cigarette.

'We forgot Shakespeare,' he beamed.

Even at this monstrously late hour my breakfast still awaited me. The laybrother even apologized for the lukewarm coffee. And presently Pére hôtelier brought in my rucksack, the wide rents of the previous day miraculously mended. All were charming. The *entente* was restored.

For the rest of the day I owned an island drenched in sunlight and lapped by the Mediterranean. I explored the deep woods of conifers, and the creeks and rocky recesses in which lay shells and madrepores, anemones and corollas, swaying and moving almost imperceptibly in the clear water like an amphibious ballet. Near one of these inlets, on a tongue of rocky land jutting into the sea, stands the lonely old tower which was an outpost of the medieval monastery. It is fortified in the manner of St. Victor at Marseilles and the church of Les-Saintes-Maries, half religious house, half fortress against marauders from the sea. Standing four-square at the water's edge, it is at once grim and pathetic, its cavernous cellars and narrow cloister into which the sun reluctantly penetrates now visited only by the occasional tourist, whose perambulation of the island is limited to a short and well-defined circuit. But nothing could be more eloquent of the Antonian desert than this empty tower. Unless it be the remains of seven small chapels dotted about the island, all built after the early desert model, four of them remaining intact. The most singular of these is the *chapelle de la Trinité*, a grey rubble oratory lost in the woods, and lost in time, for it is of the sixth century, and, according to Viollet-le-Duc, the most ancient specimen in the west, having three apses, a cupola and vaulting in the Byzantine manner. Scholarly speculation suggests that these chapels were in fact the first monasteries here. Certainly the Gallican rite was used in them, and Lérins is said to have been the first place in which the *Magnificat* was sung liturgically.

I encountered few of the forty or so monks, but when I did they nodded a silent greeting as they passed with breviary or muck-rake. I had the uncomfortable feeling that I was a trespasser in this communion of dedicated men who bowed their heads beneath the sea winds and hid their faces amid the pines or in the hard upright choir stalls or in the silence of their bare box-like cells. It is not easy to be a guest in a monastery, to live in it and yet not to be part of it, to move about freely, not subject to discipline and routine, yet always conscious of them, to be in a community and yet be more alone than any monk. One is soon faced with the choice between leaving and entering the monastery—and when one has left there is the painful process of rehabilitation in a material world.

Evening brought to the island a natural calm. From its northern shores the mountains of the mainland, now shot with silver, seemed to plunge straight into the sea. The strait lay slumbering in a milky golden light, the boats merging into the pale twilight water. The monks look across this narrow strait to a remote world of imper-fections, false glitter and seedy vice, much as Lot beheld Sodom. The summer hedonism of the Côte d'Azur invades the frontiers of this Cistercian kingdom, and these island shores are then peopled with half-naked giggling tourists. This embarrassing situation is nothing new, for the cover of an old French book on the island has a delightful if naïve caricature of a man standing like Gulliver astride the island, resisting the blandishments of all the sirens and serpents swimming towards him. But even in summer the last pleasure boat must return to the mainland—it leaves early in the evening—and Saint-Honorat is left to the monks and the innkeeper at the western end, who caters for passing fishermen.

The last boat for Cannes had sailed. But by the tiny primitive jetty a forlorn woman and two children hovered. The woman was tall and straight, the children plump and beautiful, and all were bronzed. They had wandered too far and had been left behind. There was little one could do except to wave frantically to yachts passing well offshore. Finally I took them to the inn to enlist help from Louis Szezureic, the Pole, who served as barman. Louis asked us to wait, so we sat at an alfresco café table and drank pastis. It turned out that Olive Sayre was an American and had rented a villa in Cannes for the season. Her husband was a pilot of Pan-American Airways and was then based on Hong-Kong. Consequently the world was their oyster, and they had wandered from Texas to Rio de Janeiro, from Miami to Hampshire, from Rome to Cannes.

Presently Louis turned up with a fisherman who was going back to Cannes. He would normally have charged 2,000 francs, but he took a liking to Olive and, I gathered later, did not charge her a *sou*. I waved them off from the shore, until the boat was indistinguishable from the sea. Then I went back to drink with Louis, who worked there most of the time and spent only his evenings off and occasional weekends with his family in Cannes. It was at this inn that I would get my cigarettes, which like everything else here bore an addition of some thirty francs, for transport to and from the mainland had to be paid for—at least that was the excuse, and it was useless to cavil.

I returned along the shore and turned into the monastery to partake of a solitary supper, for my companions of the previous day had left the island. Afterwards I climbed the dim stone spiral staircase in an angle of the church, groping my way into the tribune for Compline, the last Office of the day. Below me were the flickering candles and the white tonsured figures bending low. Nothing disturbed the Gregorian but the gentle rustling of woollen habits. Then the last supplication—*Salve Regina, Mater misericordiae, vita, dulcedo, et spes nostra salve.*

Presently the darkness of the desert came down over Lérins.

5

'MONASTICON GALLICANUM'

THE spring of another year found me at Honfleur on the Normandy coast, lodged in an ancient inn on the Quai St. Etienne, where my room looking over the harbour was reached with no little difficulty by the craziest of staircases. Here the table of the *patronne*, who did all the cooking herself, threatened to keep me indefinitely, as did the intriguing little town itself with its toy houses mirrored for ever in the waters of the lagoon, its acacia tree lolling against the town gate at the water's edge, its seventeenth-century salt storehouses in arched passages running off the streets, its mariners and painters and its memories of Henri de Régnier, most sensitive of minor Symbolist writers.

My immediate business, however, lay in the valley of the Seine midway between its mouth and Rouen. I ultimately reached my objective by a circuitous journey on several local 'buses—to Pont Audemer, where is the inn of Flaubert's *Madame Bovary*, across the Seine by ferry to Duclair, with ships' funnels rising above the forest, on to war-scarred Caudebec, and yet a little further beyond lush green fields and Indian files of poplars and through the early summer woods to the abbey of St. Wandrille.

Huysmans was here for a brief space, so later was Maeterlinck, the one in search of God and the other in quest of that inconsequential philosophy which emerges from his nature studies. It should not be difficult to find both in such surroundings, though it may be argued that Huysmans had 'aids' since the Benedictines were there in his time. Huysmans went to St. Wandrille at the invitation of his friend Dom Besse of Ligugé, who in 1895 had been given the charge of restoring the derelict abbey. Dom Besse was no ordinary monk. He was the founder (in 1905) and editor of the academic *Revue Mabillon*, he traced the history of Oriental monachism in *Les Moines d'Orient avant le concile de Chalcédoine*, and he was an authority on art and literature. As the Abbé Felletin he is described for us in Huysmans's *L'Oblat* : 'Robust, the blood near the surface of the cheeks and making them look like the peel of apricots, the nose protuberant and mobile when he smiled, the eyes light blue and the lips full, this monk exuded an atmosphere of tranquil piety, the joy of a healthy and unselfish soul, a soul that smells good.' But Dom Besse was in trouble. He had spent too much money on his beloved St. Wandrille, and the authorities packed him off to the abbey of Silos in Spain.

St. Wandrille was not re-occupied by the Benedictines until 1931, and though some of the buildings have been adapted for use the medieval ruins remain much as in Huysmans's time. So too does the landscape, with the little Fontenelle stream trickling into the hills, the long alleys of secular trees, the vista of forest flowing away beyond the vast buildings and the timber-framed village. Curling stalks of stone and petrified foliage cling to the elegant tall shafts and segments of pirouetting arches of the ruined church, a high tangle of Gothic suspended in mid-air, while an occasional archway enriched with the abbey crest stands out of the turf.

In the new chapel there is an almost Cistercian austerity and a hint of the *avant-garde* movement in French sacred art. There are chandeliers of wrought iron, and on the low high altar is nothing but six candlesticks in line, behind it on the wall a rood, the Christ lifeless and impersonal and a little distorted. The tonsured monks were singing the Office and wisps of smoke from burning gums pirouetted above the heads of the excursionists out from Rouen for the day. These people also filled the gatehouse shop, just beyond the Abbé de Jarente's great Rococo and cartouched doorway, where they bought beads, photographs and books and products made by the monks themselves, sweets and—furniture polish. There is a touch of whimsy and not a little hazard in such a coupling of products, though if one is aware of monastic ingenuity one is also happily aware of monastic integrity.

In a Louis XV parlour several of us met the abbot, Dom Gabriel Gontard, tall, handsome and white-haired, wearing a black skullcap and a gold pectoral cross dangling upon his breast. My two companions collapsed on their knees to kiss the great emerald on his right hand. Conversation was brief. The abbot bid us welcome, and for me he had a word for England. Then he deputed a young, thin,

angelic monk to show us over the abbey, a Baedeker round of
seventeenth- or eighteenth-century classical buildings with perspectives of wrought-iron staircases and Gothic oratories. On a
night in 1944 Allied bombs damaged the west wing. One monk was
killed and several injured. There were no Germans in the building,
but there was an ordinance dump a kilometre or so away. Of the
original buildings the fifteenth-century cloister survives intact, its
great arcades of traceried light throwing filigreed patterns on the
paving. In one of these cloister walks a lavabo of almost a century
later is let into the wall, panelled and tabernacled and as rich as the
chantry chapels it resembles. There are the polished oak floor of the
Louis XV chapter house, the dark curving stone vaults of the crypt,
the bookworm congestion of the cramped library—the library which
has treasures. Brother Maurus showed us a copy of the polyglot
Bible in eight volumes, printed in 1569-73 by Christopher Plantin
in Antwerp, bound in green leather and stamped with the arms of
the Hohenburg family, the text in Hebrew, Latin and Greek. It was
for a time in the possession of Hermann Goering, the Nazi leader,
who is believed to have found it in a Polish university during the
war, and it was recovered at Berchtesgarden in 1945 by soldiers of
the French 2nd Armoured Division.

Out into the courtyard where prim mansard roofs and sharp
dormers chaperone the more capricious Gothic remnants, and so to
the workshops and laboratories with their moulds and tanks of wax
for sweets and polishes. Thus is the forty-eighth chapter of the Rule
of St. Benedict fulfilled, for monks must work, both on principle and
in order to support themselves. There is no welfare state in the
monastery. The production of secular commodities, however, is an
external accomplishment, and the monk's business is purely with
his immortal soul, as he is reminded by the crucifix which stands
not only in the laboratories but also above furnace, cooking range
and carpenter's bench.

A bell pealed, and Brother Maurus led us into the refectory,
where high, arcaded, Norman walls soared to an open timber roof.
A novice brought a silver ewer and a basin, and the abbot sprinkled
a little water over our hands, which the novice dried with a towel.
The monks, ranged in two long lines, were now chanting the grace,
and the abbot gave the signal for the meal to commence. The monks
tucked their napkins into their collars while we three intruders

placed ours discreetly over our laps. In an arc of light in a hanging pulpit hollowed out of a wall the lector stood reading from Holy Writ. Only the shuffling of the discreet aproned servers carrying in tureens of steaming amber-coloured soup and the intermittent scraping of cutlery on the dishes disturbed the peculiar falsetto voice of the reader. The meal ended spasmodically, the reading abruptly at the abbot's signalling tap on the table with a small mallet, and the chant of thanksgiving began. Still chanting, the monks filed out and into the church.

My unknown companions, I gathered, were staying in the monastery, but I had arranged to spend the night in Brionne further south, where I arrived early in the evening. Brionne is among the smallest of country townships, with a satisfying quality which, however, is not immediately revealed. In the single square the market was just folding up, the gay striped awnings coming down. From the window of the inn I could see these manoeuvres. A few hard-bargaining peasant women were still ensconced on their haunches amid mounds of dresses, ironmongery and fruit, but others were already coaxing the horses between the shafts of their carts and traps. *Madame Bovary* seemed to be very real. The inn itself had window boxes of geraniums, and from the courtyard where speckled trout were imprisoned in a glass tank one could see the donjon of a ruined château on a grassy hillock. The long street bending sharply at the Hôtel de Ville is filled with timber-framed houses with plastered fronts, and flowers hang everywhere, cascading from painted bird-cages and even from old sabots suspended from windows.

After dinner I sat drinking coffee and calvados with Gerard Raoult in the bistro of which he is *patron*, from whom I learned a great deal about the mysteries of cider and *crûs*. Here too were the *petit peuple*, shrewd, humorous, essentially civilized, and far from being the suspicious, sordid and narrow characters, somewhat in-articulate, with little knack of expressing themselves save through the ballot box, of Zola's novels. The café had the timid mouldings of what approximated to our own Regency period, and opposite was the contemporary Hôtel de Ville with perron and great sculptured figures of human deities, a little stiff, in the pediment, while open arched undercrofts adjoining contained the fish market. In a top window the *concierge* was arranging flower boxes on the sill, while his wife was hanging washing from another window. Here was *la Normandie inconnue* and the essential France.

Next morning I was on the road to Le Bec Hellouin a few kilo-metres away, driven thence by a friend of Monsieur Raoult who was going that way. The village of Bec Hellouin lies at the confluence of two streams, the valley flanked by wooded hills. A straggling village green is surrounded by magpie-coloured cottages and an *auberge* or two. Beyond this, in a cul-de-sac, lies another green hemmed in on the far side by a high girdling wall, and beyond that wall stands all that remains of the powerful Norman abbey of Bec, which sent three of its priors, Lanfranc, Anselm and Theobald, to become Arch-bishops of Canterbury, Gundulf (who designed the Tower of London) and two others to become Bishops of Rochester, and yet nine more of its monks to become abbots of major English abbeys. The decisive influence of Bec on English medieval history may never be fully assessed. Today all that remains of the medieval building is a splendid belfry tower, as powerful and dogmatic as a papal bull, begun in 1467, and some arcaded fragments of the church, while the gatehouse with its turrets of the same period leads to the former Abbot's Lodging which in the eighteenth century was converted into a desirable miniature château.

The domestic buildings are a reconstruction of seventeenth- or eighteenth-century date, for which the Congregation of St. Maur was responsible. The last abbot before the French Revolution was the infamous Talleyrand, four times turncoat, President of the Revolutionary National Assembly, Minister under the Directory, Minister under Napoleon's Consulate, and Minister under the Empire. But a few years before the suppression at the Revolution Dom Martène was there, to give us the Costumary of Bec in his *De Antiquis Monachorum Ritibus*. When the State took over, the monas-tery was transformed into a cavalry mounting depot.

Though I knew that Benedictine monks were once again at Bec, since 1948, I was not prepared for the white habit, which I finally encountered after a long search through the apparently deserted warren of buildings. They are Olivetans, Benedictines of the Con-gregation of Monte Oliveto in Italy. On them has fallen the heavy task of living up to the traditions of Lanfranc and Anselm, and of putting the neglected buildings in good order, though in the latter respect they have the assistance of the Department of Historical

Monuments. There were, it appeared, but a handful of them, and one was then at Monte Oliveto. It was Dom Bernard who showed me over the estate.

In a temporary chapel set up in an old granary the newest trends in French sacred art were again apparent. Cloister, dormitory, refectory and chapter house were not yet in normal use, and there was something hollow in their Rococo flourishes, their swags and scrolls and delicate wrought-iron staircases. In the immense and beautifully vaulted refectory erected by the Maurists horse troughs still lined the walls, for the cavalry stables were here for close on a century and a half. During the last war it became a veterinary hospital, and the rest of the buildings were occupied by the Pioneer Corps. The stalls and mangers, at least, have gone, and the chaos has been reduced. The vegetable gardens have been replanted and the fields tilled, and there are fish in the monastery stream. In an attempt at economic survival the monks have also made a modest beginning in ceramics. But Bec was full of ghosts, and I was gripped by the poignant medieval past with its paradox of splendour and misery. One could not go back, and yet the present often seemed as agonizingly unreal. There was something pathetic about this restoration.

Southward in the Orne country north-east of Sées spring was getting into its stride and there was a gossamer of greenery. Great dappled Percherons, ungainly and yet somehow graceful, though lacking the bearded fetlocks which distinguish the Clydesdale and Suffolk Punch, were at work in the fields. At the village of Soligny, where timber-cutting was in evidence, the road came out on to a terrace beside a church, revealing a landscape which, dipping and rising, was shot with a multitude of varying greens. I asked an old labourer the way to La Grande Trappe, *la monastère*. He shrugged his shoulders. '*Tout à droite*, past the calvary.' He stood staring in the road.

'They're dead up there, all dead,' he said. 'Nothing smells worse than dead men, m'sieur. I know—I was at Verdun.'

Taken aback as I was by this anticlericalism, which is quite often encountered among the urban proletariat but rarely among the country peasants, I stood listening to him for he seemed anxious to talk. He was a groom and had recently been working at Haras-les-Pins, the State horse-breeding establishment not far away. He had also worked for Marcel Boussac, he hastened to point out. Boussac?

Yes, the internationally-known owner and breeder of fine race-horses, surely I had heard of him? Before I had time to frame a suitable reply he shuffled off.

Beyond the lonely calvary I proceeded with some apprehension. This was, after all, La Trappe, a name which had once sent a shudder through Europe. The last human habitation seemed to have been left behind me. The sky had clouded over and it was fast becoming dark. A miserable drizzle soon made the thick surrounding oak woods into nebulous, grey, oppressive walls. Somewhere a bell tolled on a penitential note. Presently a vast drab building appeared out of the mist, and at close range, despite the night, I could see that it was a modern Gothic essay in Puginesque-Viollet-le-Duc manner.

I rang the bell at the gatehouse, then again, and again. Still nobody came. Then a comet of light shot out from somewhere, and a harsh voice called out '*Qui est là—moment.*' The door opened just a little, furtively, and remained so. A bearded head poked around it and inquired what I wanted. I explained briefly my business and produced a letter which was taken by an unseen hand. The door closed again.

It seemed as though I stood there for an hour, though it was probably no more than ten minutes. Heavy boots sounded on paving and the door opened, wide open this time. Light flooded out into the night. The porter was accompanied by a tall heavily-built man who smiled a greeting and shouldered my rucksack and bid me follow him. Gimcrack Gothic mouldings rose above us, and as we climbed a staircase a light flickered on the shining baldness of a tonsured head.

'Here is your cell,' said the monk, whose name turned out to be Père Stéphan, 'I will fetch you for supper in ten minutes.'

I knew that the community had long retired, and I was not hungry. I declined the supper, and he left with a short bow. I was alone again, in La Trappe, where even after de Rancé's time the abstraction of mind practised here was said to be so great that some of the monks had forgotten the days of the week, and their minds were so occupied by holy contemplation that, like the Therapeutae of old, they were said often to have broken out in their sleep with prayers and Alleluias.

Among those who came here in later years was Charles de

Subiaco, the cradle of Western monasticism

(*Leonard Von Matt*)

Mass being celebrated in an English abbey

(*Pictorial Press, Ltd.*)

Fruit-picking at Quarr Abbey,
Isle of Wight

(By courtesy of the Abbot)

The Cistercian abbey of Poblet in Spain
(*By courtesy of the Spanish State Tourist Office, Madrid*)

A potter at work in an English monastery
(*Cheltenham Newspaper Co., Ltd.*)

A Carthusian in his cell; Valsainte, Switzerland

Working on scientific instruments at the Sacro Eremo, Camaldoli

(*By courtesy of the Italian State Tourist Office*)

Monks are read to
during meals

(*Pictorial Press, Ltd.*)

The Benedictine
abbey of Beuron,
Germany

(*Edouard Renner,
Frankfurt*)

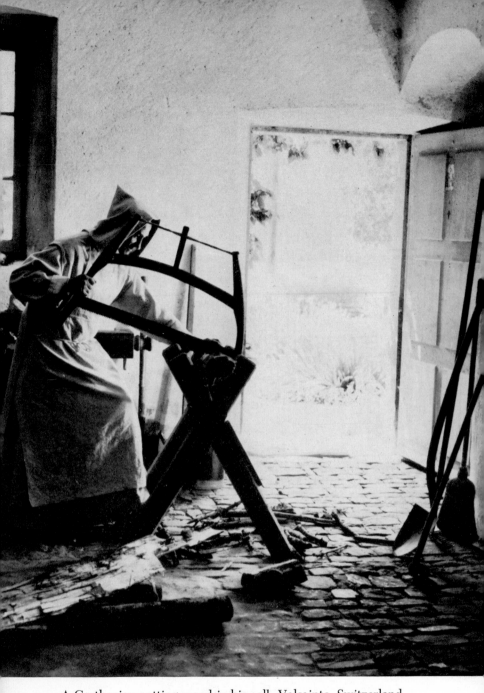

A Carthusian cutting wood in his cell; Valsainte, Switzerland

Silos, Spain. Old pharmacies are commonly found in European monasteries

(By courtesy of the Spanish State Tourist Office, Madrid)

Scent distillery at Caldey Abbey, Wales

(Squibbs' Studios, Tenby)

The Holy
Mountain of
Montserrat,
Spain

(*Leonard Von
Matt*)

Franciscan
friars in pro-
cession at
Assisi

(*Leonard Von
Matt*)

A Carthusian reading; Miraflores, Spain

(*Leonard Von Matt*)

Guadalupe Abbey, Spain: The Cloister
(*By courtesy of the Spanish State Tourist Office, Madrid*)

Guadalupe Abbey, Spain

(*By courtesy of the Spanish State Tourist Office, Madrid*)

A Camaldolese
monk at the Sacro
Eremo, Camaldoli

*(By courtesy of the
Italian State Tourist
Office)*

The monastery on
the site of St. Bene-
dict's cave, Subiaco

*(Photograph Orlandi,
Subiaco)*

Wood-carving
in an English
Benedictine
monastery

*(Pictorial Press,
Ltd.)*

Farm work on
Caldey Island,
Wales

*(B.B.C. photo-
graph)*

The great baroque sanctuary of Einsiedeln, Switzerland

(*Leonard Von Matt*)

Foucauld, soldier, explorer and hermit. He arrived on the Feast of the Trinity in May 1889 to test his vocation before becoming a novice in the Trappist abbey of Notre-Dame des Neiges in the Cevennes, amid those forests of sweet chestnut originally planted by the Benedictines, the monastery of Robert Louis Stevenson's travels with a donkey. But de Foucauld was destined for greater things, and for martyrdom in a desert far removed from this one. Three years later Huysmans was here for a week, his first real attempt to break from the corrupt secular mysticism of Paris. It was at La Trappe that he found the only alternative to moral suicide. It was an ordeal, the food of a kind which threatened to poison his pampered palate, the surreptitious smoking of cigarettes in the woods, the getting up in the middle of freezing nights, a disciplined routine by the clock. But it worked, and Huysmans was a new man.

Huysmans was at least provided with pens and writing paper and a few books, placed there for his arrival. The surface of my own desk was as bare as the billiard table it resembled. Chair, bed, washstand and prie-dieu completed the furnishing, while a distracting Christ in agony with a flaming heart like a pin cushion looked from the wall. I made a quick visit to the church. Except for the light of a sanctuary lamp it was dark, but I could see quite clearly a youngish man kneeling in prayer. When I returned to the distilled light of the cell Père Stéphan was there. There was quite a stubble on his face; the communal electric shave must have been due. I asked him about a monk with whom I had corresponded some years ago but I was assured that he was in paradise.

'Sleep well,' said Père Stéphan.

'I doubt I shall sleep at all,' I replied.

'Pray yourself to sleep, and should you wake let your thoughts again seek God. Thus your sleep will be turned to prayer, and your prayer to sleep.'

He smiled and bowed slightly and was gone.

The value of silence is lost to the modern world, which rushes forward with violence to what is regarded as the fullness of life. Yet it is silence which brings us nearer to that fullness. And so with these monks who have clamped a vice upon their tongues, for the devil may lie in the tongue, and the words which signify the life of the soul cannot be expressed in earthly language. The silence of the monastery, however, does not always rest lightly upon the passing stranger. It may be balm or it may be torment.

My sleep, such as it was, was ended by the clamouring bell of 2 a.m. The monks, who sleep in their habits, would already be rising from their straw and boards and gliding towards the church. I hastened in the same direction, with no little difficulty since the guesthouse was outside the monastic enclosure and the darkness was an unrelieved pall. For a few moments the white waxen figures were immobile in silent adoration. Then standing in darkness they recited the Matins and Lauds of Our Lady. This is never sung and there are never lights. Meditation was followed by the canonical Matins and Lauds, also recited, sung only on Sundays and holy days. I began to feel stiff and cold, and I stole back to my cell to regain lost sleep. The Trappist has no opportunity to regain lost sleep, not since de Rancé savagely twisted the Cistercian horarium.

At breakfast in the parlour I encountered the man I had glimpsed in the shadows of the church the previous evening. He was probably in his early forties, good-looking in a Rod la Roque-ish sort of way. He immediately began conversation, alternating between French and a highly Americanized English. It appeared that he lived in America, in Denver, where he was an automobile salesman and where he had gone after being discharged from the Free French Army at the end of the war. He had made enough money to visit France for a long holiday, and he was devoting his time to a strange quest.

His parents were dead, and he had been an only child. He volunteered the further information that there had been five great loves in his life, and that for some time he had had an irresistible urge to know what had happened to them. He had come back to France to find out, possibly to ask one of them to marry him. It was a strange story and reminded me not a little of Marcel Carné's film *Un Carnet de Bal*. His quest had led him from Paris to the Côte d'Azur, from there to Bordeaux, and now he was on his way back to Paris. He had little more than two weeks to go, and one woman still to find. One had died, one had married, another was the mistress of a painter, and the fourth was—frankly, he preferred not to speak of her. . . . And the fifth? There was yet time, but his hopes were fading. Maybe he had been foolish; after all, he said, American women were very kind. . . .

At Mass I saw him again, with bowed head and a look of eternity, but once outside and it was not long before he returned to the subject. It was Péguy, I think, who held that everything begins in mysticism and ends in sex.

Before I left La Trappe I walked about several small lakes, stagnant and sombre. Nearby, pigs rooted among the weeds, and beyond there were bullocks treading slowly in a meadow. I paid my last respects to Armand-Jean la Bouthillier de Rancé, first abbot of La Trappe, and then departed. Père Stéphan saw me off. I liked him and felt curious about him. Was he earnestly trying to become a saint while continuing to be flesh and blood? It was not difficult to guess what was taking place in his soul, but what was in his mind was another matter. An unenclosed mind in an enclosed body?

By the time I reached Avallon in the Yonne it was summer. In this town of granite-bound ramparts high above the swift-flowing Cousin it is the arts of war, not the arts of peace, that are remembered. It is Sebastien Vauban, the military architect and engineer to Louis XIV, who is here commemorated by monument and inscribed tablet, not the gentle Carthusian Saint Hugh who was born here and after becoming procurator of the Grande Chartreuse was sent to rule the first English charterhouse in the Selwood Forest, finally becoming Bishop of Lincoln. The Chapeau Rouge where Napoleon spent a night on his return from Elba has become the admirable Hôtel de Poste, in which the traveller may be invited to sleep in the Imperial bedroom. Having no need of such luxuries and such a dubious honour I made my way towards the woods of Morvan, discovering en route the deserted ruins of a priory of the Bonshommes, its Romanesque church and cloister garth with well and calvary hidden in overgrown fields and now given over to prolific and enormous orange-coloured snails.

The narrow lanes of the Côte d'Or threaded at length across the flat Burgundian landscape staked low with the grape and brought me to Vougeot, to whose vineyard gates General Berthon ordered his troops always to present arms. The château stood alone, its pyramidal turrets pricking the cobalt sky, its airy courtyard leading to the great cellar of the medieval abbots of Citeaux, aisled and timbered like a church, and its ancient wine presses, immense Heath-Robinson-like contraptions, still *in situ*. Here at the annual

Gargantuan feast of the Chevaliers du Tastevin there are trumpeters in hunting pink, the Chevaliers in red and gold robes, and orators praising Bacchus from a barrel-decorated platform; there are platters of sucking pigs roasted whole and a model in nougat of a medieval wine press. But now Vougeot was deserted, a prosaic enough landscape with little hint of its riches.

Beyond Nuits St. Georges, on the road to Citeaux, there was an aged *curé* slowly plodding towards the abbey. His emaciated figure was crowned with a face as lined as the map of France itself, and his *soutane* was dusty and threadbare. He was, he said, a professor of Dijon University, a teacher of Greek, and he was temporarily in this area with a contingent of orphaned children on holiday from Dijon. It was his charge, every few days, to walk to Citeaux to obtain bread and cheese from the abbey. It seemed strange that there were no supplies nearer his base and that he was compelled to hobble all this distance. There was something about him that recalled Saint Vincent de Paul, the Monsieur Vincent of an excellent French film.

We parted at the gatehouse shop of Citeaux, where an enormous white-habited monk was weighing the large round flat monastery cheeses for the casual purchasers, villagers of the region who drifted in. Some of these customers asked the monk for a blessing, which he bestowed with the same equanimity as he sold the cheese. It made a somewhat incongruous picture, yet the pattern was pleasantly opposed to the sullen indifference and stolidity encountered in the emporia of our own spoiled Anglo-Saxon merchants. Nor are blessings and cheeses the only commodities purveyed here, for there are caramels and bonbons, booklets and picture cards, all products of Cistercian industry.

Little remains that one can identify with St. Bernard and the birthplace of the Cistercian Order. Medieval Citeaux has vanished as completely as a Pacific atoll under atomic bombardment. There remains a single medieval heavily-buttressed building, formerly the library, and a small building of the Renaissance. In the former were housed those splendid illuminated manuscripts written under Stephen Harding, including the *Moralia in Job*, with its remarkable drawings, now with most of Citeaux's books in the city library of Dijon. A substantial building of the eighteenth century contains the cloister walk and now houses the monastery proper. Of the medieval church with its tombs of the Dukes of Burgundy there is no trace, and the former cemetery of the monks is now a miniature plain of potato and cabbage patches. The new Citeaux was opened in 1898, a move due to the energy of Dom Jean-Baptiste Chautard and the generosity of the Baroness de la Roche Taillée, and it continues to take its place at the head of the Cistercian world, which conforms very largely, however, to the de Rancé reforms of La Trappe. The community now numbers about eighty, most of whom were called up during the last war, though all returned safely.

Cistercian austerity and order distinguish a rather ugly modern church of indeterminate style, redeemed externally only by the last lingering blossoms of a spreading almond tree. The soaring vaulted whiteness of cloister and refectory is nicely balanced by staircases with scrolled wrought-iron balustrades. One admires again and again the wrought iron of the Renaissance, but here at Citeaux there is a sense of continuity, for the community has an ironworker whose products would be in great demand in the art jungles of the world. Frère Denis is an artist of the Rococo, as may be seen in his reliquary with three reclining human figures symbolizing Faith, Hope and Charity and in his lectern in the chapter house. In the latter, however, he was equally influenced by medieval Cistercian manuscripts, by the flowing cipher initials of the *Moralia in Job* and other miniatures with their grotesque figures branching out of a tree.

The work of studio and farm is in the ancient tradition of Citeaux, and in the self-abnegation and almost perpetual silence the rigorous pruning of human faculty has endured. I left Citeaux, however, with a profound feeling of frustration and a feeling that I had arrived too late, eight centuries too late.

A little to the east of the Beaujolais hills, between the Saône and the Ain, lies a terrain which is unknown to even the most inquisitive travellers—the Dombes. It is a country of marsh and mere as intriguing as the Camargue in the Rhône delta, with which it has some affinity. I had left Bourg along the road to Lyons, and now, at the village of St. Paul-de-Varax, where a Romanesque church stood near the highway, I struck eastward. As the day wore on it became clear that my directions had been false or that I had misunderstood them, for I was hopelessly lost on a gloomy alluvial plain. Behind me were the pale smoky humps of the Jura. On all sides steel-coloured lakes fanned out and dissolved in a murky drizzle. There was the shimmer of dead waters. Occasionally a solitary farmstead, apparently inaccessible, stood out of the flat land.

At a place called St. Nizier-le-Désert, which was very much of the desert, an old crone did her best to help me. Obviously I had turned off the Lyons road too soon. I should have gone on towards Villars-les-Dombes and taken the Chalamont road. Now there was little point in going back and I had perforce to complete my circle. A lonely road struck southward through the wilderness, through marshland interspersed with meres and forests of birch. A mist rose from the sodden ground and percolated into my own soul.

It was dusk when I found my way into the Trappist abbey of Notre-Dame des Dombes. The community had retired to their hard cots and I was greeted with a grumble by a surprised monk who, however, hastily prepared a meal for me, and, smiling now, gave me his blessing before he deposited me in a cell for the night. I was by now in a somewhat melancholy and introspective state of mind. The monastery, which I had as yet barely seen, had the brooding quality of the watery wilderness in which it was lost. I thought of the denizens of those marshland villages, and I wished them the peaceful night that the monk had wished me. *Que le Seigneur tout Puissant vous accorde une nuit tranquille.*

Morning broke on a landscape rather more sylvan and cheerful than I had imagined. The monastery bells had dispersed all the dark spirits and Alleluias rang out in the neo-Gothic chapel. Hot coffee, fresh bread and interested and friendly monks dispelled the melancholy of the previous day. Though a modern foundation this was no ordinary community. Not for nothing had the French Government conferred the Cross of the Legion of Honour upon it, for its resistance to the Gestapo in the last war was little short of heroic. In 1943 Père Bernard, the cellarer, was arrested by the Gestapo, who had to wait for him to disrobe since he was celebrating a Mass for the feast of the Immaculate Conception. Père Bernard was a friend of the Maquis; that was enough for the Gestapo who promptly packed him off to concentration camps at Nordhausen and Belsen, where he died. The sympathy of the monks with the Resistance brought other unwelcome visits from the Nazis, who on one occasion lined the community against a wall and viciously interrogated them with the persuasion of a battery of tommy-guns. The monastery was then searched, some prisoners were taken—and the monks continued as before.

These Cistercians are as much at home in the bull-pen as in choir. The standard of agriculture is high, and the yield of honey is prolific. The head beekeeper, Père Marie Dugat, has evolved a technique which may revolutionize the science of the apiary, and his skyscraper hives contain up to seven queens.

It was Friday, and for my solitary lunch there was fish from a nearby lake, one of the hundreds of meres that sprig this plain of the Dombes. The serving brother remarked that the fish was a rare dish, and he suggested that the lakes of the Dombes teemed with rare aquatic creatures. Eels were common and were sometimes eaten here. If, however, this prompted me to look forward to an adventure of the palate I was quickly disillusioned.

I left the abbey early next morning, since I wished to walk across country as far as Meximieux in order to see more of this strange country. The hamlet of Le Plantay was as deserted as its tiny wayside burial ground. Beyond, there was a single forest flanking the road, and then nothing but a flat plain open to heaven. There were meres on all sides and some straw-coloured beds of rushes at the water's edge. The silence was broken only by the scurried flight of wild duck. In all that day I came upon but two more hamlets, Versailleux and St. Eloi, and a few isolated farmhouses, here called a *mas*, the Provençal terminology, thus strangely confirming the feeling that I was in the Camargue. Evening found me in Pérouges, perched upon its hummock and looking over a landscape which though not spectacular was certainly more pampered than the Dombes.

Pérouges has a double ring of medieval fortifications, and the ancient houses hemming the narrow cobbled ways may have been built by merchants from Perugia. Abandoned in the seventeenth century, grass grew in its streets and it became another Les Baux. Even now from a distance it might be one of those *villages abandonnées* so common in the south. In the last war the Maquis found refuge here, as did refugees from the north. They stayed, and Pérouges became alive again, its houses restored one by one. In the ancient and delightful inn Monsieur Thibault cosseted me with a luxury to which I had been unaccustomed for some time. The stars came out high above the ramparts and the fortified church to which goes a Christmas Eve torchlight procession, preceded by musicians.

There was a decided cretin-like quality about some of the people in this area, and it was not surprising to hear from an innkeeper the story of a friend's *débâcle*. He met him one day coming from his work in the fields.

'I'm dead,' he said.

'What on earth do you mean—you're dead ?' asked the innkeeper.

'I'm dead, I tell you, dead.'

The next day he met him again.

'Ah, I'm mad,' said the labourer with slow emphasis, 'I'm mad.'

That same day he presented himself at the nearest asylum, and he has been there ever since.

From Meximieux a kilometre or so away it was possible to get transport by various stages to Belley, where from the Promenade a statue of Brillat-Savarin, of *La Physiologie du Goût*, looks towards the Alps, and where at the former Jesuit college is another statue to yet another local immortal whose *Méditations* marked the true beginning of Romantic poetry in France—Alphonse Lamartine.

My objective now lay on the shores of Lac du Bourget, a journey of which the last stage had to be made on foot. A bend in the road, and there were the dark granite hills sidling into the water. Below me at the water's edge, on a long low promontory, stood the compact buildings, dormered and turreted, of the Abbaye d'Hautecombe. A medieval Cistercian foundation abandoned at the Revolution, it was rebuilt in the eighteenth century in a mild classical style. Later it became the home of Charles-Félix, King of Sardinia and Count of Savoy, and in 1922 it passed to the Benedictines.

The façade of the chapel, almost the only portion of the medieval monastery to survive, is a fussy but attractive work in Flamboyant Gothic. Internally the building is a reconstruction of 1824-43, carried out under Charles-Félix, who seems to have adopted the cathedral of Milan as a model and the Piedmontese Ernest Melano as architect. Consequently it is a riotous fantasy of ornament with a decided flavour of Strawberry Hill Gothic and not a little of the Rococo. It was virtually designed as a mausoleum for the Counts of Savoy, whose tombs and petrified figures, with an air of panache, overcrowd this tiny arena. Most of the monuments are the work of Benoît Cacciatori, a pupil of Canova, including that of Charles-Félix himself, who sits enthroned, sceptre in hand, and a highly successful Pietà after Michelangelo. That of Charles-Félix's queen, Marie-Christine de Bourbon, daughter of Ferdinand IV of Naples and sister-in-law of Louis-Philippe, is by the sculptor Jean

Albertoni of Turin. It is a work of much artistic excellence and one of no little historical significance, for eleven years after her death, in 1860, Savoy was united to France. The queen spent a great part of her life in the abbey (it was not then a monastery), and her simple rooms retain their modest 1820 furniture, striped wallpapers and draped hangings surrounding long windows overlooking the lake.

The chapel indeed is so like an annexe to a royal palace that it comes as a surprise when the monks file in to sing their Office and the Gregorian rises to the gimcrack ornaments that fill the choir arches. The visitors, however, are more likely to be in the shops admiring the little bottles of perfume distilled by the monks, phials of lavender and cyclamen labelled with the abbey crest. In the cloister the ledges of the Gothic arcades are piled with baskets of beans and tomatoes, and a monk in a battered soft straw hat is drawing water from a pump in the cloister garden. The scene resembles a fragment of genre painting. A monk coming down the wide stone staircase turned out to have been at the abbey of Farnborough in Hampshire, and he it was who showed me the mural paintings of last century, by an Italian, in the refectory.

A paddle-steamer was about to leave the little jetty for Aix-les-Bains, and I waited for it at the water's edge, loitering amid a copse of trees below the abbey's whitewashed walls and shuttered windows. On this narrow strip of earth there were wild sweet peas, and on the shingle lay numerous tiny fish, *perchettes*, swept up on the stony shore to die. The steamer was almost deserted, and within half an hour it was moored beside the stone jetty of the Vieux Port of Aix-les-Bains. There was a huddle of fishing boats and yachts, and a group of restaurants half hidden by a canopy of bleached plane trees. Aix itself lies well back from this southern extremity of the lake, the town crowded with Colonel Blimps who flounder in the brine of the thermal temples, an impressive range of new buildings of functional type mixed up with some Second Empire beauties and Roman monuments. Night in Aix was a confusing experience, and the half-drowned world of the Dombes might never have existed.

I had toyed with the idea of going up to the abbey of Tamié near Albertville and then on to the St. Bernard Hospice on the Swiss frontier. A few years earlier I had met one of the monks, strictly a canon, of the latter when he had come down into the valley on skis.

So dedicated to God and his fellow men was Jules Detry, however, that he would now in all probability be back in Tibet. Père Detry was no ordinary priest. A former cadet in the Royal Navy, amateur light-heavyweight boxer of Belgium, ju-jitsu expert, swordsman, rifle-shot and explorer, he vacillated between Savoy and his new hospice at the summit of the 12,000-foot Latsa Pass in Tibet. I finally decided to go southward to the Grande Chartreuse in Dauphiné, cradle and mother-house of the Carthusians.

From the Boulevard de la Colonne in Chambéry, dominated by an Asiatic piece of confectionery in the form of a monument like a palm tree with the life-size head and trunk and legs of an elephant on each of its four faces, a 'bus leaves for St. Laurent du Pont. Mild country gives way to stonier terrain, and St. Laurent stands at the head of the first valley. Most of the stone houses in this village were rebuilt under the Carthusians after the fire of 1854. Today the chief industry of the villagers, apart from woodcutting, is the preparation of perfumes, but up to the beginning of the century the people worked on the estates and industries of the Grande Chartreuse. On the suppression of the monastery in 1903 thirty workmen here were receiving pensions after long service, so that the Carthusians may be regarded as pioneers of the old-age-pension scheme.

Beyond St. Laurent it was a stiff climb to the gorge of the Guiers-Mort, enclosed on all sides by bastions of limestone and forests of fir. Below, the Guier stream boiled over its rocky bed. About Fourvoirie I came upon an old disused forge, possibly of the eighteenth century, though it is known that the Carthusians had forges as early as the Middle Ages in this area, and they were perhaps the first in France to work with steel. Iron fireplaces made in these forges, identified by the symbol of the Dolphin in the design, are still to be seen in old châteaux of the Isère valley. At Fourvoirie too is the laboratory and storehouse of the Chartreuse liqueur, a plain building, much of it raised since the avalanche of 1935.

Here cowled white-habited monks were at work among the great copper stills of the distillery and the massive oak casks up to 12,000 litres in the cellar, like some alchemists in an old engraving. The origin of the liqueur is obscure. According to one tradition the recipe was given to the Carthusians of Paris in 1605 by the Marshal d'Estrées, brother of Gabrielle, the mistress of Henri IV. They in turn passed it, in 1735, to the Grande Chartreuse, where it was perfected in the pharmacy by Frère Jerome Maubec. The elixir was soon in demand over a large area, and every week Frère Charles would pack a mule and sell the liqueur in Chambéry and Grenoble. Rousseau, visiting the Chartreuse, wrote in the monastery album: 'I have found here rare plants, and virtues still more rare.' It is these rare plants that give Chartreuse its quality. There are reputed to be one hundred and thirty ingredients, including carnations, absinthium and the young buds of pine trees, but the secret is well kept. There appear to be but two copies of the exact recipe in existence, one in the possession of the Père-General of the Order, and the other, sealed, deposited in a bank. In 1903 anticlericalism banished from France the greatest of all monastic liqueurs, but since the return of the Carthusians it has the blessing of Church and State and the approbation of the medical profession.

There were now whips of wind and arrows of rain, though they soon passed. The mountains closed in, higher and bleaker, and decayed fangs of rock leered against the sky. The Grande Chartreuse valley and other cross valleys here form an enclosed world of secrecy, which before the laying of roads must have been a wilderness. Early last century travellers making their way with mules reported that the monastery gateway was decorated with the heads of bears killed in these valleys. Soon I had passed the Entrée du Désert and the bridge named after Saint Bruno, familiar from engravings of the Romantic period, and after passing through several small tunnels came into the meadows dominated by the high Grand-Som.

The charcoal-coloured high-pitched slate roofs and turrets of the vast monastery shimmered in a transient pale sunlight. On the green before the main gateway several groups of tourists frolicked with deplorable levity. Some of them, girls included, were lying almost full-length on the ground beside the gate in an attempt to peer underneath it, giggling as they did so. It is this kind of unsympathetic behaviour that has almost driven the Carthusians from their ancient retreat, and it was with some embarrassment that I pulled on the bell. The onlookers smirked and jeered at what they obviously considered to be senile optimism on my part. The heavy gate creaked open and a brown-smocked laybrother appeared. He scanned my letters of introduction and admitted me. There was a moment's silence from the knot of people, and then they broke out into sarcastic banter. The gate swung to, and I was in the courtyard of the Grande Chartreuse.

The tall, lean, pale monk to whom I was introduced was the prior and the Père-General of the Order, and he had spent four years at the English charterhouse of Parkminster. His own community now numbered twenty-six priests and twenty-four brothers, among them a Chinese from Australia and two Americans who were serving their novitiate before going out to a new charterhouse to be established in Vermont, the first on the other side of the Atlantic. Guests are not encouraged in Carthusian monasteries, and it was a privilege to have the prior himself as my mentor.

It was clear that the buildings were not fully restored and furnished, for the monks had returned only in 1940, and in the interim period since the expulsion of 1903 the monastery had been sanatorium, school, museum and tourist peepshow. The Government were by this time at their wits' end to know what to do with it, and it was even offered to the League of Nations as a house of rest for 'tired intellectuals'. It was a stroke of genius, and irony, to recall the monks, then in Spain, in the year of France's downfall.

The great hall of the General Chapter is hung with paintings of the life of Saint Bruno, copies of those done by Lesueur for the *chartreuse* of Paris and now in the Louvre (where Lesueur worked on the queen's winter quarters). Many paintings have disappeared since 1903. Along the frieze of this hall were spaces which, the prior said, were to be filled with oil portraits of the Pères-Generals of the Order. The great statue of Bruno by the sculptor Foyatier is still here. The library lost most of its precious books to the Municipal Library of Grenoble, but one notices splendid newer editions of Denys de Ryckel, and, in fact, a large proportion of this library is a *Bibliotheca Cartusiana*, for the Carthusians can claim some eight hundred writers.

The whitewashed cloisters, of fourteenth- and sixteenth-century date, though the vaulting is later, are narrow but of enormous length. Architecturally they are in the form of an elongated trapezium cut through by two transverse galleries. Off them, in the manner of the ancient *laura* of the Egyptian deserts, lead the so-called cells, which are virtually self-contained houses. In each of them a monk prays, works, eats and sleeps, living on one meal a day, with a collation in the evening, and emerging only for the Divine

Office in the church, a common meal in the refectory on Sundays and feast days, and the weekly communal walk or *spatiamentum*. With Rossetti the Carthusian can say

> I shut myself in with my soul
> And the shapes come eddying forth.

For him contemplation is the final and eternal destiny of the human soul.

Each cell, which in this Order varies only slightly from one country to another, consists of a short corridor, for exercise, leading to two rooms, one serving as a workshop and the other as a wood store. The latter usually leads on to a small garden in which the monk cultivates flowers, rarely vegetables. A flight of stone steps leads from the corridor to an anteroom and the cell proper. It is in this last that the solitary Carthusian spends most of his life, taking his meals (passed from the cloister through a hatch in the door) at a knee-hole table fixed against the wall, praying at a prie-dieu alcoved off to form a small oratory, and sleeping in an alcoved bed with straw palliasse, chaff pillow and woollen blankets. There are other cells specially reserved for the priors of foreign houses when they attend the annual Grand Chapter.

At 10.30 or 11.15 p.m. according to the canonical season, the monk is roused from his sleep—he retired at 6.30—by the *excitator* who rings a bell and leaves a lighted oil lamp at the door. The monk who sleeps in his underclothing covered by a light night-cowl, is quickly dressed, makes the sign of the Cross, kisses his crucifix, and takes the little lamp into his 'oratory' to make the prescribed devotions. The great bell then summons him to the church. He then puts out the oil lamp, lights a small lantern of peculiar and ancient design and makes his way along the cloister. The cloister becomes for a few moments a world of shadows and flickering, smoking oil lamps, and there is but the sound of the tolling bell and the gliding procession of men alone moving on cork-soled shoes.

It is clear that there has never been any architectural or artistic magnificence at the Grande Chartreuse, and today there is indeed a suggestion of a barracks in the paucity of ornament. Even the small church, partly of the fifteenth century though remodelled and refurnished in the nineteenth, adheres to the first principles of austerity. The traditional screen, resembling the *iconastasis* of the Eastern Churches, divides the chapel in two, separating the choir of

the monks and that of the laybrothers. Over the western end is a
tribune. Carthusian churches, however, are not open to the public.

Even by day this church is one of *adagio* moods, but now its
chocolate and black and grey tones are no longer visible, for there
is only the light of the sanctuary lamp. The monks enter, in twos,
bowing profoundly to the high altar, and take their places in the
choir stalls. The novices in their *cappas* or black cloaks are barely
distinguishable. The others are quite spectral, though their white
habits may merely derive from the cloaks of local herdsmen (who
until recent years wore a garment the same shape as a cowl, called
a *mandrille*, from the Greek word signifying a sheepfold). Now the
hebdomadary priest intones the *Deus in adjutorium*, and the sonorous
voices respond with *Domine ad adjuvandum me festina*. The remainder of Matins and Lauds is sung by the light of oil lamps
carefully shaded to throw their light on the heavy brass-clamped
Psalters and Antiphonals, one volume being shared by two or three
monks. At the end of the long Office the Angelus rings, and the
monks return to their cells to perform private devotions before
retiring to their beds for the second time, a brief repose which ends
at 5.45.

The ancillary buildings and the world of husbandry flow about
the great silent monastery. There are no cattle—Carthusians are not
allowed to keep them—and the kitchen gardens are tended by the
brothers. Near the main gateway is the hospice where the traveller
can still be wined and dined without dispensation, perhaps even
now on the fried carp, eggs and potatoes on which Stendhal fared
here (was it before he wrote *La Chartreuse de Parme*?).

Beyond, in the heart of the forest, set in an arena of firs, is the
chapel of Notre-Dame de Casalibus (Our Lady of the Huts) on the
site of the first Carthusian oratory of 1084, and nearby, perched on
a rocky belvedere, is the chapel of Saint Bruno on the site of his cell.
The desert lies all about us. *O Beata Solitudo! O Solitudo Beata.*

6

'IN SOLITUDINE'

THERE is a hint of paradox in being projected on an early spring night from the streamlined railway station of Florence into a medieval world, from that glittering caravanserai into the market which the Florentines call Shanghai, where the festooned lights of the stalls flow along the Via Del' Ariento and into the Piazza S. Lorenzo. Deeper into the town the Piazza Della Republica seethes with the crowds drifting about the cafés, and the *carrozze* with their nodding white palanquins move sedately by to the trot of intelligent horses whose heads are plumed with feathers. Nearby, in the Piazza Della Signoria pedlars hawk giant sponges in the spray of the fountain guarded by Neptune and his tritons. One walks haphazardly across the ancient city, weaving mental images out of the half-seen domes and campaniles cresting the sky and treading softly through the deserted colonnades of the dark canyon of the Uffizi palace to come abruptly upon the black waters of the Arno.

With morning these towering palaces become golden fortresses, church façades are seen to be zebra-striped, and everywhere flowers seem suddenly to have blossomed. The Duomo is a mental as well as a visual experience. Having taken in Brunelleschi's gigantic dome and Giotto's campanile the eye is obsessed by the polychrome exterior, like an immense set of dominoes or a confectioner's display of lozenges in chocolate, ivory, pink and green. It might be regarded as the Jazz decoration of the Middle Ages, and it was the first of such experiments in the area. It is a joy to look upon, but within it is chilly and barren.

Like San Marco, Santa Maria Novella still belongs to the Dominicans, though the original convent now houses both a cinema and a barrack square. More unexpected is the convent pharmacy, in secular hands for the past century. It is hidden in a side street and

there is no external clue to its character. Through a classical vestibule one enters into a series of salons of *c*. 1612 with frescoed vaulted
ceilings, Gothic furniture, portraits of Dominican priors and ornate
gilded cabinets displaying ancient herbals, Faenza porcelain and
rows of orris-root tonics from the white sweet-smelling flower of the
Iris florentina. An earlier chamber is covered with frescoes attributed
to Giotto.

Giotto's most mature and consummate work is probably his last
great series of frescoes in the Bardi and Peruzzi chapels of Santa
Croce. Santa Croce is the largest if not the most beautiful Franciscan
church in Italy, rich in such tombs as those of Michelangelo,
Machiavelli and Galileo. In one of the buildings adjoining a Brunelleschi cloister is a Leather School conducted by the Franciscans,
where pupils from modest Florentine families are taught by artisan
teachers. The art may be regarded as essentially Florentine, having
its origin in the Middle Ages. Every phase of work can be seen in
the school, from shaping the leather to the egg-white and oil
smearing, from the spreading of the 22 carat gold leaves to the
actual gilding with tools heated up to the right degree on the gas
jets.

The greater monasteries hover on the edge of the city—San
Miniato, Monte Senario and the *certosa* of Galluzzo, and we would
linger in the last, the fortified house of the Carthusians upon its
cypress-pointed hill, founded by Niccola Acciauoli, the friend of
Petrarch and Boccaccio. Just before the last war the prior was an
Englishman, Dom Sebastian Maccabe, later prior of Pavia. I climbed
thence with a local friend of the prior, making one of his periodical
visits. He had fought under Marshal Graziani in the African desert,
where he was captured by the Americans and interned in a prison
camp in the United States. He returned to find that the Nazis had
killed his brother and his friends the Carthusian monks of Lucca.
He made an imaginary machine-gun of his hands and pointed it in
a sweeping circle. It seemed unreal in this scented sunlit garden. He
apologized for Italy's part in the war. 'It was a big mistake,' he said,
'*un grande sbaglio*.' Upon the terraced steps of the monastery I left
him to find his friend. There were twenty-six monks representing
eight nations. One of them, aged and halting, took me under his
wing.

The reception rooms leading off the outer court are enriched with stuccowork, frescoed ceilings and contemporary furniture, which has been used there by several popes and by the Emperor Charles V, and with old engravings and oil portraits of the Carthusian hierarchy. The church, entered from this court, is a festive triumph of marble and sculpture and paint, and it is traditionally divided into two choirs for monks and laybrethren, that of the former containing stalls decorated with intarsio work. Adjoining it is a large chapel in the form of a Greek cross to designs by Orcagna. A stone staircase descends to a series of underground chapels in which are marble pavement tombs of the Acciauoli family. These are attributed to Orcagna and his pupils, though one is now said to be by Donatello, with richly sculptured marginal reliefs of fruit and flowers by Luca Giordano.

The great cloister is a garden fragrant with lavender and other herbs, and here too are the simple crosses of the dead. The Carthusian sings the psalm *In exitu Israel* at the grave of his brother, for death is but the great day of deliverance, the *janua caeli*—the door of Eternal Life. The silent cells are ranged about, and though they are basically on the plan of those at the Grande Chartreuse they have a more exotic note, with open loggias filled with flower pots and sometimes, as in the prior's cell, a cluster of vines. On the cloister arcades are carved medallions of prophets, saints and sibyls by Giovanni Della Robbia and his school.

We came upon the prior, who was talking about the invaders. I sympathized. The compulsory admission of tourists to a State Monument such as this must be most distracting.

'No, no, not those,' said the prior, 'we are used to them. No, no —the termites, the white ants.'

These termites have, it appears, invaded the entire city, but the *certosa* was the first victim, possibly because of the neighbouring woods, and scientific chemical action has been necessary to combat them.

A little terrace outside the monastery leads to the pharmacy where products of the monks' labours can be purchased, Certosino liqueur, chocolate, *pasticche di China* or pastel sweets, and soaps scented with almond and marshmallow.

There are other *certose* in Italy, and their founder St. Bruno is buried at La Torre in Calabria. While the Carthusians have recently gained ground in Spain, however, they have lost it in Italy, and their historic houses of Pavia and Trisulti have now been handed over to the Carmelites and Cistercians respectively, while that of Calci has become a house of Dutch vocations.

A few days later I was on my way to Camaldoli, driving through the upper Arno valley and changing 'buses at Bibbiena and again at a lonely hamlet. It was a long journey, and by now there were but two fellow passengers, both local foresters. The 'bus, climbing ever higher into the mountains of the Castentino, deposited the last forester at the village of Serravalle, retraced its tracks for a while and then shot up towards the forest of pines which closed in the head of the valley. This was a journey out of time, remote as a dream, and only this rumbling crazy vehicle disturbed the silent and inanimate landscape. Though it was April, winter still held these mountains. There was snow in the hollows and a glacial wind from the peaks. The Archiano, tributary of the Arno, boiling between moss-grown rocks, gleamed white in the uncertain light of early evening. Suddenly the chauffeur pointed ahead, and turning to his solitary passenger cried, '*Ecco Camaldoli*'.

Half castle, half villa or farm, it stands in an Etruscan glade, its walls dropping sharply where it hangs over the ravine. Its white walls and pantiled roofs have the patina of age and an unmistakable suggestion of aloofness and denial, clearly a place which is not for those who would be cossetted. Even its *foresteria* or guesthouse then lay a mournful wreck, though reclamation lies ahead, for the Government is now restoring its ancient monuments, Camaldoli among them.

The prior, Dom Albertino Butozzi, soon installed me in a monk's cell, where the mountain air was warmed by a fire of faggots hastily lighted by one of the *contadini*. After supper with the little community in the refectory (a sparse but adequate meal of macaroni soup, salami and salad, local walnuts and the monastery wine, a little sour for it had been a bad year), I was privileged to meet the Prior General of the Congregation, Dom Anselmo Giabanni. He normally resided in the Sacro Eremo higher up the mountain but was now convalescing here and watching building operations. I had, at supper, sat beside this patrician figure of powerful presence, whose vigorous black beard contrasted so strikingly with the Camaldolese white habit, and now, in one of the parlours, he was anxious to know of English monasteries, to talk of mutual acquaintances and of plans for a large-scale restoration of Camaldoli. The night air was scented with the burning pine logs in my primitive stove, and the silence was broken only by the ancient fountain of Fonte Buono on the roadside beneath my window.

The early history of Camaldoli and its foundation by St. Romuald of Ravenna (*c.* 950-1027) is well known, the initial source being the biographical work by Romuald's disciple Peter Damian, whose manuscript *Vita B. Romualdi eremitae et eremiticae vitae institutoris* was later (1520) printed at Camaldoli. Romuald was virtually the founder of Fonte Avellana, the congregation of hermits, and Camaldoli. Fonte Avellana early came under the influence of Peter Damian, but it was not until half a century after Romuald's death in 1072 that the Camaldolesi were formally constituted and given a Rule. By now there was a hospice at Fonte Buono, and this became the present cenobitic monastery of Camaldoli.

A younger contemporary of Romuald and one influenced by him was St. John Gualbert of Florence (*c.* 990-1073), who, like Romuald, became a monk of San Miniato and left it for Camaldoli, only to leave there in order to found a cenobitic house at Vallombrosa. Don Diego de Franchi in his *Historia del Patriarcha S. Giovangualberto* records that for a long time the two institutes maintained such fraternal relations that a Camaldolese visiting Vallombrosa would take off his own and put on a Vallombrosan habit, the same custom prevailing when a Vallombrosan visited Camaldoli.

Medieval development stressed the cenobitic rather than the eremitic elements, and Camaldoli became known for its scholars rather than its hermits. Among the former was a General of the Order, Ambrogio Traversari, later known as St. Ambrose of Camaldoli (1386-1439). Not for nothing was he dubbed *il famoso Greco*, for he spoke Greek fluently, translated many of the Greek Fathers into humanist Latin, and was employed by the papacy at the Council of Basle and on monastic reform, which he described in his *Hodoeporicon*. He was also largely responsible for collecting the celebrated library which was finally dispersed at the end of last century, many volumes of which can be seen in Florence. Other Camaldolese scholars included Augustinus Florentius, whose *Historiarum Camaldulensium* was published in Florence in 1575, and Guido Grandi, author of *Dissertationes Camaldulenses* and *Historia dell' ordine Camald*. Such was the literary industry that in the fifteenth century the monk Maurus Lapi copied out over a thousand manuscripts in less than fifty years.

The monastery was suppressed in 1866, and it became the property of the State Woods and Forests Department. Half a century ago it was the Grande Albergo, a romantic retreat for those English travellers making the Victorian—and Edwardian—Grand Tour, though a few aged and infirm monks occupied a wing. The more recent history of Camaldoli is linked with a heartening revival, though there was a period of uncertainty during the last war when it lay directly on the Gothic Line. Field-Marshal Kesselring established his headquarters at nearby Serravalle, but he had sufficient imagination to declare the monastery a protected monument. The changing fortunes in this theatre of war drove some five hundred refugees into the monastery, where they spent some time cramped in the *foresteria*, while among the few Allied men who escaped from the German prison camp in Florence to be sheltered here was Major-General Neame, V.C.

Little remains of the original buildings, but the *foresteria* encloses the original cloister, of eleventh-century construction, the arcades having columns with simply carved bases and capitals supporting arches. The remainder was destroyed by fire in 1203, and the existing fabric is largely of fifteenth- and eighteenth-century reconstruction. The church was rebuilt in 1523 but was restored and much altered in 1772-76. The decor, indeed, is of the latter date, in a mild Baroque, with apsidal chapels flanking the nave and a sculptured and frescoed vault, all picked out in white and gold, while there are three oil paintings attributed to Vasari.

The main cloister is an eighteenth-century platitude, a playground now for the thirty or so boys schooled and accommodated here, and the older cells on the ground floor are no longer in normal use. The cells of the monks now lead off the spacious vaulted passages above, where, strangely departing from monastic usage, is the refectory (though this is not rare in Italy and is to be found at Monte Cassino). The refectory has Renaissance richly carved lavabos in the antechamber, and, within, a fifteenth-century coffered wood ceiling divided into caissons enriched with cherubs, fleurs-de-lis and insignia. There are several such ceilings of the *cinquecento*, including that of the pharmacy, with its carved cabinets displaying old porcelain and alembics.

There is no lack of continuity in the production of tonics and liqueurs, and today the pharmacy sends out Laurus, Lacrima d'Abete, based on essence of local pines, and Elixir dell' Eremita, which resembles Chartreuse in bouquet and taste. The excellence of the forests in this part of the Castentino is largely due to the earlier cultivation of the trees by the monks of Camaldoli, and since the forests have come into the charge of the Government these trees— the great firs (the local *abete*), the beeches, oaks and chestnut groves —still flourish. At their farm below on the plain the monks now cultivate extensive vineyards and tobacco crops, on which the Government has a monopoly.

Camaldoli or Fonte Buono, from the excellent fountain there, is a hamlet merely, and besides the monastery there are two modest *albergos*, catering for the foresters but also out to catch summer visitors, and a State Forestry Department villa housing a small collection of local fauna and flora. Beyond lie the far-flung mountains and forests, threaded with silver cascades and starred with pale yellow primroses and celandines which thrust their heads through the close matting of fir needles. Slim green lizards dart among the uncurling ferns, and even in April snow lies thick in sheltered glades and on the very threshold of the Sacro Eremo near the summit. A roughly paved path all but follows the course of the Archiano, that stream which rises above the hermitage and which Dante knew, as he knew the Sacro Eremo:

> . . . *appiè del Castentino*
> *Traversa un' acqua c'ha nome l'Archiano*
> *Che sovra l'Eremo nasce in Appenino.*
> (*Purg.*, 5).

The Eremo itself is a miniature Antonian desert, in plan like the *laura* of the ancient Copts. It is heavily gated against the world, if the world can be said to dwell in this mountain fastness, and within the walled enclosure, beyond the forecourt, is ranged the double row of cells flanking a paved path. Here live the Hermits of the West, at present twenty-two of them, including three recluses, a much larger community than that normally at Fonte Buono below.

St. Romuald was wise enough to give his monks the advantages of the eremitical life without its disadvantages, as did St. Bruno after him, and indeed the Camaldolese hermits have more affinity

with the Carthusians than with any other western body of monks.
Nor is the *horarium* greatly dissimilar, from the rising at 1.30 a.m.
for Matins and Lauds in the church until Compline about an hour
before sunset, with meals taken in the solitude of the cells, and the
occasional communal gatherings and walks outside the enclosure
approximating to the Carthusian *spatiamentum*.

Here I met Dom Ildebrando Billi, a monk of some linguistic
attainments and one with a deep interest in the *Sancta Sophia* of our
own Augustine Baker. Together we made the round of the Eremo.
The forecourt with its offices, *foresteria* and laybrothers' quarters is
dominated by the church. This is much smaller than that of Fonte
Buono, though the grey and white façade and twin campanile
towers would appear to have been designed by the same architect.
Internally, however, there is a greater exuberance of the Baroque,
and it glows with gilt and fresco and sculptured cherubim and has
an intriguing rood-screen of gilt filigree designed like a triumphal
arch. There is a Chapel of St. Romuald, and another chapel with a
Della Robbia altarpiece, while the little chapter house has one of the
coffered ceilings so much in evidence in the monastery below. The
church is said to have been decorated by the gold-loving Neapoli-
tans, and it is considered by the hermits to be too ornate for their
purpose. The cells, with their pantiled roofs and high-walled
gardens, resemble bungalows. Each has four rooms—a small hall or
lobby, a living-room containing an alcoved bed, table and fireplace
(with a hatch through which food is passed), a little oratory with an
altar and a prie-dieu, and a study containing a writing table and a
small library. One of these cells is never inhabited. It is the cell
of St. Romuald, on the same plan as the others but its rooms
are wainscoted with later panelling. The novices live in cells
located in another enclosure, the entrance to which is always kept
locked.

In the summer of 1468 some of the leading scholars of the
Italian Renaissance spent some days here in learned discussion.
Among them was Cristoforo Landini (1424-92), the humanist and
author of neo-Platonic dialogues and a commentary on Dante, to
whose *Disputationes camaldulenses* we owe our knowledge of the
gathering. The first to arrive were the two young Medici, Lorenzo
and Giuliano, Donato Acciajuoli, the author of a commentary on
Aristotle, Alemanno Rinucinni, who translated some of Plutarch's

Lives, and several others. Before long the Prior of the Eremo, Mariotto, said to have been a pupil of the Prior General, Ambrosio Traversari, brought in two men who were celebrities of the period. One was Leon Battista Alberti (1404-72), the other Marsilio Ficino (1433-99).

Alberti seems to have had the versatility of Leonardo da Vinci. His published works include *Della famiglia*, a treatise on matrimony, paternal duties and the education of children, a comedy, and some of the earliest treatises on painting, sculpture and architecture, while his known architectural works include the façade of Santa Maria Novella in Florence. Ficino was one of the greatest Hellenists of his age, translating Plato into Latin and generally attempting to reconcile philosophy with religion, with the result that he was accused of heresy. He taught Greek in the Academy of Florence, where his friend Landini taught Latin. Both Ficino and Landini are represented in the fresco by Domenico Ghirlandaio in Santa Maria Novella.

This then was the circle of men who met at the Sacro Eremo in that summer of 1468, when the Republic of Florence followed the example of the Republic of Venice, and the vogue for Plato stimulated a new and intensive interest in Virgil and Horace, Dante and Petrarch. And the chief subject of discussion, after Mass and beneath the beech trees, was, appropriately enough, the contemplative life, which was lauded by all present, thus according both with Plato's ideality and the Christian exaltation of Mary above Martha.

By the end of the century, however, all the monasteries of the Camaldolese Order had abandoned the solitary life except the Sacro Eremo. The return to the primitive ideals of St. Romuald was entirely due to Paolo Giustiniani (1476-1528). A philosopher and theologian, he early entered the Sacro Eremo, where he was soon elected prior, but his views involved him in conflict with heads of other houses of the Order, and he ultimately sought and received Papal permission to form a new eremitical congregation which would be exempt from the jurisdiction of the General of the Camaldolesi. In 1523 his Congregation was established and the first general chapter held at a hermitage near Ancona, but it was not until 1667 that it was formally organized into the Congregation of Monte Corona, from the hermitage of that name in the valley of the

Tiber. Since 1861 the mother-house has been at Frascati, near Rome. Two later Congregations, those of Turin in Italy and Notre-Dame de Consolation in France were short-lived.

While the Congregation of Monte Corona is numerically stronger than that of Camaldoli the latter has enjoyed a marked resurgence in recent years, though it has lost the hermitage of Roquebrune in southern France, which in 1947 became a Discalced Carmelite 'desert'. Today there are, in addition to the Sacro Eremo and the monastery at Fonte Buono, hermitages at Fano and Fontevellana, the cenobitic house of San Gregorio in Rome, and the college or *alumnate* at Buonsolazzo near Florence. The prior told me that a new foundation was about to be made in Sardinia.

Siena on its triune hill girdled by vineyards and olive groves is a medieval splendour, with a hint of the Byzantine in its minarets and ancient echoing walls. The clamour of its streets is stilled in the Campo, that shell-shaped arena of rosy Sienese brick, bright and fiery in the southern sun, filled on one side with the soaring Mangia tower and the Palazzo Publico, heavy with torch-holders and barred windows, squatting beside it. And beyond it, like an iced bridal cake, lies the Duomo.

I lunched that day in a tiny parlour of the Sanctuario di Santa Caterina in the steep Via Benincasa, the narrow street perpetuating the name of Catherine of Siena's family and still, as in her day, the home of the dyers. The rooms of Catherine's house have long been converted into oratories, and this memorial is in the custody of two monks of Monte Oliveto, Dom Augustino and Fra Gaetano. The upper entrance is gained by a cloistered court which leads on to four chapels, the first containing an excellent statue of the saint by Nerocchio and some realistic frescoes by Pacchia, and the second, her former cell, displaying her veil and hair shirt, pillow, lantern and other relics.

St. Catherine, with Dante, Petrarch and Boccaccio, was undoubtedly one of the great writers of the *trecento* ; her letters are militantly devotional, and her *Libro della Divina Dottrina* embodies the essence of her mystical teaching. But she was, too, an important figure in the political and social life of Italy. She campaigned for a Crusade, persuaded Pope Gregory XI to return to Rome, and devoted her energies to counselling the princes of Europe to uphold

Urban VI. It is consequently a little disturbing to find her head in a marble reliquary in the fortress-like church of S. Domenico.

A local 'bus left Siena by the Porta Romana to shoot through wooded country with cypress-pointed hills alternating with vineyards and olive patches. It halted a while in the little square of Asciano and then continued to the point in mid-country where I was to drop off.

The country had changed to an almost volcanic-looking desert of clay, sterile and forbidding, the spectral humps and clefts ranging across an asbestos wilderness as far as the eye could see. Presently a clump of trees sheltered a cool lane which trickled through a fortified gatehouse of old Sienese brick, with, above the archway, a polychrome terracotta of Madonna and Child by no less an artist than Giovanni della Robbia. The lane dipped down to the monastery, its vast fiery reddish walls turreted and arcaded, and its church campanile cresting a turquoise sky above a light screen of cypresses. Like a great bastion it jutted out into a ravine, and the sloping earth, for here it *was* earth, was cultivated with terraced gardens and allotments. This, then, was the oasis of Monte Oliveto Maggiore, home of the first Olivetans.

The white box of my cell, for I was accommodated in the monks' quarters, opened off a long high corridor lined with such cells, and the window looked over the sharply indented valley, the vines and patches of maize. There was a broad writing desk for my convenience, and on the walls hung a gilt-framed picture of Bernardo Tolomei, founder of the Benedictine Congregation of Monte Oliveto, in contemplation. I was not long alone, for there were friends to show me over the maze of labyrinthine buildings. There were the Dutch Dom Gerard Kuppel, about to make a foundation in Louisiana, the first outside Europe, the coloured American (or should one say Colonial?) Dom Renato Holmes, then on 'vacation' from the Benedictine college of San Anselmo in Rome, and Dom Bernard, monk of Bec in France.

In Olivetan houses guests do not dine in the monastic refectory. Consequently I dined alone in a suite of once elegant but now faded reception rooms, where Fra Celestino, who had been a laybrother here for thirty years, studied my comfort with almost sybaritic attention, refilling the brimming carafe of the local equivalent of *vin rosé* and heaping my plates with excellent macaroni soup, salami and vegetables, and fruit. Compline with the white-habited community was held in the crypt. We filed out of the great church, now in near darkness except for points of pale flickering candlelight, into the silence and solitude of our cells.

In 1313 Bernardo Tolomei and his companions Patrizio Patrizi and Ambrogio Piccolomini, formerly associated with the charitable works of the Hospital della Scala in Siena, went out into the white desert about what was then Accona, where they established a hermitage. Others joined them, and six years later, clothed in white habits by the Camaldolese abbot of Sasso, they made their solemn profession in the cathedral of Arezzo. Thus it is from that year, 1319, that the foundation of the Congregation of Olivetan Benedictines dates. During the plague that swept Italy in the middle of that century the convent of Monte Oliveto at Accona continually went into Siena to succour the afflicted, with dire consequences, for in 1348 abbot Bernardo Tolomei with eighty of his religious perished of the disease. It was generally maintained that Tolomei was buried in the Olivetan house at Siena, but his body is also reputed to have been transferred to Monte Oliveto in 1554. Whatever the truth of this his final resting-place is unknown. He was later beatified but the cause for his canonization was left in abeyance, despite the fact that by the end of the fifteenth century there were some hundred Olivetan houses in Italy. The standard biography is still the *Vie du Bernardo Tolomei* by Maréchaux, published in Paris in 1888 and later in Rome.

The morning bells called to Mass, and in the basilica the *contadini,* the estate labourers and their wives, sombrely dressed in black, gathered in a group at the end of the nave nearest the choir. The monks stood in their richly-carved stalls at the western end, a flowing of white habits against the polished pale chocolate woodwork. The southern light streamed in upon snowy Baroque walls, upon soaring pillar and Corinthian capital and moulded cornice. The Gregorian seemed to rise from all sides, and in the choir splendid vestments moved through a smoky veil of incense.

Presently the great church was almost deserted, and one could appraise it in detail. The structure is largely sixteenth century with some remodelling of about 1772. The Olivetans were formerly celebrated for their inlaid woodwork, and the choir stalls with their magnificent *intarsio* and *intagliata* are from the hand of Fra Giovanni da Verona (1502-05), who also executed the reading desk. Unfortunately they are now badly worm-eaten. These are not the original stalls, however, which were removed to the choir in the Duomo of Siena in 1813, when these were brought in from the now lost Olivetan house in Siena. The Duomo choir stalls are also the work of Giovanni da Verona. The modern abbot's throne and sedilia were carved by a monk of Bec (an Olivetan house since its restoration in 1948). The charming sacristy with its suggestion of the *quattrocento* is enriched with medallion portraits of the founders, and its architectural counterpart on the other side of the church is now a chapel largely used by the laybrothers. Though one may love the shimmering Baroque world of light, joy and triumph, one regrets the loss of the original church with its Late Medieval glories described in the *Commentarii* of Aeneas Sylvius Piccolomini (later Pius II, the crusading pope of the *Bulla Retractationis*), who spent several days here searching for the tombs of his ancestors. Pius II was something of a versatile genius, and his tale of *Euryalus and Lucrezia* is still popular. For the later history of Monte Oliveto one must turn to Secondo Lancelotti's *Historiae Olivetanae*, published in Venice in 1623.

Of several cloisters the greatest is that wholly frescoed on three sides by Luca Signorelli of Cortona, who may be regarded as the forerunner of Michelangelo and whose best work is at Orvieto, and Bazzi of Siena, commonly known as Sodoma. These frescoes comprise thirty-five panels depicting the life of St. Benedict as related by Pope Gregory the Great in his *Dialogues*, though there are several incidents not to be found in Gregory. They were begun by Signorelli in 1497, but Sodoma, beginning eight years later, painted by far the greatest part. In the embodiment of sensuous grace and beauty, Sodoma, much of whose work may be seen in the galleries and churches of Siena, has been considered a serious rival to Raphael. According to Vasari he painted—well, badly or indifferently—in proportion to his payment, a strange and somewhat violent artist who kept badgers, apes, asses, tortoises and other creatures in his house.

This is not the best Italian art of the period, but for those of us without exacting criteria it is a glorious vision. We are back at the very beginning of western monachism. Here, among other incidents, all realistically set out, are Benedict leaving home, the Broken

Cribble, the Temptation of the Monks, the Reception of the novices Maurus and Placidus, the Malice of Florentius, the Humbling of Totila, the Destruction of Monte Cassino, and lastly Benedict releasing some chained peasants. The series is probably incomplete for St. Benedict's death is not here recorded. Possibly the end of this haunting saga lies beneath the plaster on nearby walls.

The original pharmacy, rich in majolica and other pottery, opens out as an antechamber at the far end of the library, itself a museum. Today the new pharmacy below sends out a creditable cognac, a medicinal liqueur *Flora di Monte Oliveto* (made from some twenty-eight local plants), and *Balsamo oliveto*, an ointment for skin diseases.

The vast monastic refectory is also enriched with frescoes of the *quattrocento*, and by the entrance is an elaborate marble lavatorium. After the evening meal the white figures would file out of the refectory and stand about in groups like wraiths, and my friends, after Fra Celestino had done with me, would walk with me in the dim cloister. I would not see them again that day except for a fleeting glimpse at Compline. The long Olivetan day begins at 5 a.m. and ends at 9.15 at night.

With Dom Bernard and Dom Gerard I later explored the grounds, where there are chill damp grottoes in the shelving ledges of the ravine, among them the cave with its natural bed of hard rock which may once have racked the shoulders of Bernardo Tolomei. In the tangle of ancient gardens are many chapels, some of them built like rotundas. One of these, dedicated to St. Scolastica, has a beautiful Annunciation carved by Fra Antonio da Bologna (1515). They are rarely used, and they now resemble the mournful and neglected follies in deserted English parks. Most of them are locked, but through a grille or a hole in a worm-eaten door one can look into a tiny spectral arena with pale distracting figures.

The tomb-like silence of these chapels is today pierced by the shouting of some fifty exuberant boys who are accommodated here. The *contadini* and their families who work on the estate bring the total number of human beings at Monte Oliveto to something like a hundred and forty, for a great deal of secular labour is still employed. Some of these labourers can be seen about the largely derelict and extensive buildings which formerly housed the stables, and which until recently were divided into various sections bearing tablets with the names of the chief towns of Italy.

In one of the workshops here incunabula and manuscripts, engravings and prints are scientifically restored, cleaned and if necessary rebound under the direction of Dom Mario Pinzutti, who is a biochemist. There are only six such institutions in Europe, so that work is received from far afield. In the workshop, or 'the clinic' as the monks call it, is a unique collection of some five thousand bookbinding tools, some of them dating from the time of the Medici, and others new, made by the monks themselves.

The policy of the Italian Government where the monasteries are concerned is deplorable enough, but it is better that monks should, even as custodians, have back their ancient houses rather than lose them altogether. The official scheduling of many monasteries as National Monuments greatly inconveniences the life and work of the religious communities occupying them, but the *Opus Dei is* maintained. Sometimes Government control has a few advantages. At Monte Oliveto, for example, the Government has diverted wholesome water all the way from Buonconvento, while new roads and paving are now under construction all round the monastery. The last abbot of the old régime ended by the Risorgimento was Abbate di Negro, of the family of S. Catherine of Genoa, who died in 1897. From that time Monte Oliveto was a suppressed convent with a handful of monks acting as custodians. Gradually controls have been relaxed, and the recent Olivetan revival augurs well for the future.

Several days later a burly young laybrother drove me to Asciano station where I boarded an overcrowded local train for Perugia, passing along the shores of gloomy Lake Trasimeno. A brief halt in Perugia, loitering in the Corso and the Piazza del Duomo (though this is now, somewhat grotesquely, the Fourth of November Square) before catching a 'bus for Assisi. In the valleys cypresses gave way to sequences of slender poplars, and olive groves and vineyards were caught up in a mosaic at the foot of hills which had a Grecian cast of melancholy beauty and the same purity of modelling. This bright Umbrian landscape is perhaps best seen in early spring, when every line is revealed like a thread of silver and there is a curiously Pre-Raphaelite look about it.

The hill town of Assisi is visible from afar, and I alighted at the outlying village that has grown about the Franciscan monastery of Santa Maria degli Angeli, where I was to be lodged for a few days.

The vast basilica was begun to designs by Vignola, one of the leaders of the Baroque, in the sixteenth century, though much of the interior was rebuilt after the earthquake of 1832. It has some features of interest, but everything is dwarfed into insignificance by the tiny and archaic chapel of the Porziuncola, the Sion of the Franciscan world, for it is the very oratory of St. Francis himself, once lost in the forest but now built about with ostentation. Below, in the crypt, lies his death cell.

At Santa Maria degli Angeli there is a hospice for both sexes. Fra Paolo, a jovial and stocky little friar, greeted me and showed me into my room off a long corridor. The original convent refectory, a frescoed hall, now served as both refectory and lounge for guests. Writing materials, timetables and magazines were provided on a table. The place was surprisingly full, and Italian and French pilgrims, women predominating, were here in strength. A French Franciscan arrived shepherding his flock of excited and voluble women. At supper everyone stood to say grace, and then fell to on generous portions of *minestrone*, spaghetti, roast veal and potatoes, followed by cake, fruit and local wine in plenty. Only a narrow cloister divided this abundance from abstinence. Fra Paolo, ever smiling, loquacious and quick in movement, directed his servers with military precision; one might have thought him a worldly friar did one not catch him unawares in the church, motionless in prayer, head bent, his knees on the hard flagstones. He seemed always pleased with life. I told him so. He smiled.

'*Qui si è contenti*—here one is happy, *signore*.'

It was Easter. Assisi lay dark upon its hill. Late into the night of Maundy Thursday the people of Santa Maria degli Angeli flocked into the basilica. They came out of the Cinema Modernissimo, the cafés and the barbers' shops. They loitered outside the butcher's shop dressed with flowers, with its notice *Buona Pasqua* and, in the open doorway, a beribboned live black lamb in a basket laid upon a bed of grass. Outside a decaying Renaissance building the village band could be heard practising for the morrow. In a café bar the television screen was interpreting the Passion from Italian frescoes. A few customers sat entranced, a few played cards, and two were lulled into sleep, pillowing their heads upon their arms across the table. The Passion went on to its bitter end, and the café was silent save for the occasional hissing of steam in the *espresso* coffee machine.

On the morning of Good Friday Santa Maria degli Angeli and Assisi went about their normal business. Carpenters were making great cart wheels. Women balanced giant Easter cakes upon their heads. Painted carts drawn by oxen or mules trundled along the hot white road into Assisi. The little town swarmed with people parading before the haunting Giottos and Cimabues in the monastery church of San Francesco terraced upon the flank of the stony hill. These people made their obeisances before the tomb of Saint Francis, who lies surrounded by his henchmen Ruffino, Angelo and Masseo in the dark crypt with its great silver lamps, and then they went on to Santa Chiara at the other end of the town to kneel before the age-blackened body of Saint Clare, sister in poverty of Francis and first abbess of the Order she founded. They wandered among the churches with their rose windows and their balconied lofts like opera boxes. They noticed, perhaps, the muleteers, the stonecutters and the bearded craftsman in the little majolica factory. Down among the olive groves they found the convent of S. Damiano, where Francis had written the 'Canticle to the Sun', and on the stony heights of Monte Subiaso they were given a vision of the medieval world in the hermitage of the Carceri.

Overnight the Holy Sepulchres in all the town churches had been stripped of the jewelled candlelights and the massed glowing flowers, and these chapels now lay sombre and stark. In the lower church of San Francesco the life-size figure of the crucified Christ, covered with a thin black veil, rested on a gilded catafalque draped with black velvet. At sunset a procession arrived from the cathedral with clergy and Confraternities carrying the image of the Sorrowful Mother in search of her dead Son. The streets were now lined with people. There were no lights in the town, but high on all the walls flames of burning tallow in iron sconces sizzled and flared in the breeze. The waiting crowds flowed from the gates of San Francesco.

Presently the procession returned from the monastery to the cathedral. It was led by a drummer beating a muffled drum, followed by the crucifix borne aloft. Then came the clergy and Confraternities in their brilliant coloured capes, each carrying a long lighted candle. And now came the *Crociferi* or cross-bearers, the barefoot penitents in their *cagoules* or hoods with slits pierced for the eyes, with halters about their necks, each bent under the weight of an immense heavy cross. Choirboys carried the emblems of the

Passion. The only sounds were those of the muffled drum, the clap-clap of sandals and the sizzling of burning fat in the sconces. The bier of the dead Christ was followed by the figure of the Madonna, thus interpreting the medieval legend that the latter, afflicted and unconsoled, searched for her dead Son on a night in spring. From a detailed description of the procession written in 1300 (preserved in the archives of the Confraternity of St. Stephen) it is evident that here is the medieval procession complete in every detail.

Finally there came the friars and their flocks and the pilgrims, all singing on the wind. The procession, carrying me with it, surged through the narrow streets, along the Via San Francesco, the Via del Seminario, the Via Portica, beneath the ancient archway now surmounted with an illuminated cross, and into the little Piazza del Commune. Diadems of candlelight sparkled high on balconies and window-ledges. Nuns stood grouped about their open convent doors. In the still open shops could be seen rich interiors not noticed by day—an original eighteenth-century pharmacy, ornate wrought-iron lamps in a butcher's shop.

In the Piazza even the clock face on the tower of the Roman temple of Minerva was in darkness, and lighted sconces in the portico touched the antique columns with silver. (One notices a decided change in public taste since the time of Goethe, who visited Assisi solely to see the Minerva, completely ignoring San Francesco —today it is the Minerva that is unfairly cold-shouldered.) The procession now climbed the hillside and disappeared into the precincts of the cathedral. Assisi switched on its lights, and once more the cafés began to hum.

Down on the plain in the semi-darkness of Santa Maria degli Angeli things were only just beginning. The great west doors of the basilica were thrown open, revealing the tiny primitive chapel of the Porziuncola like a barque afloat on this wide Baroque sea. Out of the darkness of the village came the halting strains of the local band. As ten o'clock chimed a procession entered the basilica.

The pattern was much the same as at San Francesco, but here there were no penitents. As before, the Confraternities, splendidly habited, and the bier of the dead Christ surrounded by a guard of honour carrying magnificent lamp-standards. The band, reading by candlelight, played the procession in. Then came the friars of Santa

Maria degli Angeli, carrying intriguing little lanterns of coloured parchment. The bier and the Madonna came to rest before the Porziuncola. The friars, Fra Paolo among them, still with their lanterns, stood in a singing group. The people of Santa Maria made their last orisons. Gradually the basilica emptied. Almost the last to pay his tribute was the local Chief of Police. Then the great doors closed to. Presently all Santa Maria degli Angeli lay in darkness.

The streamlined C.I.T. coach flashed along the road to Rome. Foligno, Trevi, Spoleto, one grey rock-bound hill-town after another, were left behind until the road navigated a series of valleys with dried-up river beds and sparse foliage. When night fell there were but half a dozen passengers, and the coach hurtled alarmingly through the darkness. It was a long drive. The stewardess curled herself up on the back seat and tried to sleep for a while. There was a brief halt in the warm lighted oasis of Terni. Furtively, almost reluctantly, Rome gathered shape as we sped through its suburbs.

Now the last passenger had disembarked, and the stewardess had jumped off at the company's offices, leaving instructions with the driver to drop me at my destination. This, however, was by no means certain, though I told the driver to take me to the monastery of San Gregorio. That was easier said than done, and the driver, weaving through Rome's crowded streets, halted every few moments to shout an inquiry at passers-by. Finally he pulled up abruptly and threw out his arms in despair.

'It is impossible, *signore*.'

'Very well, drop me here. I'll make my own way.'

Inquiries from several shopkeepers eventually established me on the dark and deserted Coelian hill. Two white spectral figures, obviously Camaldolese monks, flitted by. A bend in the road, and I was climbing the wide flight of steps and passing into the colonnaded court of San Gregorio. A vestibule door was ajar, and there was a glimpse of white figures along a tiled passage. Presently a monk with a sharp jet-black beard jutting from his white cowl, a startling figure which in the gloom of the court was decidedly Moorish, came out with a lantern and peeped at my letter of introduction, to which I added a verbal message from Camaldoli. He seemed extremely suspicious and finally shook his head.

'We have no room. Tomorrow, perhaps, or the next day.'

And with that he, too, disappeared down the steps on what must have been a prescribed nocturnal exercise for the community.

Thus abandoned, I was compelled to wander into the night. A road below the monastery brought me face to face with the Colosseum, a dark tyrannical monster tiered with patches of sky showing through its galleried apertures. From it flowed Mussolini's broad Via dell' Impero, cut through the ancillary buildings of the Roman Forum, and even in the darkness the capitals and broken columns could be distinguished. Fortunately the Olivetan monastery of S. Francesca Romana was at hand. Dom Bernard of Monte Oliveto had suggested that I might call there. Beyond the immense arches of Constantine's basilica, however, the convent lay in utter darkness and there was not the slightest sign of life. Either the bell no longer worked or the place was deserted.

I looked about for a *pensione* and entered the first to be encountered, just off the Via dell' Impero. As I stepped inside a woman hissed and leered from the shadows. The place was small and shabby but it would do. The fat *padrone* took me up a narrow staircase and into a tight room. He threw wide the window.

'There, *signore*, the finest view in Rome.'

It may well have been. The Vittorio Emmanuele monument, its lofty colonnades and flying chariots floodlighted, stood out like a vast piece of gleaming confectionery, and about it the tall columns of the Forum rose in a well of soft light. Later I mingled with the crowds along the Corso.

The next day I set out for Tre Fontane, calling on the way at the Benedictine basilica of San Paolo Fuori le Mura, which as its name implies is, or was, outside the walls of Rome. Some of its magnificence is little more than a century old, but the medieval cloister with its twisted shafts and its mosaics by the Cosmati, is intact. Peasants stood bathed in the golden light and they swarmed about the entrance to the sacristy to see priests about parochial matters or to make offerings. Somewhere here may still lie the remains of St. Paul, whose body was placed by Constantine in a coffin of solid bronze and around which the first church here was built. This much is asserted in the *Liber Pontificalis*, and when the archaeologist Lanciani descended into the tomb in 1891 he found a marble slab engraved with the words Paulo Apostolo Mart.

From here the Via Laurentina flows into the country. In the

distance are the deserted colonnades and half-finished pavilions of
Mussolini's exhibition buildings, a monument of Fascism and
political bankruptcy. A wooded lane leads to the abbey of Tre
Fontane, the once deserted fever-ridden marshland where St. Paul
was led to execution, and where three fountains are said to mark the
places where the martyr's head fell. In 1868 the estate was given to
some French Trappists (though the community has since acquired
Italian characteristics). They reclaimed this wilderness devastated
by malaria, and in so doing thirty of their number perished. The
heady scent of the eucalyptus trees they planted is everywhere, and
the dried leaves are used in the preparation of liqueurs and tonics,
chief of which is Eucalyptine, a satisfying concoction once one has
got over the initial taste of cough drops. There is also Kinol-Trap,
made of old Marsala, quinine and eucalyptus, and an aromatic
vinegar. Olive oil, honey and chocolate are other monastic products,
while an annual total of some forty tons of grain is, or was until
recently, given to the Government, in addition to the daily distribu-
tion of about one hundred gallons of milk to local children and
infirm.

Beyond the ancient gateway, groves of these health-giving trees
shade three chapels, the largest of them partly medieval, now the
monastic church, the second a Renaissance circular building and the
third, with classical façade, housing the three fountains, each now
covered by a small altar. A knot of people loitered about the garden.
It was Easter Sunday.

At the gatehouse I inquired if I might be given a room. A
bearded and somewhat irate monk gave me not only a chilly reception but almost what might best be described in American slang as a
'grilling'. Why had I not written? Why did I want to stay there?
Where had I come from and where was I going? This embarrassing
monologue—for I was given little opportunity to say anything—was
ended by an interruption from a passer-by who hovered at the open
door.

'What seems to be the trouble?' he asked, in English. I told him.
He uttered a few words to the monk, took my arm and gently but
firmly led me away.

'They are not kind here,' he said simply.

He was of middle height, stocky, spruce. His name was (let us
say) Richard Jackson, he was an Australian, and he was not yet

thirty. He had left Australia to become a Trappist at Tre Fontane. He was there for five years but had recently left before taking his final vows, for he felt that his vocation lay elsewhere. He was now living in Rome on what remained of his dwindling 'bank roll', and he had come out here on one of his periodical visits to look up old acquaintances. If all this surprised me the rest of his story was quite incredible, for he said that he was founding a new religious Order.

'Let's eat. We can talk about it,' said Jackson.

We lunched at a nearby workers' restaurant on the edge of the monastery estate. Jackson knew everyone and was shaking hands all round. Over the spaghetti and rough local wine he talked, crisply and with conviction. He held strong views on the wealth of the Church and he was an ardent advocate of what he termed White Communism. St. Francis, *il poverello*, might have found in him a strong henchman, but Jackson was not interested in twentieth-century Franciscanism. He did, however, wish to take religion into the world, into the homes of the people. He had drawn up in manuscript provisional Constitutions based on the teaching of St. Marie-Louis de Montfort and designed for families living in groups and under vows. The Order, or more correctly Institution, was to be called The Company of Mary, and it would have three branches—a Secular Society, a Families Society and a Regular Society.

No one would ever have associated such a man with such a project. Worldly, even slick, with more of a dance musician than a mystic in his appearance, it was incredible that he was spending his meagre savings and the whole of his time daily interviewing priests and others to gain official support.

After lunch we called at the Workers' Social Centre, the club-house of the *contadini* who work on the abbey estate, where some thirty families are employed. Five years at the monastery had made Jackson well known and obviously well liked. In the simple club room most of the young men were playing billiards. The president was the former abbey carpenter, a likeable young firebrand who had fallen out with his employers.

'This is Giovanni,' said Jackson.

'*Buon giorno.*'

The conversation made it clear that all these workers were Communists—except on Sundays and feast days. Giovanni opened a bottle of the abbey *liquori* and we toasted each other. The Pope

was about to give his annual Easter Sunday address from the balcony
of St. Peter's, and it was being broadcast.

'Perhaps you would like to hear it, *signore*,' said Giovanni.

He switched on. The words came slowly, gently, over the loud-
speaker. Jackson translated patches of it for me.

'A new day begins to dawn, and the darkness of travail and
misery shall soon be dispelled. . . .'

Giovanni switched off.

'*Papa politico* always says the same things,' he smiled.

Jackson had not yet finished looking up his friends, and now we
went to the nearby Grotto of the Apparition, one of the puzzolano
pits with which the hills about the abbey are honeycombed. At the
entrance he shook hands with the custodian. Benches had been
placed in the enclosure, and the grotto itself, now containing a
statue of the Madonna, was railed off. Jackson explained that in
1947 a child had seen the Madonna here, and the miracle was now
recognized by the Church.

'It used to be called the Grotto of Sin, for the German soldiers
used to take the girls into it.'

There was a handful of pilgrims. A woman kneeled, sobbing
and almost hysterical, while she urged her daughter to scoop out
handfuls of earth from between the bars.

'Maudlin sentiment,' growled Jackson, though he clearly
believed in the miracle.

We caught a 'bus into town, and since I was still in search of
lodgings Jackson suggested that I go with him to his own retreat
with the Piccole Suore della Sacra Familia in the Viale Vaticano.
The convent of the Little Sisters of the Holy Family turned out to
be a nineteenth-century villa facing the high precinct wall of the
Vatican. Here, after close scrutiny by Sister Maddalena, whose soft
graceful beauty allied to strength and purpose somehow reminded
me of a Hollywood film star, I was given a spacious room for a few
days. There were no demands beyond being in by a certain time at
night, for the gate was always locked and had to be opened by one
of the nuns, all of whom rose at 5 a.m. Even this, however, gave way
to an arrangement whereby I could enter another way without disturbing anyone.

I saw but little more of Jackson, and that mostly in the evenings,
when we would exchange confidences and he would tell me of his

interviews to further his project. The days were filled with wanderings among antique columns and marble basilicas and Palladian
palazzos and the still more ancient odours of poverty.

Soon I was being carried across the Campagna on my way to
Subiaco. The cowboys, the water buffaloes and the fields of Indian
corn have gone, and this is now a ramshackle country in which
industry is oddly mixed with a few ploughing oxen and patches of
parched waste land. The vague blue shapes of Tivoli on the edge of
the Sabine hills gradually became tangible, and suddenly we were
there, sweeping along the avenues of plane trees into the town, the
Roman Tiber praised by Horace. Any romantic imaginings, however, any visions of Augustus Hare, were smothered by the new
civilization superimposed here, by the noisy motor-scooters and the
hoardings. From the road nothing was visible of the temples and
cascades, the Villa d'Este and the luxuriant gardens. Rather did
I think of those Camaldolese monks, no longer here, who were
visited by Lamennais, who in his *Affaires de Rome* referred to these
monks at their devotions, still and silent, 'giving no outward sign of
life, wrapped in their long white cloaks, like the praying statues of
old tombs'.

In Subiaco itself swarthy men were riding mules laden with
panniers. Women walked gracefully balancing heavy baskets and
even milk churns upon their heads. Beyond the town the road
followed the banks of the Anio, shot through a narrow gorge, turned
sharply by an old bridge and climbed the brown mountainside of the
valley, surrounded by olive groves, fields of maize and vines that
twisted from tree to tree. On these higher rocky slopes a few scattered ilex trees and oaks found a precarious sustenance. A zigzag
road led up to the abbey.

In the abbey square goats and donkeys were tethered, munching
greedily. My arrangements had already been made, so that a monk
soon conducted me from the porter's lodge through a cloister where
crowns of ivy festooned the columns and into the guesthouse. The
abbey of Santa Scholastica was one of twelve founded by St.
Benedict in the neighbourhood. Actually, however, the present
buildings of Santa Scholastica embody the remains of three Benedictine monasteries, the first, in which I was lodged, being largely
an eighteenth-century reconstruction, the second rebuilt in the
Gothic, while of the third there remains little more than a small

Romanesque cloister with mosaics of the school of the Cosmati. The
abbey church has a Romanesque campanile, but the interior is a dull,
grey, classical platitude.

The history of the monastery is as violent as that of Subiaco,
with which its fortunes were linked. We have earlier observed that
Benedict was compelled to flee to Cassino. His successors here seem
to have been tyrants, abbots who became barons and held both temporal and spiritual power. During the great Schism the Avignon
pope sent a friend of his as abbot. The latter established a brothel in
the monastery and gathered about him monks of a like sensuality.
On his death the ascetic François Adhemar became abbot, and he
forthwith hanged seven of the offending monks upside down over a
slow fire. The same abbot had fifteen young men of the town hung
on gibbets for mildly insulting the monks. The reaction of the
townspeople was swift and terrible; they set fire to the monastery,
killed the monks and threw the abbot out of a window. The reign of
the Colonna family at Subiaco was as odious as that of the Borgias,
and it was during this period that the Cenci matricide of Shelley's
play took place at Subiaco. The last Cardinal-abbot of the Colonna
dynasty lived here openly with his mistress Arthemise, who replaced
him in charge of the abbey during his absence. The feudal tyranny of
the Cardinal-abbots of Subiaco lasted until the middle of the
eighteenth century. It is a sad story, and it is even sadder that it
belongs to a terrain where the Benedictine ideal was born. Yet no
one knew better than Benedict how fallible is man.

I had found my way into a workshop with a printing press,
which recalled the fact that in 1465 the Germans Arnold Pannartz
and Conrad Schweinheim printed here the first book published in
Italy. Nearby was the pharmacy, filled with mysterious bottles,
phials and relics and a skull or two. The brother in charge noticed
my declining hair and cried out, too joyfully, I thought, 'Un calvo—
we have just the thing.' He produced a bottle of *Aqua di Betulla*, an
old scalp tonic made from the bark of birch trees. I looked at his own
shriven crown but realized that monastic ordinance encourages hair
only on the chin and not on the pate.

A bell tolled for dinner. The refectory was small and overcrowded. I sat beside the high table at which were seated two abbots,
Dom Emmanuel Caronti, Abbot-General of the Cassinese Congregation, to which this monastery belongs, and Dom Laurence

Salvi, abbot of Santa Scholastica, who being an abbot *nullius* (having
the rights and privileges of a bishop) wore a purple *zuchetto* instead
of the black one common to most abbots. The food was frugal but
adequate, and I noticed that many of the monks seemed to have a
dispensation from flesh meat.

Afterwards I wandered about the gardens, the boxwood hedges,
lavender trees and fishponds, until a storm blew up and fell on the
abbey with considerable force. As I stood talking to Dom Emmanuel
in the cloister, howling freezing winds shattered a glass door at our
feet.

Next morning, after taking *mixtum* (bread broken in weak coffee
and hot milk) with the monks, I climbed up to the Sacro Speco or
sacred cave, the little monastery built over St. Benedict's cell in the
rock, the cradle of western monachism. It hangs on the edge of a
towering cliff, indeed it is fastened to the very face of the rock, like
a hanging convent in Palestine or on Mount Athos, with great
buttressing arches dropping to a patch of garden. Upward beyond
the ilex trees, where the raven (Benedict's own symbol) croaks, and
along the mounting steps to the narrow ledge where is the entrance
to the grotto.

The caves, converted into chapels, are almost one upon the
other, and in the dim light of candles and sanctuary lamps the
medieval frescoes by an unknown master glow with a smouldering
fire. In Benedict's own cave a figure of the saint, attributed to no less
a sculptor than Bernini, contemplates the cross. The little monastery
is tenanted by a handful of solitaries who leave the abbey below for
specified periods to lead a stricter more eremitical life, so that it
recalls the Sacro Eremo of Camaldoli. The cells are virtually small
cottages, and the monks eat and sleep and study here, each cultivating a little garden and the flowers arranged along the window sills,
and having no other company than, perhaps, a pet canary.

In this area is the medieval Basilian abbey of Grottaferrata, one
of the extremely few monasteries in Italy which, though owing
allegiance to the Pope, still preserve the rites of the Greek Orthodox
Church. There are, too, the Cistercian abbeys of Casamari and
Fossanuova [1] on the edge of the Pontine Marshes. The latter was
almost the earliest Cistercian monastery in Italy, and Thomas
Aquinas died there. There was little time to see all these, and I

<hr>

[1] Now Franciscan.

decided to go straight to Monte Cassino. It was necessary to be in Subiaco at an alarmingly early hour, as I complained to one of the monks.

'*Chi dorme non piglia pesci*,' returned that wise one, 'He who sleeps doesn't catch fish.'

From the new railway station of Cassino the Viale Dante led into the town. On the outskirts there were acres of rubble and ashen ruins looking like ancient monuments. In the town itself a new landscape of buildings stuccoed in white, pink and yellow was taking shape, and an incomplete piazza arcaded on one side recalled the new Coventry. I had already heard much of Senatore Restagno, the Mayor of Cassino, who was making such a determined bid for rehabilitation. In this new oasis the agony was already forgotten. From below, the great abbey of Monte Cassino looked virtually intact, a gleaming palace of sugar icing. An almost empty 'bus followed the road which spirals up the holy mountain, through orange and lemon groves, vineyards and terraced gardens to the monastery hanging above its crown of sere oak woods.

A group of small bony peasants hovered in the outer court. A monk unlocked a door and out filed a row of young seminarians in black soutanes and Roman round hats. The porter told me to wait for the monk who would be responsible for my welfare. It was some little time before Dom Raffaele Caracciolo appeared. He was youngish and ascetic looking and he greeted me affably. We passed into the enclosure and several small courts and then we entered—a lift. This must be the only Benedictine elevator in the world, I suggested.

'Ah, but in America, perhaps?' smiled Dom Raffaele.

There was as yet no guesthouse so that I was to be immured in the heart of the new monastery. We paced an immense corridor, some two hundred yards long, and in the middle of it was my cell.

Dom Raffaele seemed to be staring at my clothes.

'You wish to say Mass—you have brought your habit?'

This completely staggered me. I stood there like a tongue-tied schoolboy. He repeated his question.

'I'm afraid I don't quite understand, Father,' I managed to get out.

'It is the custom to wear ordinary clothes in England, yes? You are a priest, are you not?'

So that was it. There had been a misunderstanding and they had expected a priest. Apologies from both sides, and then we both laughed.

It was clear that the new Monte Cassino, the aristocrat of Benedictine monasteries, was to be somewhat revolutionary where material comfort was concerned. My spacious cell had a porcelain washing basin with tiled background, and on an enormous escritoire stood a reading lamp of the latest functional design. From my window I could see the jagged peaks of mountains purple in shadow and, further off, the snowy white crests of others ringing the plain, while far below everything was reduced to microscopic proportions, the river meandering in loops, the toy farmsteads, the thin glistening lines of the railway swooping across the plain into the hills.

Presently Dom Paolo, a Maltese who has been on the mountain for half a century, came to see me. He was obviously happy to speak English again, and his eyes beamed through the thick lens of his spectacles. A friend of his in the community, Dom Maurus Inguanez, was also a Maltese and was now permanently in Malta as librarian of the Royal Malta Library. It was he, said Dom Paolo, who before the bombing of the abbey, acting on his own initiative, smuggled out many of the most valuable manuscripts in his personal luggage, including a number of holographs of Shelley and Keats. The wartime abbot, Dom Gregorio Diamare, also saved much of the archives and works of art when the battle line began to approach the holy mountain. Even after the destruction of the abbey, when all the monks had left for other monasteries, Abbot Diamare, then aged seventy-nine, continued his welfare work among the stricken civilians of the town. Finally, when further work was impossible, he led a group of wounded and infirm through the German lines to safety. A year later, just before his death, he laid the foundation stone of the new abbey.

'Yes, war is an ugly business,' said Dom Paolo, '*un bruto affare*,' he repeated, lapsing into Italian. 'But come, let me show you the new Monte Cassino.'

Without Dom Paolo I might easily have been lost in the vast honeycomb of buildings. We began in the basilica, now like a workmen's yard, while my mentor commented on the restoration. Plans were drawn up by a monk of the community, Dom Angelo Pantoni, who was working in collaboration with an architect-engineer. The new abbey is almost an exact replica of that which existed on the eve of the bombardment in 1944. Decoration of the rebuilt basilica was now nearing completion, the original features reproduced in inlaid marbles, sculpture, frescoes and gilded stucco-work. Much of this craftsmanship was being done on the site under the direction of the monk-sculptor Dom Francesco Vignelli. The component parts of the high altar, embodying portions of that attributed to Michelangelo, where laid ready for assembling. Below it would rest the silver and bronze casket designed to house the remains of St. Benedict and his sister Scholastica discovered in the ruins in 1950, when Roman and pre-Roman walls were found beneath the tomb. A shell which fell immediately alongside the tomb did not explode. Almost the only innovation in the basilica is the entrance doors with bronze reliefs by the Rome sculptor Canonici depicting the four destructions of Monte Cassino—by the Lombards in 572, the Saracens about 880, the French and Spanish, fighting for possession of the Two Sicilies in the fifteenth century, and that of 1944.

Of the five cloistered quadrangles only one, the cloister of the Priors, was completed. The cloister of the Benefactors fronting the basilica awaited the statues of saints, popes and sovereigns. The three cloisters linked together at the entrance, the central one containing the celebrated Loggia del Paradiso of Bramante, were being restored by an army of artisans, and a giant crane swung blocks of marble and stone through the air.

Dom Paolo had occasionally to halt and I had to take his arm when descending steps. He was indeed an ailing man, and the days of his youth when he had first professed the vows of St. Benedict were far behind. His kindness was thus a little embarrassing.

At supper in the refectory I was the sole guest at the table of the abbot, Dom Ildephonsus Rea. Aproned brothers wheeled in the steaming courses on trolleys, first boiled cabbage, then a succulent filleted fish with olives, and finally fruit. At 8.15 p.m. the bells rang for Compline. Since the basilica was not yet ready, the community used the subterranean chapel of the Torretta or tower. This is a relic of the Roman settlement of Arx Cassini, but there are also the Cyclopean blocks of pre-Roman walls, and there is little doubt that the first Christian church here superseded a temple of Apollo.

The main chapel here is now enriched with a life-sized bronze group portraying the dying Benedict with his disciples, executed by the sculptor Selva and given by Dr. Adenauer. Here too were laid the relics of Saints Benedict and Scholastica, exposed in long glass cases, the bones separated and pieced together by archaeologists and surgeons, awaiting the completion of the tomb. Monte Cassino thus ignores the old controversy over the rival claim of the French abbey of Fleury-sur-Loire to possess the relics of the great Patriarch. The findings of the experts, with much scientific apparatus, have been published in a quarto volume *Il Sepulchro di S. Benedetto*. The weight of historical documentary evidence in favour of the Fleury tradition cannot be ignored, though it is just possible that when, in the seventh century, the French monk Aygulfus and his companions removed what they thought were the remains of the two saints from the then abandoned Monte Cassino to safe keeping in Gaul—they may have rifled the wrong tomb. It is all very confusing and unsatisfactory.

Everyone, then, being assembled, let them say Compline ; and when that is finished, let none be allowed to speak to anyone. Thus the forty-second chapter of St. Benedict's Rule, which he wrote here in this very monastery. The silence of the Torretta accompanied me all the way to my cell. Through the window I could see the town, a diadem of lights far below. I seemed to hang in space. Was all this perhaps an anachronism? Could the past really exist? Certainly the way to the future lay down there, whether one liked it or not. Somehow it was like staring into one's destiny and finding all ways of escape cut off.

On a high plateau near the monastery is the elaborate cemetery of the Polish soldiers who climbed the mountain under a hail of fire, their crosses looking towards the great abbey. It was not until I left Monte Cassino that I found the British cemetery on the road to Rome. An English gardener and half a dozen workmen were busy between the long narrow aisles of white headstones on which the sun now shone. It was as yet incomplete, lacking the standard monument and pavilion, but its very simplicity was eloquent. It had the bright Italian sky for a dome, and the slow husbandry of the fields was at hand, the plodding yoked oxen, the labourers with their scythes, the women bending over the olive trees.

My road, however, lay in the opposite direction, the road to Naples and beyond.

To be catapulted into the oriental violence of Naples after the siesta of the holy mountain was a bewildering experience. Crowds jostled along the Corso Umberto, the Via Toledo and the Partenope. Olive-skinned girls like Egyptians, their ears and wrists cascading with ornaments, sidled out of Baroque chapels in Saracenic alleys. Everywhere were the shoeblacks, their elaborate chairs glittering with brass medallions, a type of folk art perhaps allied to the barrel organ and the painted carts of Sicily. Naples is no more Italian than Marseilles is French—both are cities of the Levant, melting-pots of the Mediterranean—and it belongs equally to the classical world and to Africa. Noted for philosophers and gangsters, both are to be seen drinking Lachryma Christi, the sweet white wine from the soil of Vesuvius, in the *trattorie* of Santa Lucia and sipping their coffee in the Galleria. Near the latter is the opera house of San Carlo, a Pompeian study in grey and white, and adjoining it is the royal palace, a product of the Spanish period, in red and grey enriched with niches of sculptured figures. Opposite sweeps the semi-circular Piazza Plebiscito with its Bourbon statues and the curving colonnades of San Francesco di Paola. Beyond lies the San Guiseppe Carita quarter filled with monumental Fascist architecture. Cultures and civilizations are crowded one upon the other like palimpsest.

From the Via Roma the little cable railway of the popular song *Funiculi, Funicula* swings to the heights of the Vomero quarter, dominated by the former Carthusian monastery of San Martino, now a National Museum, atop a precipice which drops to the monastic vineyard and slithers down again into the town. No longer a living monastery, it is yet rich in the *seicento* arts and these may serve as a fitting prelude to the authentic south. The treasury walls are lined with vestment presses of inlaid and painted wood, and overhead is a splendid series of frescoes by Luca Giordano, while the church preserves a host of Neapolitan paintings and much sculpture by Cosimo Fansaga, who was responsible for the cloister garden and its statuary.

Logically, one is led on to Monte Vergine, Padula and La Cava. This proved to be more difficult than it seemed. Neither train nor 'bus to Avellino was available. As I stood making inquiries outside the station an evil-looking tout who had obviously overheard my conversation persuaded me, with promises of immediate transport, to follow him. On the edge of the square the tout introduced me, if the abrupt encounter could be termed an introduction, to a man who was driving to Avellino within a few minutes and would take me for a reasonable fare. Four other men now appeared and crowded into the tiny vintage car. None of them inspired the slightest degree of confidence. Memories of gangster films crowded into my mind and I had the unpleasant feeling that I was being taken 'for a ride'. When the car lurched forward the tout stood on the running-board and demanded concrete recognition of his services.

The journey proved uneventful, and we sped through the fertile Campania and its little towns in air that became decidedly crisp. It was snowing before we reached the mountains about Avellino, a prosaic enough town, where it had apparently been snowing for several days. The zigzag mountain road to Monte Vergine, where snow lies for six months of the year, was said to be dangerous and perhaps blocked, and it was with difficulty that I persuaded a driver to go. Some refused point-blank to go at all, others were willing— for an astronomical price. I had almost abandoned my project when, later in the day, a meek little man volunteered to take me without robbing me.

We set off on the steep climb, and once out of the foothills the mountain was camouflaged with considerable snow. At the last hamlet we were held up by a funeral which occupied the entire road, the mourners and confraternities of women in voluminous black garments down to the ground, spreadeagled out in military forma- tion, each carrying a banner or a wreath on a stave. The obstacle could not be negotiated for some time, and the driver cursed unfeelingly. The road grew steeper and more precarious. There were high snow drifts and sheets of ice. Even the thick chestnut woods resembled great snow caps. And on the summit, nearly 2,500 feet higher than Monte Cassino, stood the monastery of Monte Vergine where the first hermits had cut down the grove of Cybele.

The pile of buildings looked drab and neglected, a range of cubes of no aesthetic merit, ostensibly of eighteenth- nineteenth-century date. The place seemed quite deserted. Snow was falling steadily and the mist and cold struck through my clothes. I crossed the courtyard on packed snow and ice with fresh snow squelching over my ankles, mounted a wide flight of steps and found myself in the zebra-striped atrium of the basilica. Two quite bald and shrivelled monks in white habits loitered in this arena, and one of them shuffled off like a mandarin to find someone who would take charge of the strange visitor. I was then quickly dealt with by a more virile monk who conducted me through a reception room into a suite of rooms to which I was given the key. Then I was alone.

My suite of rooms, parlour, bedroom and toilet room, must surely have normally been designed for dignitaries. Like the reception room with its chandelier and bowl of goldfish, they were now shabby, the fabrics almost threadbare, but were filled with heavy antique furniture and paintings. Adjoining the suite was the Salone di ricevimento, an empty Baroque apartment like a ballroom with elaborate coved ceiling and enormous gilt medallion pictures. All this lay outside the locked gate to the monastic enclosure.

The abbey of Monte Vergine was founded for a new body of hermits by St. Guglielmo of Vercelli early in the twelfth century. Later it adopted the Benedictine rule and now belongs to the Cassinese Congregation. The community has retained its original white habit, the only Benedictines to do so with the single exception of those of Prinknash Abbey in England (though the Olivetans and Camaldolese, now grouped under the Benedictine aegis, also wear white habits).

I seemed to have the entire place to myself, *outside* the monastic enclosure, that is, for I had not yet been bidden beyond it. The basilica, a seventeenth-century Baroque temple, was now as cold as a refrigerator, and the figures of monuments and tombs, suggesting the proximity of the Roman world, seemed to add to the chilliness. The stylized tomb of Catherine II has medallion portraits of her. More poignant is the Roman marble sarcophagus destined for King Manfred, the son of Frederick II, who fell at Benevento. The most distracting is not a tomb or monument at all but the mummified body, exposed in a glass case, of Fra Giulio di Nardo, a monk of the abbey who died in 1601 and has since been beatified. The walls about are covered with *ex votos* and the photographs of perhaps thousands of pilgrims to the monastery. The high altar of mosaic is set against a pulpitum or monastic screen with flanking doorways into the choir, where are excellent highly carved stalls. The Chapel of the Madonna, a riot of modern marble and intagliata work, has a celebrated picture of the Virgin, a quite-Byzantine composition which has been freely copied.

Mercifully, I was able to warm up with coffee which was hot but had little else to commend it in the monastery café-bar across the courtyard, where an *espresso* machine hissed and backfired under the persuasion of Fra Modesto and a secular employee. The decor of the café is new and sophisticated, such as may be found in the town below, and the most intriguing refreshments purveyed here are the half-dozen different liqueurs, one of them based on aniseed, made by the monks at the Loreto near the foot of the mountain.

My solitary supper was taken in a small square whitewashed chamber adjoining the monastic refectory, and through a pane of glass above a hatch I could see the heads of monks passing to and fro. A window overlooked the court, and outside it hung giant icicles like stalactites. The food was quite unpalatable, and altogether I was now suffering from frustration. The rule of segregation seemed to be persisting for too long, and, quite unreasonably, I began to resent it.

I managed to find my way into the darkened church for Compline, only to find that here too I was to be alone, for the monks had gathered in the Coretto di Notte, the monastic night chapel inside the enclosure. This overlooked the Chapel of the Madonna by an opened window like a grille high at one end, facing the altar. A sacristan lighted a candle for me, and I knelt there alone in the gloom and the icy cold, the candlelight flickering on the patterned marbles and the golden Madonna looking straight at me, while the chant flared and died and the whispered *Amens* floated like sighs through that high open window.

It snowed all night. From my room I could see the monastery beacon light flashing round like a lighthouse lantern.

Next morning the handful of monks began to take some notice of me, and Fra Modesto showed me over the rest of the monastery. There was not very much of it. I had already glimpsed the small plain cloister, and now we mounted to the wide Corridoio del Crocifisso off which run the cells. The chapel where the monks had sung the previous night is only large enough to contain the monks' stalls and the altar. Resting above the stalls, on either side, are rows of imposing reliquary caskets, some seventy of them, including an arm of St. Luke and the remains of St. Costanza, patron saint of Capri. From there to the treasures of the library with its great medieval triune chair covered with almost-Saracenic ornament, and those of the sacristy with its ciborium in Cosmati work presented by Charles Martell of Sicily in 1290.

We crossed the outer court and then waded shin-deep in snow to a site at the side of the basilica.

'There are so many pilgrims that the basilica must be extended,' said Fra Modesto. 'Here there will be a new wing. The façade will have a rose window, and there will be a plain lantern tower over the centre. A campanile will stand alone, and there will be steps and statues and gardens. You will not know the old Monte Vergine.'

Parties of skiers were now arriving to make sport on a slope behind the monastery. These were not the pilgrims I had expected, those who at Whitsun donned traditional costume and went up the mountain carrying staves decorated with fruit and flowers as in the ancient Bacchanalia, though it appeared that the September pilgrimages were ardent enough, many arriving barefoot and crawling on hands and knees up the basilica steps and across the marble floor to the high altar.

A lone skier returning to Avellino by car offered to take me to the Loreto, the *ospizio*, where the abbot and the older brethren live. The weather at Monte Vergine is too severe for even the younger monks to stay longer than a few weeks at a time, and most of the community of about sixty live at the lower house.

The Loreto, designed by Domenicantonio Vaccaro, a pupil of Vanvitelli, is an early eighteenth-century octagon built around a central court, and it was originally the abbatial palace. Internally it is as near southern Rococo as anything could be, from the reception room recalling that at the higher monastery to the room of the archives with its inlaid walnut cabinets filled with such rarities as the letters of St. Jerome. In the abbatial apartments are late Empire furnishings, Flemish tapestries and portraits of the Bourbon kings, among them that 'King Bomba' (Ferdinando II) who with his family frequently stayed here. The splendid pharmacy is lined with cabinets filled with majolica vases from Capodimonte and Piedmont and with antique medicaments.

I spent that night on the way to Salerno at the monastery of Corpo di Cava, hidden in its gorge out of sight of the towered and castled hills. The curious inlaid stalls and abbatial throne in the chapter house originally belonged to the former *certosa* of Padula

and thus prepared me for the morrow's journey across bleak mountain country. Padula was wrecked by an earthquake and finally
sacked by the French in the time of Napoleon, and in our own
equally unstable time it became Campo 35, a prisoner-of-war camp
for British officers. Today Italian war orphans play in the vast
arcaded courts and climb warily up Vanvitelli's immense Baroque
staircase with apertures open to sun and wind.

The snows had gone. A furtive moon rode over a medieval
cloister. Before me lay the whole of the south, the classical world on
which the medieval lay superimposed.

7

THE BAROQUE WORLD

O N the edge of Canton Fribourg the walled town of Murten (French Morat) stands at the edge of a reedy bird-haunted lake poisoned by the ox-red algae. Down its long arcaded street, visible from a café terrace at breakfast, came a travelling circus, the animals two by two, to pass through the Bernese gate and pitch camp outside the city walls. From the solid comforts of a hotel fashioned out of the patrician house of the de Diesbach de Liebistorf family I went forth to the exploration of Fribourg and the heart of the Canton. It was midsummer of another year, and the foothills wore a velvet of greenery.

Fribourg itself, German-looking but French-speaking, is a little Rome, another Quebec. Its theological tradition dates from Peter Canisius, the Jesuit born in time to become one of the leaders of the counter-reformation, though he was canonized only in 1925, and who now lies in the Jesuit church here. The University maintains the tradition, now coloured with Jacques Maritain-ism, and the new building designed by Fernand Dumas is itself a classic of modern architecture. The Chancellor, Herr Kanzler Aepli, to whom I had an introduction though he was away, was said to be an Anglophile and had introduced some English methods into his seat of learning.

The functional buildings of the University do not sit too happily in this medieval and Renaissance town filled with fountains of considerable artistic merit and with innumerable convents and churches. One recalls the Ursuline and Augustinian convents, the Visitation convent with its coffered dome and beautiful wrought-iron grille, and several Franciscan houses, including that of the Cordeliers with its medieval cloisters and frescoes and its splendid altarpiece by the *maître à l'oeillet*, so called since this unidentified painter always signed his work with representations of two carnations. It was there that I met young Pater Alexis Vez, who had just celebrated his first Solemn Mass, and whose sister was then in a convent school in Kent.

The hillside huddle of ramparts and towers plunges down to the river, and across a bridge lies a flat spit of land almost islanded by the river which loops around it on three sides. The town might almost be a hundred miles away. There is a Capuchin nunnery with simple belfry and Baroque chapel, and beyond it the Cistercian nunnery of Maigrauge with Romanesque capitals and whitewashed walls and a hidden singing choir. I spoke to Sister Portress through the gatehouse grille and asked for a drink, for it was a hot day. She apologized and directed me to a farmhouse, where an aged couple took me into a cellar and drew a draught of cold Obstwein.

The road to Valsainte is long and not easily found, and few travellers find their way into the no-man's-land between Gruyères and Lake Thun. Skirting Gruyères itself only the hilltop castle is visible, and the country is one of low-lying pasturage in the radiant valley of the Sarine. The farms about here offer excellent honey, and the cowman rounding up his cattle may sing or chant the old *Ranz des Vaches*, beloved of Berlioz. Beyond Bulle, on the way to the Juan Pass, a narrow rough road streaks away from the highway, which is here carried by a steel arched bridge over the river, and climbs into the hills. The track, still climbing, becomes rougher, until beyond the rock-bound village of Cerniat it threatens to peter out. Here there is likely to be rain-mist or snow for much of the year.

In a hollow of these mountains, with dark pine forests edging up the slopes from the foothills, stands the *chartreuse* of Valsainte. It was suppressed early in the eighteenth century and restored last century. In the interim it acquired a heroic reputation as the brief home of those exiled Trappists who, under Dom Augustine de Lestrange, here lived on roots, leaves and black bread. At the gatehouse I was handed over to Frater Meinrad, young and handsome, though his pallor told of abstinence and lack of sleep. He hailed from the Grisons and had been at Valsainte for six years. We crossed the outer court, knelt in the small prim church and then entered the labyrinth.

My companion said that in winter Valsainte was a refrigerator. Even now in high summer it was decidedly cool. This was perhaps the most austere Carthusian monastery I had seen, the long but narrow cloisters white and bare and cold, *les rues d'une ville de glace*, as Pierre van der Meer de Walcheren puts it. And in the centre the plain black crosses of the dead.

'We live here as our Order did at the beginning—*Cartusia numquam reformata, quia numquam deformata,*' said Frater Meinrad.

Without reform, without stain. . . . It is no mean boast. So high is the standard that today there are but a score of Carthusian monasteries in the world. Frater Meinrad and his fellow novices, French, Swiss and three Americans destined for the new monastery at Sky Farm in Vermont, serve a strange apprenticeship, studying the arts of self-abnegation, preparing for death. There are few dispensations, and though the cells here seem to be somewhat larger than many Carthusian cells they seem also to be gloomier. Above each entrance door is a letter of the alphabet and a quotation from the Scriptures: *Conversatio nostra in coelis est.* The plan differs slightly from the norm. One enters on the first floor. Downstairs is a woodcutting bench and a carpenter's lathe, and this workroom leads on to a garden with cultivated flowers and espaliered pears on the enclosing walls. Upstairs, on the second floor, is the cell proper divided into study, oratory and a curtained bed rather like those to be seen in Breton cottages.

Valsainte is the *Paradis Blanc* of Pierre van der Meer de Walcheren, the Dutch writer who followed Nietzsche until he visited the Trappist monastery of Westmalle in Belgium, an experience which set him on the thorny road to Catholicism. He was influenced by his friend Léon Bloy and he became an oblate of the Benedictine abbey of Oosterhout in Holland. It has recently been rumoured that he has himself entered a monastery.

The sun hung poised in an empty sky when a few days later I arrived at Sion in the heart of the Valais. Climbing out of the Sahara-like apricot-growing plain of the Rhône valley, one ascends a long lateral valley to climb ever higher into the remote and ancient world which lies beneath the polar wastes of Arolla. Life here bears an Homeric impress, and there is no room for those who would be cossetted. In summer the villages depend for their water upon the primitive troughs or wooden pipes fed from a stream which rises high up at glacier level, and such is the terrain that barley and rye must often be grown above 6,000 feet. Life is thus reduced to elementals, yet mountain inhabitants of the Valais have created a communal life and a peasant art of singular interest.

This Valaisian world is mirrored in the pages of Charles Ferdinand Ramuz (1878-1947), who may well prove to be the most powerful and original Swiss writer since Rousseau. He was a poet and a cosmic visionary, and one must look beyond those descriptive novels and essays which classify him as a regional writer. He was indeed a regional writer but in the best sense, that is, in the sense in which Frédéric Mistral was a regional writer, and in his *Journal*, his *Vues sur le Valais, La Grande Peur dans la Montagne* and other novels he gives us the key to a land of archaic village-kingdoms where the changing seasons compel migratory movements in the struggle for existence.

Evolène, on the high narrow road to Arolla, is such a village-kingdom, with more than a suggestion of a matriarchy. It has all the elements common to the most spectacular (though so often spurious) folders doled out to tourists, and from the balcony of a chalet one sees the pines, the tilted burnt-up landscape below the timber line, the costumed women labouring on the land, the mules with overflowing panniers, and the arctic pyramid of the Dent Blanche rising like a spectre in the background. The sturdy chalets and byres standing four-square are of horizontal unsplit timbers, fir or larch, sometimes enriched with carving.

There is often a cretin-like quality (quickly dispelled upon acquaintance) about this heavily goitred peasantry which is enhanced by the habitually worn costume. The women wear the same black dress and stockings all the week, but on Sundays the cotton apron and fichu and sometimes a jacket of alpaca with silvered lapels are worn. Finery is not favoured by the men, not even by the three Pierres—Pierre Bovier, who makes excellent ice-axes, Pierre Georges, the woodcarver, and Pierre Vallette, the local poet.

More eloquent of mountain piety than the rebuilt church of Evolène is the nearby village chapel of Pannaz, of 1711, with an arcaded porch on the Italian model and a disturbing Pietà. In summer the shelving landscape between Pannaz and Evolène, the habitat of lizards, grasshoppers and snakes with black and white intaglio designs, is filled with the thick-set figures of women who are never far removed from the cares of husbandry. The stony mule path to Arolla can be negotiated by one of the jeeps introduced here since the war, a helter-skelter ride through basaltic wastes dotted with little Edens. Arolla is a hamlet merely with a vast white-elephant hotel. Flanking the valley are forests of cembra pines or *aroles*, and the valley plunges into the glacier world of Mont Collon, a formidable bastion. From here it is fourteen hours on foot into Italy. Strangers hazarding a winter trek have reached eternity in less time.

North-east of Sion lies another hidden valley, the eagle-haunted Lötschental, which peters out into yet another glacial world. A century and a half ago it was referred to as 'a little Siberia, with its bears, chamois, marmots and half-wild population'. There are today the first signs of an invasion from without, but the valley, like the monk, is still dominated by the medieval cycle of times and seasons, traditions and beliefs, and nowhere in Europe is the Catholic year observed with greater gusto. A thousand years before Karl Marx the people of the Lötschental organized their society on the lines of a naturally developed collectivism. Kippel and other villages have communal dairies where all pool their milk and receive butter and cheese according to their contribution. Each morning the freshly-made butter is stamped with the sign of the Cross. In winter the cheeses are stored, and there are vintage cheeses as there are vintage wines. In Ferden there are cheeses which are centenarians. It was once the custom at the birth of a child to set aside a cheese which would be kept to be eaten at the funeral in old age of that same person.

These villages, Ferden, Kippel, Wiler and others, have hoary chocolate- and charcoal-coloured dwellings engraved with elegant inscriptions in old German. This mastery of wood, the common material, is also reflected in the farm implements—the sleigh-like *zuge*, milk pails, churns, ladles and spoons. A flattened churn of local pinewood, beautifully shaped and polished, is strapped to the back for carrying the milk from the pastures to the village. The bearded craftsmen of Wiler carve weird highly-painted masks of wood, often quite diabolical and decidedly African or Polynesian in feeling, which are traditionally associated with local folk dances.

The church of Kippel stands in a sea of wooden crosses, those of husbands and wives painted blue, those of unmarried persons black. In the Valais colours have marked liturgical significance. This is the focal point of the great procession which moves through the streets, planted with flowering branches of acacia, at Corpus Christi. The men wear uniforms brought back by old campaigners who

served with the armies of France, Italy and Spain a century and two
centuries ago—the helmets with scarlet plumes, enormous epaul-
ettes, breastplates and baldrics of white leather laid cross-wise on
the breast. A white train of village maidens bear banners and statues
garlanded like tiered bridal cakes, and in their wake come the women
in their best costume, wearing those vast busby like hats which seem
related to the shakos and helmets of the Grenadiers.

North of the Lötschental, itself a fitting testing-ground for
hermits, lies a terrain authentically associated with hermits. Near
the abbey of Engelberg, a town of Edwardian survivals, is Sachseln,
where is buried that Bruder Klaus who was Nicholas von der
Flue and who from 1467 lived in a hermitage and survived without
food or drink for twenty years. It was also said that he made an
annual appearance at Einsiedeln without ever having been seen on
the road in either direction. At Einsiedeln itself stands another great
Benedictine abbey, Our Lady of the Hermits, girdled with the white
radiance of villas and chapels and the summer slopes rich in the rare
yellow saxifrage, marsh orchid and the dwarf birch. This was the
town of Paracelsus, the supreme Magus of Europe, the 'ass of
Einsiedeln' as his enemies called him. He would not recognize the
shoddy and amorphous collection of buildings and emporia which
still cater for the 'crowd of palmers and votaries' whom Gibbon saw
here and which now crowd into the Klosterplatz before the most
lyrical building in Switzerland. There is little hint of this lyricism,
however, from without, though the Baroque planning and symmetry
of church and flanking buildings is itself admirable, while there is a
hint of theatrical decor in the foreground hemicycle of arcades facing
pavilion-like fountains of black marble.

Einsiedeln (itself meaning 'hermitage') was founded in 934 on
the site of the cell inhabited by the hermit Meinrad. The present
abbey is the sixth on the site, and none of its predecessors could have
compared with it. Designed by the Bavarian Caspar Moosbrugger,
a laybrother of the abbey, the monastery was reconstructed from the
year 1719. The church belongs to the Rococo world of Bavaria and
the Danube, and it achieves an almost incredible degree of unity and
harmony in view of the fact that some hundreds of artists and craftsmen were employed on it. The humanity of the statues belongs to
Johann Baptist Babel, the cunning art of the stuccatore belongs to
Egid Quiram Asam, the brilliant limpid frescoes of the cupolas to

his brother Cosmas Damian, the dominating high altar to the Italians Torricelli and Pozzi and the allegorical side altars to an Italian sculptor who worked much in the Germanic countries, Diego Carlone.

For many this is a new experience, both visually and mentally, a new dimension, a relaxation of the senses after the discipline of the Gothic. The sacred mysteries are given a new setting, and if this has more than a hint of the secular world it is ultimately both convincing and logical. Here is hope, joy and triumph, sharply contrasting with the lament and despair of the cold dark minsters of the Gothic north.

Set near the western end is the Gnadenkapelle on the site of Meinrad's cell, the Porziuncola of Einsiedeln, though unlike the Assisi chapel this is a classical temple of gleaming black marble housing the medieval Black Madonna, dressed as a queen, crowned and standing in a foam of frothy clouds. Goethe, surprisingly, in his Memoirs praised its predecessor and said that it moved him to serious reflection. Vespers were just ending, and now the monks in their black choir habits, preceded by the young seminarians, came two by two across the great shimmering gold and ivory opera-house to kneel in pairs inside the chapel, singing the *Salve Regina*, as they do each day, year in, year out.

Pater Frederick, the tall, lean distinguished monk whom I encountered here resembled a schoolmaster rather than a monk, so that it was not surprising to learn that he taught English to the some three hundred students in the college attached to the abbey. He had stayed with the Benedictines of Ramsgate ('What a strange town!') nearly half a century ago, and he had visited the monastery on Caldey Island. It was an Englishman, he told me, who initiated the Swiss American Congregation when in 1853 the monastery sent out to the United States a band of monks led by Dom Bede O'Connor, a Londoner by birth and an Irishman by descent.

'That is one of the great moments in our history,' smiled Pater Frederick. 'There are others. . . .' And he proceeded to describe them, how at the Reformation the last monk had gone over to the reformer Zwingli and the people brought a new abbot from St. Gall, and how at the French Revolution, when the monks had fled, invaders took prisoner the sole remaining monk, Pater Martin du Fay de Lavallaz, a former officer in a Valaisan regiment. Such a moment too was that when the Swiss Benedictine Congregation was organized by Pater Augustine of this monastery early in the seventeenth century. Today Einsiedeln, the mother-house of the Congregation, has about one hundred and thirty-five monks and over fifty laybrothers, and though their activities are spread over education and the humanities, agriculture and the arts, the pattern of holiness is still to be found. Such were the qualities of Frater Meinrad Eugster, who worked in the tailoring shop and died in 1925, that, like the earlier Meinrad, he may soon be raised to the altar.

The apartments of abbot, cellarer and guests are contained in a wing of the monastery known as the Court, deriving its name from the time when the Abbots of Einsiedeln bore the title of Prince of the Holy Roman Empire and exercised temporal power over the territory of the dark forest. In the Fürstensaal or Hall of the Princes are life-size oil portraits of the Emperors and Sovereigns who have been associated with the abbey, from William I, grandfather of the last Kaiser, to Napoleon III and the Empress Eugénie, by Winterhalter, from Franz Joseph and Elizabeth of Austria to Carol of Roumania and his queen Carmen Sylva, all figures of tragedy or frustration. The elegant stuccoed embellishments of the Fürstensaal are extended to library and guest room, where there are some imaginary landscapes by the Bavarian Joseph Anton Feuchtmayer.

In winter the guest may be lulled by the soporific fumes of a peat fire (as he is with the Irish Benedictine nuns of Kylemore in Connemara), for this is the fuel, cut from the pine-girdled and soggy plateau, that drives the great monastery, the boilerhouses, kitchens, bakery, laundry and much else. There is here the entire gamut of industry, even to breeding those horses for which Einsiedeln is noted; they are indeed far more useful than tractors in this mountain country, and the abbey retains over seventy of them for its own purposes.

Other abbeys of the Congregation are those at Engelberg and Disentis, the latter largely rebuilt by Einsiedeln's architect Caspar Moosbrugger, though in its Merovingian crypt it has what no other Benedictine abbey in Switzerland can show. Pater Maurus Carnot, who earlier this century wrote excellent folk tales and folk dramas in the Romansch language of this region, was a monk of this abbey. It is not surprising that the great abbey of St. Gall near the Bodensee has long been secularized, for as a Protestant town St. Gall formed an independent miniature state in the midst of monastic territory down to the days of Napoleon.

It was the hermit Gall, a pupil of St. Columban, who gave his name to this abbey, of which the first ground plan, dated about the year 820, the earliest Benedictine plan in existence, may still be seen in the former abbey library. It was in that first monastery that the medieval drama which we call the Miracle or Passion Play may have had its origin, for one of its main forms can be traced back to the ninth century *Quem quaeritis?* a chanted dialogue introduced into the Easter service here. Three choristers representing the three Marys walked up to the altar, which stood for the empty tomb, and were there met by a fourth who answered them in the words of the angel: 'He is not here. He is risen.'

Today St. Gall's vast buildings are converted to secular use, but the church, designed by Giovanno Bagnato, who was responsible for some excellent public buildings in this area, remains a monument of the Rococo and is the peer of Einsiedeln. The attendant craftsmen are much in evidence, and the elegant hand of Feuchtmayer is to be seen in choir stalls and confessionals, though we may be more intrigued by the library of the Gigl brothers, with its curving balconies and enriched painted ceilings and its gleaming floor of polished walnut, set with scrolls and radiating stars, over which we glide in cloth overshoes, a sanctum which prepares us for the festive monastic libraries of Austria.

Summer had passed, and the succeeding winter had barely ended when I crossed the frontier into Austria. Indeed a phenomenally fierce winter was persisting through March into the first days of April. Salzburg barely resembled, as it normally does, a radiant city of the Italian south thrusting itself into the Germanic north. It lay bleak and grey and lifeless, with an almost monotonous quality about its Baroque domes and towers, and arrows and slings of silver rain fell upon its stone paving. The ancient cemetery garden alone, sandwiched between the catacombed rock face and the abbey of St. Peter, was an oasis of greenery and colour, and the mimosa sprinkled its canary-coloured balls of chenille upon a variety of tombstones which cavorted and pirouetted into all manner of shapes. And near the cemetery gates there was refuge and refreshment in the Peter-skeller, the tavern belonging to the monks.

The most engaging if not the most virtuous personality associated with St. Peter's was probably Marcus Sitticus, Prince and

Archbishop of Salzburg, who established the University in 1617 and placed it under the direction of the Benedictines. He also strengthened the city fortifications, imprisoned his predecessor (whose country seat he then re-named Schloss Mirabel), and built for himself, and for his beautiful plump mistress, a country palace at Hellbronn. This Prince of the Church was as wilfully mischievous as a schoolboy, and at Hellbronn he contrived practical jokes in the garden which took the form of hidden fountains and jets of water which deluged his unsuspecting guests, and they are still there to soak the unwary visitor. He was also guilty of other extravagances, and altogether his conduct was not entirely reconcilable with the spirit of St. Benedict.

Snow was falling when I made my way through the Salzkammergut *en route* for the Danube. Chancing to come upon the deep Traunsee I followed its banks to the almost deserted village of Traunkirchen set idyllically on a spit of land facing the steep Traunstein plunging precipitately into the lake. At the end of this tiny peninsula a former convent church stands at the water's edge, filled with cartouched shell-like altars and dominated by a remarkable Rococo pulpit built like the barque of St. Peter and draped with overhanging fish nets of gold. Generations of Traunkirchen fishermen lie beneath Rococo iron crosses in the beautiful churchyard against the lake wall, and with them lie many others who became soldiers and died for the Reich at Stalingrad.

All about are the little jetties and the boatbuilding yards, almost microscopic when seen from the Calvary hill or the high chapel-crowned hummock near the shore. At Corpus Christi the people don traditional costume and go in a procession of boats over the lake. The old boatbuilder Herr Enichelmeier was the first to greet me with '*Grüss Gott!*' and one old woman was so surprised by this early visitor in the snow that she murmured '*Frohe Ostern*', for it was Easter.

I settled in at the arcaded and balconied Hotel Post. That night the proprietor Franz Gröller entertained two of his friends, and I shared their table. Seppe Angele, who lived in the vicinity, was a quiet man with lunar features beneath whitening hair. Fritz Schuster, who lived at Gmunden at the head of the lake, was a boisterous businessman, a sprinter and high-jumper, leaner and more trim of body than his full-figured companions. Fritz and

Franz had been soldiers together throughout the war, and now the latter brought out his war photograph album. This was the war from the other side of the fence—the occupation of Paris and of the Channel Islands, and the tide of battle flowing across Europe to the end. Franz was never without his camera, and so here he was, with Fritz, under the Eiffel Tower, in Jersey, in Normandy. Two dead French soldiers lay beside a country lane. Franz turned the page rather quickly, a little apologetically. He murmured that he was sorry. War was stupid—but it *was* war. But the war was over. Let us eat and drink and be merry. For tomorrow?

'*Man weiss nicht,*' shrugged Seppe, 'no one knows.'

The years of doubt and pain were over, and the people could speak their minds. The wine ran and the tongues with it, in a speech that is German with the harsher sounds softened, a *lingua franca*. We swore allegiance and friendship. There was laughter and back-thumping at Traunkirchen in the snow that night.

Travelling still northward one may see a brilliant example of the combined work of Jakob Prandtauer and the Carlone family for the Benedictines. It is strange that Kremsmunster is rarely visited for it lies on the Pyhrnbahn railway, at one time the second big link between Prague and Trieste. There is nothing else in the somnolent little town, however, and the station set well away suggests a country halt, where in the inn the Franz Kafka peasants blow noisily upon their *gulasch*, which they eat with those hoops of bread called *ringbrot*. These Austrian abbeys are among the most ancient in Europe, and Kremsmunster was founded by that rival of Charlmagne, the Bavarian Duke Tassilo III, whose giant statue may be seen on the Bruckentor Gate of the abbey. Under the Carlovingians the monastery colonized Upper Austria, and there was a well-known scribes' school here *c.* 1300. In the fifteenth century the Austrian Benedictine abbeys followed the salutary example of the Congregation of St. Justine of Padua, and they were grouped into two federations, a division which lasted until the end of the eighteenth century. These federations were almost destroyed by the oppressive reign of Josef II and the laws forbidding the reception of novices, but they revived and in 1889 were formed into two new Congregations.

Kremsmunster is notable in that the Baroque is represented in all its stages over a century and a half, a curious cross-section of art evolution. Its most remarkable feature is probably the eight-storey functional-type meteorological building, now housing natural science collections. Built in 1748-58 to designs by Dom Anselm Diesink, it seems to anticipate the skyscraper and it was in fact then regarded as the highest building in Europe. At the beginning of the present century the research and discoveries of Dom Reselhuber and Dom Schwab brought them international repute.

This element of surprise is not yet exhausted, for the enclosed fishponds begun by Carlone and extended by Prandtauer must be unique. These ponds like elaborate swimming pools in the Bahamas are surrounded with open arcades, and they are decorated with fountain statues in which St. Peter and other Apostles are mixed up with marine deities and symbols; each preserve has its separate lock and key, and the fish, according to my mentor Dom Egbert, were said to have been summoned to their meals by the ringing of a bell.

Dom Egbert is the librarian, so that his main province is the delightful library with ceiling frescoes by that Diego Francesco Carlone whose work is also to be seen in the refectory and Kaisersaal here, as it is to be encountered in the monasteries of Weingarten and Einsiedeln and the University Church of Salzburg. In the library, which has points of contact with that of St. Florian, the rare *Codex millenarius* of *c.* 800 may be singled out. The Kaisersaal here resembles a Rococo drawing-room and is more satisfactory, certainly more intimate, than the megalomania of St. Florian's Marmorsaal. One may be more intrigued, however, by the deserted musty galleries filled with curious antiques and rare treasures, among them the great *Tassilokelch* or goblet and the thirteenth-century *flabellum* or liturgical fan, perhaps the finest in existence. Economic pressure has compelled the monks to sell much in recent years, and the Reydams tapestries are now in the Metropolitan Museum of New York.

The church and the vast vaulted cloisters were obviously designed for a greater number than the eighty monks who can today be mustered, including those in the parishes. Of this community nearly all but a token handful left in charge served in the forces of the Reich, and eight of them fell on foreign fields. That the prosperity of the community is now assured is hinted at in the wine cellars, to which one descends in a mine-like cage, where are aisles

of great casks, carved and enriched, filled with the good elixir which
is sold all over Austria.

At Linz an arctic wind hurtled down the Danube. A flurry of
snow fell upon the Hauptplatz and turned the spikes of the curious
Trinity Column, like a totem pole, into icicles. Dark silent steamers
were moored in the lee of the arcaded buildings on the waterfront,
where the people crowded into the Stadtkeller. Gaunt functional
buildings by Peter Behrens stood strangely beside patrician houses
of the time when Mozart dedicated a new symphony to his friends
here. The Iron Curtain falls heavily a few miles to the north, so that
there is always a certain amount of tension here, and at five o'clock
one morning a posse of police banged upon every bedroom door of
the inn where I was staying and took away passports or credentials
for examination.

Near Linz, close to the southern bank of the Danube, is the
village of Wilhering dominated by the lemon and cream stuccoed
abbey of the Cistercians. Conversation with Pater Valentine, whose
slight frame was covered with a clerical-grey raincoat over his habit
as protection against the polar wind, and whose thick unruly grey
hair had no semblance of a tonsure, made it clear that the abbey
belongs to the Common Observance. A medieval foundation, it is
ostensibly a monastery of the eighteenth century when it was largely
rebuilt. Its claustral buildings are of a somewhat stock classicism,
and it is in the church, begun in 1733, that all conscious artistic effort
is concentrated.

Wilhering is almost entirely the work of the Altomonte family,
who originated in Genoa but later settled in Vienna, and who were
responsible for the ceiling paintings in the library of Admont Abbey
and the Marmorsaal of the Vienna Belvedere, and for the Trinity
Column in the town of Baden. Andreas designed this church of
Wilhering, Bartolomeo painted the frescoes and Martino the altar
panels. The stuccowork is by several hands, notably Joseph Anton
Feuchtmayer, who worked largely on Bavarian monasteries and did
such excellent work at Einsiedeln and St. Gall.

The genius of Wilhering's church lies in its knowing where to
draw the line; a little more exuberance, a little more conscious effort
and all were lost. As it is, it is a glorious vision, its flashing whiteness
and flickering colours having a luminosity which startles the eyes.
Cherubs and angels strain and almost leap from their cornices and

pillars into the light, shell-like picture frames and door frames suggest a Louis XV boudoir, and both pulpit and organ-case are highly festive. The decorative detail boils and foams ever upward until the entire building seems to be dissociated from terra firma.

Not all of Wilhering is on this note of inconsequential unreality. In the refectory and chapter house the Rococo is so mild as to be identified with the early Baroque, while there is a down-to-earth note in the farm buildings and in the husbandry of the fields. As a further recall to reality the church vestibule contains the photographs of the fallen sons of the parish, thirty-five of them in the last war alone, of which a high proportion now lie under the forest of black unnamed crosses of Austrian soldiers killed *im Russland*. While these young men were dying on foreign fields their grateful compatriot Adolf Hitler confiscated their abbey, though the community escaped the worse fate of the Trappists at Engelhartszell up-river.

The true Baroque world—though it has left Bernini and Borromini far behind—is to be found less than a score of miles away, beyond Linz, in the Augustinian abbey of St. Florian. From the suburb of Ebelsberg a tram like a narrow-gauge railway ploughs through fields hemmed with wild flowers. The village of St. Florian is a yellow stuccoed landscape of inns and cottages, the colour and depth of which were enhanced by driving snow when I saw it, so that the entire composition had the appeal of a Pieter Breughel painting. The monastery buildings are terraced immediately above the village, like a long level escarpment, and its conceits and artifice are not revealed until one has approached the principal façade and entered the courtyard with its clipped shrubs.

The uniform composition of church and monastery was begun in 1686 by Carl Antonio Carlone, a member of a Como family of craftsmen who greatly enriched Austria and who are to be encountered in several of these Danube monasteries. On Carlone's death in 1708 his architectural leadership was followed by Jakob Prandtauer, whose genius was responsible for some notable compromises and additions and who is also represented at Kremsmunster and Melk. Here at St. Florian he designed the main portal, the summer refectory, the many-pillored Kaisersaal (the frescoes by Bartolomeo Altomonte, who died at St. Florian) and much else. His happiest inspiration is the open staircase hall with its series of two-storeyed arcaded openings and its flashing-white ceremonial double staircase with lovely wrought-iron gates on every landing. Here conscious art is added to the pleasure of geometry.

The elaborate series of state apartments all but outdo Schonbrunn and the Vienna Hof burg, frescoed with the chase as well as the pilgrimage, and each having a magnificent *ofen* or stove to correspond with the colour scheme. These culminate in fantasy in the Prinz-Eugen Zimmer, which has stuccoed war trophies from no less a hand than that of Johann Michael Feichtmayr and a gilded Rococo bed with almost life-size figures of Turkish pirates. This vast reception suite is an unexpected extension of the monastic world, its splendours designed for the Holy Roman Emperor should he come, while Kaiser and Kaiserin, among them Maria Theresa herself, held audience here.

One returns to the monastic norm in the church, though the same note of magnificence persists. To the Carlone family goes most of the credit, for Carl Antonio designed it and Bartolomeo executed the beautiful stuccoes. It is a pure Baroque product and is enriched with painted ceilings and elaborate choir stalls. The organ here is notable in itself but has greater significance in the fact that for many years it responded to the touch of a resident organist who became one of the great composers of the romantic century.

Anton Bruckner was a choirboy at St. Florian and he returned there as organist and music teacher in 1845. Converted by Wagner from classicism to romanticism, the victim of rival factions and the sneers of Brahms, and, despite his intense belief, of his own spiritual malaise, Bruckner made his mark and was given a room by the Emperor in the Vienna Belvedere. Such honours came only after twenty-three long years at St. Florian, where he composed the D Minor Mass and his first symphony, living in a small monkish room where his humble brass bedstead and pathetic belongings remain. He lies now in an elaborate tomb in an honoured place in the crypt, though it has a distracting backcloth in the form of a whitened sepulchre, a vast mound of skulls of early Christian martyrs.

That sepulchre may point a facile moral, and the Emperor's suite may become meaningless. It may be that there is sanity only in the iron crosses in the outer court and in those few memorials of St. Florian's vanished Gothic world, among them the thirteenth-century woodcarvings of Florian himself, who is seen again in a miniature in the Missal of Abbot Heinrich von Marbach (1306).

The innate enthusiasm of the Austrians for drama and music dates from the sixteenth century, and the religious Orders, notably Benedictines and Jesuits, did much to direct it. At Lambach is the only remaining monastery theatre in the country. I would never have seen it had it not been for Pater Egbert, who conducted me up a long staircase into a warren of gloomy offices and flats now occupying part of the monastery. Among these flats was one tenanted by a professor whose wife gave us the key to an adjoining lumber room. This turned out to be a disused theatre of the Baroque, largely of painted timber, the stage *décor* having flanking human figures in classical draperies, columns supporting a cornice, and other decoration, all painted in sharp relief. As at Kremsmunster it combined refined operas with allegorical productions and apocalyptic visions of the transitoriness of worldly things, and the opening play early in the year 1770 was *Lustiger Hochzeitsfertung* (*The Merry Wedding Feast*), at which Marie Antoinette, who was by chance passing the night in the town, is said to have been present.

This tradition concerning Marie Antoinette seems a little dubious, for at Melk amid the cherry orchards lower down the Danube we are reminded that on 21 April 1770, the year of the Lambach theatre, she left Austria for ever on her journey to France to marry the Dauphin, her brother Josef II accompanying her as far as Melk where he said goodbye to her. A leisurely arrival on a winter's night at the little Wachau railway station of Emmersdorf on the northern shore of the Danube is an experience. At this rural halt Christine Brunner (her name is inscribed over the booking-office) will issue a ticket or serve refreshment or sell provisions, after which she will probably go out with a rush broom to clear the line of her strutting turkeys. The ferry crosses the great river in darkness. Lights twinkle on the opposite shore. Nearly a mile of walking brings one across the bridge over the Melk river into the little town of the Nibelungenlied. Yellow lamplight plays on drifting snow, on the Baroque Post House with its stuccoed portrait medallions, trophies and Imperial eagles, and on low huddled inns, among them the Weisser Rössl, where an attack of 'flu compelled me to stay.

With morning light comes the revelation, for Melk is dominated by its abbey as by a mighty fortress, its vast complex of buildings spreadeagled across a rocky belvedere and terminating in a curving and colonnaded terrace enclosing a forecourt flanked by summer pavilions. The reforms instituted by Nicholaus von Cusa in 1451 were of far more than local significance, but one is apt to be more impressed by the changes made under Abbot Berthold Dietmayr in 1702, since these resulted in what is seen today. There are immense monasteries in Bavaria, but nothing quite like this is to be found elsewhere in Europe outside Russia and, possibly, Spain.

The form of Melk owes much, it seems, to the ambitious abbot, but it must finally be regarded as the masterpiece of Jakob Prandtauer (1660-1726), whose portrait in oils is to be seen here, a glum, lethargic, heavily built man, his great girth swathed in a grey military frock coat with white cuffs, with which a white stock is worn. We have already encountered him at St. Florian and Kremsmunster, and may do so again at St. Polten and the episcopal palace of Linz. He designed a number of minor buildings but he was not really comfortable on small-scale works, and Melk is an essay in megalomania, recalling, perhaps, our own Sir John Vanbrugh, who was building Blenheim at the same time and who indeed died in the same year as Prandtauer.

There is more drama here than at St. Florian but there is the same note of eighteenth-century absolutism. It is difficult to select the most attractive or significant of Melk's salient features. There is the staircase hall with its ornamental effigies by Lorenzo Matielli, the interminable Kaiser Corridor, white and silent and receding into distance, the splendid library in gold and pale blue with its gallery, on caryatides and Pobel's symbolic figures of the four faculties, Natural Science, Philosophy, Law and Medicine, the vast Marmorsaal with its coved ceiling painted in perspective with 'The Triumph of Reason' by Paul Troger, and, not least, the cathedral-like church with embellished organ loft, gilded filigreed balconies, curved golden pulpit like a royal opera box, and, among the quite-Rococo caskets, a reliquary of St. Columban, who was hanged as a suspected spy at nearby Durnstein when on his way to the Holy Land.

There is the monotonous voice of the courier and the shuffling of worldly feet, but soon the last excursionists, Baedeker in hand, have gone (though, for a brief space, not far, since they are probably drinking the monastery wine in the simple cellar with presiding crucifix, rough-hewn tables and gravelled floor). The vast courts and galleries are silent again, until the vesper bell.

Beyond the Wachau, tasselled with apricots and peaches, with wayside calvaries alternating with vine-clad pergolas and the foot-hills terraced and staked with vines, are other Baroque monasteries, crowded into this area like grains in a tussock of corn. At Seiten-stetten the abbot's room contains paintings by the Genoese Ales-sandro Magnasco, an eccentric whose work is rare enough and whose ever-recurring theme is the monastic life, though portrayed as caricature and near-fantasy. North of the Danube lies Altenburg, where the triple domes of the library shelter a pair of brooding sphinxes and a pair of prancing winged horses. Eastward still, piled high in a pastoral setting near the southern shore of the great river, is Gottweig, which, had it been completed to those designs by Lukas von Hildebrandt (architect of the Vienna Belvedere) still to be seen in the archives of the Vienna Library, might have outshone both St. Florian and Melk.

At Klosterneuburg is the abbey transformed after 1730 by the Emperor Karl VI, with his glass-covered private oratory and marble saloon, and the symbols of secular Imperial might surmounting the two great domes, one a model of the Austrian ducal coronet and the other a model of the German Imperial crown. Nearby, from the last spur of the Alps, the cliff called Leopoldsberg, one looks on the Baroque city of Vienna.

8

ROCOCO

M Y wanderings along the Danube between Passau and Vienna had prompted me to see the source of that mighty river at Donaueschingen in Swabia, where the spring is contained by a sculptured basin in the grounds of the schloss, and small boys attempt with magnets or tins fixed on long rods to fish out the coins thrown in by visitors. I stayed that night in Möhringen, a village in the flat Danube valley near Tuttlingen. Peasant women worked the gates of a small level-crossing, and other women in black head-shawls brandished long whips as they drove the cattle down the street. This is a farming community. In what might be called wide lanes branching off the single street are rows of small farmsteads with the living quarters adjoining and over the cow byres, an arrangement to be found until recently in the Welsh 'longhouse'. Mark Twain said that the farmer of this area measured his wealth by the size of his muck heap, and here in Möhringen these gigantic salubrious mounds stand before the front doors.

Elsewhere in the village are a small Rathaus of 1698, a nonde-script church, a ponderous eminently Teutonic war memorial heavily sculptured with a barbaric figure comparable to St. George and the dragon, tragically heavy with names, a couple of inns and a small brewery. The brewery may be surprising but does not mean that this is any more than a small village, for in Germany breweries are omnipresent—Bavaria alone has some eighteen hundred. Foun-tains and troughs for cattle and horses are of filigreed enriched design, of iron painted in grey and silver, one surmounted with a cherub, another with an eagle, and yet another with a colourful amost life-size figure of the half-naked Moor, with bow and sheath of arrows, after which the village is named.

Since early afternoon some obscure jubilee celebrations in connection with Höhner the accordionist had been in progress. In a clearing at the foot of the village near the Danube canal a timber platform was rigged up, surrounded by long trestle tables and benches filled with old and young. The village band and various groups of accordionists from the area frequently played, beer ran freely, and at night there was dancing. Girls with Gretchen plaits gathered in giggling groups, coyly looking on at others dancing with strapping youths in leather knickerbockers. For there were only youths—and old men. The rest had gone, and only their names remained on that barbaric war memorial.

The next day I followed the meandering Danube, not yet fully-fledged, beyond the little town of Tuttlingen to Beuron, lying below the last southern spurs of the Swabian Alps, the high-flung rock buttresses suspended in a tangle of midsummer woods. Village and meadows are dominated by the great Benedictine abbey, its church tower like a white minaret with a black hat and seen from afar as one comes along the lanes and the woodland paths sprigged with pale blue corncockles. The pleasant short village street is virtually an overflow of the abbey for it is part of the monastic estate. There is a handful of inns, all belonging to the monastery, of which the newly refurbished Hotel Pelikan is of streamlined design and has a hint of Mayfair in its decor. Three nuns sat there in their black habits, strangely sombre and exiled amid a knot of elderly visitors who were drinking Jesuitgarten wine.

Peasants milled about the porter's lodge. I was admitted by a black monolith of a monk and told to wait. Presently a tall bespectacled monk, smiling, hand outstretched, strode towards me.

'Oh, *Sie sind Englisch!*' he exclaimed and then lapsed into English, 'Ah, you are English! Do you know Fort Augustus—in Scotland?'

I did. It appeared that Dom Bernard Happle had taught in the Benedictine school there, as he had taught in Korea. He might also have taught in Japan, for just before the war Beuron made a foundation there though it was abandoned. I was to see him again, but now he handed me over to a bearded laybrother who took me to a cell above the cloister. My window framed a crown of rock cliffs set above the valley, the woodlands tumbling to this luxuriant oasis. The monastery buildings filled the foreground, and beyond flowed a vista of white villas and a white ribbon of road disappearing into the hills. This then was Beuron, which I had wanted to see ever since, as a youth, I was enthralled by a book about the life here, *Ein Tag im Kloster* by Dom Sebastian van Oer, as I was by the strange revival of Christian art which flourished here from about 1870 to the beginning of the Great War.

An eleventh-century Augustinian monastery, Beuron was suppressed in 1803 and restored by the Benedictines in 1863, when it became the mother-house of the new Congregation of Beuron. The development of this abbey was arrested about ten years later by Bismarck's *Kulturkampf*, which forced the monks to leave, to return in 1884. During this brief period of exile they made foundations in Belgium, Styria, Prague and Erdington on the edge of Birmingham (which housed Beuron monks until 1922, though little remains to speak for them), and since they had already begun to carry out a religious decorative art after what was held to be a more Christian inspiration they were able to express themselves in most of these places, as they were in other monasteries later attached to their Congregation.

The warm summer days drifted by. There was so much activity in this community of some seventy choir monks and a hundred lay-brothers, in addition to the novices. Twenty monks acting as chaplains had been killed in the last war, and another twenty were missing, some of them possibly alive in Russia. The Russians and the French had taken all the abbey's machinery, so that all the existing machines in the printing shop are new, all German except for an English monotype machine which is highly praised here. A great deal of publishing is done, and the most notable work of the present time is the reconstruction and editing of old Latin texts prior to Jerome, of which the finest collection in the world is here. In this connection the world's foremost scholars are collaborating with Beuron. Prominent in this work is Dom Alban Dold, a bearded and bespectacled scientist who works principally on palimpsests and has invented a process for deciphering them.

From the printing shop I would go perhaps to the studio of Dom Hautmar, the abbey sculptor and woodcarver, and then to the tailor's or carpenter's shop, and then there was the farm, for Beuron has one of the best dairy farms in Germany and its cattle take many prizes. Much of all this work is carried out by the *barbati* or bearded laybrothers, and such is their zeal that the tailor was said to know every article of clothing in the monastery, how long each brother had worn his things and how soon they would need renewing, and who might best succeed to the use of a discarded garment, as the shoemaker knows the shape of every foot, and knows exactly where everyone wears out his shoes, and how the soles can be made to last as long as possible. One brother was at work on the roses outside the new library building, and others wearing soft summer hats like trilbies and carrying rakes over their shoulders passed back and forth across the courtyard. In 1933 Hitler prevented the building of a special workshop for the brothers, and it still stands incomplete near the cloister court.

The library was always well filled with monks at their studies and research, and this recalled such Beuron dilettante writers as Dom Ansgar Pöllmann, who here founded the literary and art review *Gottesminne*, and Dom Timotheus Kranich, who wrote two collections of verse. No one, however, seemed to open the locked section known as 'Hell', containing agnostic works and other books on the *Index Expurgatorius*.

Cloisters, refectory and dormitory are remarkable for the mural paintings and mosaics which are the earliest works of the Beuron art school. An entire chapter of the Rule of St. Benedict is dedicated 'to those who exercise an art in the monastery'. Up to the last century, however, art in monasteries had been pursued by individuals only. Certainly there was no school of painting, no school of arts and crafts. These are modern innovations, and they are almost entirely due to the Benedictine Congregation of Beuron, who restored the practice and teaching of religious art.

Their earliest works were, naturally enough, carried out on their own premises. Thus in 1869-74 they constructed and painted the chapel of St. Maurus not far from the monastery, painted the Life of St. Benedict in the abbey dormitory and restored the abbey church and refectory, adding murals and mosaics. The Beuron style caught on. Soon the monks were decorating churches and chapels throughout Germany and Austria, in Switzerland and elsewhere.

The School of Art at Beuron was not a school in the pedagogic sense of the word, but an artistic group who wished to work out a new line of action in Christian decorative art, reacting sharply from the prevailing styles. There were, however, elements of assimilation as well as of initiation, for the new style was largely based upon the art canons of ancient Egypt. Among the recurring motifs, in paint or mosaic, are the palm and acanthus, the temple and column with fluted capital, the triumphal arch, the paterae and roundels and the inscribed tablet. The general detail might almost provide the background to Verdi's *Aida*. The inspiration no doubt derives from the Desert Fathers, the first monks of the Nitria and Thebaid deserts, yet the compositions generally have such rigidity of line and are so ponderous that they seem at home in the nineteenth-century Germany of Bismarck. There is, in fact, no mistaking their Teutonic character, and, with their 'ship mosaics and porthole windows' they have been likened to the North German Lloyd Steamships. Some of these frescoes, however, paler and more ethereal than others, have a decided Pre-Raphaelite quality. The art principles of Beuron were explained by two craftsmen and teachers of the school, Dom Desiderius Lenz and Dom Anscar Pöllmann, in their respective books *Zur Asthetik der Beuroner Schule* (Vienna, 1898) and *Vom Wesen der hieratischen Kunst* (Beuron, 1905).

The movement spread. Paintings in churches at Messkirch and Constance, at Monte Cassino in Italy, the church of Emaus in Prague, chapels in Saxony and Bohemia, along the Rhine, in Stuttgart, the parish church of Schwyz and the church of the Franciscan nuns at Tubach, both in Switzerland, the Benedictine convent at Kempen, the convent chapel at Heiligenbronn. All this, with the building and decorating of numerous new churches, and important decorative work in the abbeys of Beuron, Maredsous (Belgium), Maria-Laach and Eibingen, was achieved during the period 1876-1908.

The most monumental examples of the Beuron style are Beuron itself, Maredsous, where the entire church smoulders with dark rust-red frescoes, Maria-Laach, the east end of the church wholly worked in mosaic, and Monte Cassino. It is remarkable that the only portions of Monte Cassino to survive its recent destruction were those decorated by the Beuron monks in 1880-1913 and earlier—the crypt of the basilica, completely faced with marbles and Aberdeen granite, with portraits and medallions in mosaic, the *torretta* with its highly stylized paintings, and the chapels of St. Martin and the Pietà, with more paintings and a distinctive altar-piece with carved figures.

During this period a great number of original statues were also turned out, and finally the school trained goldsmiths and produced church vessels and ornaments. Beuron in fact pursued its policy to its logical conclusion and became an artistic, cultural and liturgical centre, establishing its now celebrated *Gregorius-Haus* or School of Sacred Music in 1907. Its influence soon made itself felt in other monasteries, at Maredsous, where the School of Arts and Crafts founded in 1903 still flourishes, and at Maria-Laach, where religious *objets d'art* continue to be produced in a manner which attempts to transcend the sentimental without losing the qualities of simplicity.

The Beuron style, however, implies the existence of a religious technique, and surely there is no such technique, no style peculiar to religious art. Thus the premises on which the art of Beuron is based have been held by many to be false. If religious art is theology in graphic representation it must be both intelligible and beautiful, free from any form of eccentricity, though equally free from limitations. The plight of religious art and the loss of artistic conviction on the part of the Church are matters which have only recently begun to receive serious attention. In the late nineteenth century Church and artist had long been divorced, and the monks of Beuron pioneered their reconciliation. But the main problem is not purely aesthetic. Religious art cannot be based upon the same canons as what is called profane art, and it calls for the outward manifestation of a different attitude of mind, an attitude which comparatively few genuine artists seem capable of attaining. The power to turn narrative into symbol and symbol into ritual is as rare today as it was common in the Middle Ages. At Beuron the attempt was at least made.

The Lady Chapel of the abbey church is wholly an essay in this Beuronese art and provides a startling contrast to the remainder of the building, a late Baroque product completed in 1738. In the elegant frescoed and stuccoed ceilings there is not even a mild hint of the Rococo that was to come. Externally the church is plain to severity, though the gable above its porticoed front is enlivened by a Beuronese painting of its patron St. Martin of Tours on horseback. Gardens and trees girdle this precinct and the warm Italian south seems quite near, though in the cemetery enclosed here one is quickly recalled to the Vaterland by the memorials inscribed *Ruhe Sanft*, the *Rest Gently* of Bach's melody.

One day I walked out to the chapel of St. Maurus, the first work of the Beuron art school. It stood against its dark green backcloth

of firs, and a spring gushed before it. It was an Egyptian temple, the
vast medallion of St. Maurus and the attendant figures of Saints
Benedict and Scholastica usurping Osiris, and again I thought of
Verdi's *Aïda*. On the pastures about it grew blue salvias, vetch, wild
thyme, yarrow, scabious and knapweed, and a nearby potato patch
was thrusting up purple flowers. Opposite lay a strip of farmland
with poultry and two brilliantly coloured peacocks. I had last seen
monastic peacocks at the Premonstratensian abbey of Tongerloo in
the Belgian Campine. Presently a primitive farm waggon drawn by
slow oxen came by. An aged bearded laybrother sat on the waggon
and another trudged beside it, his legs swathed like a Saxon serf.
He looked my way and shouted '*Grüss Gott!*'

Still following the Danube valley, crossing and recrossing the
river, I came to the small town of Riedlingen, where a stork stood
perched upon the turret of the Rathaus. Presently the road wound
through foothills and entered a narrow valley filled with rain-mist.
At the end of it, nebulous in the haze, rose two spectral towers, and
soon I was in the street of Zwiefalten.

I went straight into the courtyard before the abbey church and
knocked on the door of the gatehouse. There was no bell and the
place had a deserted air. A dog growled. Since I could see no other
likely place I continued to bang until an elderly woman came out.
I asked if this were the porter's lodge, though by this time it clearly
was not. She did not seem to understand, so I said that I wished to
speak to one of the monks.

'*Keine Mönche*,' she said abruptly. She bent forward and almost
screeched in my face. '*Keine Mönche—Krankenhaus!*'

I slunk away with a muttered apology. The monastery was a
hospital. There were no monks and there had obviously been none
since 1803. I could not account for my error. Somehow I had always
imagined monks at Zwiefalten and had never troubled to confirm it,
though it would have been a simple matter to have done so. And
what had happened to the letter I had addressed to the Lord Abbot
of the Abbey of Zwiefalten? The townspeople must have been
bewildered, or else they had had a good laugh at my expense.

There was consolation in what had been the abbey church, an
excursion into a world of new perspectives and new dimensions, a
celestial arena of coral reefs and flying cherubs, of lacquered picture
frames and *trompe-l'oeil*. For this is the Rococo, the ultimate

sublimation of the Baroque, or is it perhaps a separate and distinct style deriving from the French *rocaille*? Whatever it is, it is the embodiment of the sensual in the strict sense of the word, the same innate sense of joy and colour which is reflected in the royal courts, the theatre and the peasant festival. It is hope, joy and light as against the despair, lament and shadow of the Gothic north, and who can say that there is not as much theological justification for the one as for the other?

Zwiefalten was designed by Johann Michael Fischer (1692-1766), the Bavarian master of the Baroque, architect of no less than twenty-two abbeys and thirty-two churches, in addition to many secular buildings. As a monastery builder his output was probably rivalled only by that of the later Benoit de Wez whose work is to be seen in Belgium and Flanders. Fischer's abbey churches include Otto-beuren, Diessen, Benediktbeuren and Rott am Inn. Ottobeuren is probably the most satisfying of them but Zwiefalten has a finer façade. Yet if all these churches are stripped the shells are seen to be in the traditional near-classic style of the region. The shell is merely the vehicle for the applied decoration, and Rococo is not architecture at all but the concerted effort of sculptor and stuccoist, painter and woodcarver and ironsmith.

So at Zwiefalten there is a flood of bright discordant colour, of gold capitals against a sea of grey and blue marble, and of frescoes and lacquer in greens and pinks and browns. The pulpit is a bosky copse filled with nymphs. The confessionals are sedan chairs. Altars and stalls are capricious with ornament. Everywhere there are flying angels and cherubs, *putti* with parted baby lips and flaxen Teutonic hair. The figure of the Prophet Isaias on the high altar is terrifying but is a masterpiece of movement, as are the Angels of the Flaming Sword and the Annunciation. Most of these figures are the work of the sculptor Joseph Christian of Riedlengen and Johann Michael Feichtmayr (1710-72). Feichtmayr, who did most of the stucco decoration, is one of the geniuses of the Rococo. He was one of a large family of artist-craftsmen from Wessobrunn, and his work is to be seen in many monasteries of the German south.

The Rococo is a fever of mind and emotions that cannot be sustained indefinitely, and I took a turn about the village in order to cool down. Moreover I had still to find lodgings. The single street finally loops itself about an open space resembling a square, and

I went on into the country. I descended into a ravine, at the bottom
of which was a water mill and a stream disappearing into a grotto.
The mill was said to accommodate guests, but the proprietor, an
evil-looking giant, leered and said there were no rooms. I returned
to the village and settled in a prosaic *gasthaus*.

Southward across gently undulating country with patches of
woodland is Buchau, where the church of a former nunnery, now an
orphanage, is a stranger in this area. Designed by Michael d'Ixard,
who was responsible for the abbey of St. Blasien in the Black Forest,
this has a beautiful and most unusual interior in the early classic
style, faintly reminiscent of the Netherlands and of Robert Adam's
few churches in England. An essay in black and white and gold, the
most surprising feature is the gilding of the edges or outlines of all
the white sculptured figures. Sculptured human groups surmount
the confessionals, there are portrait medallions on all the balconies,
and there is a host of giant urns. The church was quite deserted, but
through the gateway of the adjoining buildings there came a thin
line of chattering children marshalled by a nun.

Not far distant is Schussenried, in an area once inhabited by lake-
dwellers. Here the Premonstratensian monastery has become a
hospital, and it is not the Gothic church with Baroque embellishments that detains the traveller but the former library approached
by corridors and staircases drugged with ether. Undoubtedly this
is among the richest of German libraries, the sunlight flooding into
what might be mistaken for a ballroom were it not for the frescoed
Crucifixion filling the ceiling. Marble pillars support a curving
almost drunken filigreed balcony, the elegant cabinets rise to scrolled
ornaments, and there are life-size sculptured human figures on
pedestals.

The work of the Zimmermans, Dominikus the architect and his
brother Johann Baptist the painter, is also to be seen in the pilgrimage church of nearby Steinhausen. The brothers represent the
Rococo in its purest form, whether it be in the Schussenried library
or Steinhausen church, the meadow church of Wies near Oberammergau or the Festsaal of the Nymphenburg palace at Munich.
Steinhausen is an oval church, light and rather cold with egg-shell
green and pale blue. There is the merest hint of the Moorish in the
high elongated piers and narrow arched openings, but what is
remarkable is the way the ceiling is made to flow from the piers. The

illusion is created that there is no ceiling at all. Even the capitals of the piers, exuberant with carved birds, rams' heads and clustered pineapples, are part of the picture on the ceiling, on which a balustrade is both painted and stuccoed in perspective.

The Schussen river flowing south into the Bodensee passes near the Benedictine abbey of Weingarten in view of the Appenzell mountains. The little town of Weingarten flows about the nine-hundred-year-old monastery on its terrace. The cathedral-like church was built under Italian influence, though the main hand was not the Italian Frisoni but Caspar Moosbrugger, the Benedictine laybrother who designed the Swiss Einsiedeln. Of the princely designs prepared for the monastery about 1715 only the church and the great northern block were built. Neither the balancing southern block nor the enclosing gardens and pavilions ever materialized. This northern block has long been adapted to secular use—it has been castle, orphanage and barracks and is now divided into tene-ments—and the existing monastery is housed in some medieval and modern buildings on the south.

The abbey of Weingarten is of particular interest for the English. When in 1876 Bismarck's *Kulturkampf* expelled the monks from Germany the Beuron Benedictines went into exile in several countries. Among the foundations they made was one at Erdington on the edge of Birmingham, where they lived in cottages while they built the abbey and church which is now a Gothic Revival period-piece. In 1922 they were recalled to Germany to re-establish the monastic life at Weingarten, suppressed since 1803.

It was a Sunday morning when I arrived at Weingarten, and the great bells clashed antiphonally from the twin towers. The town was crowded and the taverns were full. Human caterpillars swarmed up and down the flights of steps to the abbey terrace, where a top-hatted and yellow-liveried flunkey stood at the church door. High Mass was just ending, and a flood of people engulfed me. My lungs already filling with incense, I went to the gatehouse and asked for Dom Paul Schneider.

Dom Paul was short and stocky, a pair of bushy eyebrows rising to a triumphal ogee arch above his weak bespectacled eyes. He was no longer young. As little more than a youth he had left his native Black Forest before the Great War to become a monk of Beuron at Erdington.

'It is good to see someone who knows Erdington. It is so long ago,' and he beamed through his glasses.

He linked his arm in mine, and we paced the restored Gothic cloister where recently revealed frescoes danced with medieval allegories in faded carmine, blue and yellow. He laughed when I referred to the 'spy' rumours at Erdington during the Great War. It was true that the abbot of that time (said to be a cousin of the Kaiser) was virtually interned in a Staffordshire convent, but Father Paul remembered nothing of an official search for a wireless aerial supposedly concealed about a flagpole hoisted on the abbey.

'And what has happened since then, Father?'

He laughed and shook his head doubtfully, but gradually the story of the community since its arrival here in 1922 was revealed. In 1940 the monks were expelled by the Nazis. They were still liable for military service, however, and by the end of the war eight of their number, all priests or novices, had been killed, while five more are still listed as missing *im Russland*. Those who were not called up existed as best they could, often living in private houses. In 1947 they were allowed to return to the large school adjoining the monastery, purely in the capacity of teachers, but two years later the abbey was handed back to them.

The Wurtemburg authorities have recently thoroughly restored the cloister, refectory, chapter house and dormitory, so that all these are somewhat bare and devoid of character, inclined to be purely functional in design and furnishing. The authorities have also promised to return the vast northern court to the monks when the town's housing problem has been solved. Meanwhile the community, mustering about sixty, is somewhat cramped. There is barely any garden, and it has been necessary to establish a farm half an hour's journey away.

In the little burial-ground lay several monks who had been at Erdington, among them Brother Dominic Thomas from Liverpool, who had been the community tailor, and Dom Lambert Nolle. Dom Lambert had stayed on in England as a parish priest and had also been a professor in Jerusalem. He had lived only for the hypothetical sweetness of death, and when I knew him he was chaplain to an orphanage in a delightful Elizabethan mansion in Worcestershire. The house had been sold by a millionaire from the north when his wife had run away with his architect, who appeared to have been

a local Pecksniff. Worcestershire was a long way off but a breath of
it hung about this simple cross.

All the Erdington monks were not yet dead, however, and now
I met Dom Vincent Steinhart, in his ninetieth year, hobbling with
a stick along the cloister. He was obviously touched by this contact
with the past. 'And there is Father Pius Goeppel,' he murmured,
'he too would like to see you, but he is not well—he is even older
than I.'

Dom Paul led me into the refectory and a smocked brother
brought steaming coffee. Then he told me of the activities of the
community. He was himself, with Dom Ambrosius, editing a German translation of Cardinal Newman's sermons, the work to be
produced in twelve volumes, of which eight had so far been completed and printed in Stuttgart.

The church, seen at last, with more elbow room, is of the
Baroque. It is one of the peaks of the Baroque but it is not yet
Rococo. Yet the artists of the Rococo are here, Franz Schmutzer,
Joseph Anton Feuchtmayer and Cosmas Damian Asam, though
they have not yet developed as we choose to remember them. Flung
across the bright vast temple are the vaults which Asam has turned
into a painter's canvas. The brothers Asam, however, are best considered in Munich and east of it. There are riches and surprises
enough, among them, strangely, the enshrined relics of St. Oswald,
King of Northumbria, the abbey's second patron, and the relic of
the Precious Blood, carried in procession by top-hatted horsemen
at the patronal celebrations. The pale chocolate confectionery of
choir stalls, great Baroque organ, 'perspective' iron screens like
the *tonnelle* of Einsiedeln.

Between Weingarten and Ottobeuren lies the Allgau cheese
country, a mild country diapered with scrub and trenched with
glens and miniature ravines. From Kisslegg with its castles upon its
lake I passed through Leutkirch on the slopes of brown-streaked
hills to Memmingen, where incessant rain compelled me to dash
across the market place to the shelter of an inn, seeing little more
than the Renaissance Rathaus.

Ottobeuren itself is a little town flowing about a wide oblong
market-place hemmed with old houses with sharp rakish gables,
in the centre a black marble obelisk commemorating the war of 1870,
and, nearby, the arcaded Rathaus. Beer-cellars were much in

evidence, and I entered one, its walls and vault prinked out with
fake medievalism. As I sat down a woman at an adjoining table
greeted me with that delightful and holy '*Grüss Gott!*' which for
years had been smothered, almost compulsorily, by '*Heil Hitler!*'
—and now it was back, it was on the lips of everyone.

She was no longer young and would probably never see her
fortieth summer again, yet there was a girlish bloom about her arch
full lips and slightly *retroussé* nose, her velvety brown eyes and
flaxen hair. We engaged in small talk for a while.

'You are German, *fraulein?*'

'Austrian—and not *fraulein.*'

'Forgive me.'

'*Es mocht nicht*—it does not matter. But what is a solitary Englishman doing in Ottobeuren?'

'I have arranged to stay in the monastery, a couple of days
perhaps.'

'Ah, my son has just gone into a monastery, but I do not think
he will stay there.'

'Indeed, and why not?'

'He is too, too . . . well, he likes women too much, like his father.
There is no sex in a monastery, is there? Monks and nuns are
barren, their blood turns to vinegar.'

She looked straight at me, queerly.

'*My* blood is not vinegar, *mein Herr*, but perhaps it is too late
for you to find that out. However, I am staying at the Hotel Hirsch
. . . , *Auf Wiedersehen.*'

And with that she was gone.

I decided to go to the abbey post-haste before human flesh
weakened. Indeed I was now so intent on my purpose that I
hastened past the great twin-minaretted abbey church terraced
above one end of the market place and went straight to what in this
vast complex of buildings appeared to be the gatehouse. There I was
put into a parlour to wait until Fratre Ulrich came along. This young
novice, tall and mildly handsome, his dark wavy hair not yet
expelled by monastic shears, had been here only eighteen months,
and he hailed from Hamburg, which, he reminded me, had long
commercial associations with England. He conducted me through
the cloisters, up a grand staircase and along a corridor filled with
cells, each with a Rococo medallion of its patron saint above the door.

'*Hier ist Ihr Zimmer,*' said Fratre Ulrich, 'I will see you presently.' He smiled and glided away.

My cell resembled a small suite of rooms. The living-room was filled with furniture, including a broad desk with modern reading lamp, and for winter there was an enriched lead *ofen* or stove, while the structural enrichments of the room included a moulded plaster ceiling, a painted medallion over the door, and several oil paintings on the walls framed by stuccoed garlands with cherubs' heads. Two small rooms opened out of this, a study overlooking the hills, and, behind it, the bedroom, which had communicating window-like glass panels which opened so that fresh air and light flooded through from the study.

An eighth-century foundation, the Benedictine abbey of Otto-beuren, belonging to the Bavarian Congregation, was one of three restored early in the last century by the efforts of King Ludwig I to strengthen the concordat between the Vatican and Bavaria. The monastic church, which I now entered, was rebuilt between 1748 and 1792 to the designs of Johann Michael Fischer, and it is perhaps the most significant church of the Rococo in Germany.

Ottobeuren, equally with Zwiefalten, is an efflorescence of colour and decoration which boils and foams in mounting fury. Painting and sculpture are crowded with movement. Everywhere are airborne seraphs, and pink-cheeked *putti* swarm over the pulpit. These are Feichtmayr's figures, and they are as cunning as his work at Zwiefalten. There are leaping angels with their cloaks blowing behind them in a frenzy of wind, angels naked but for a disturbed loincloth, while a cherub holds out a garland as though he were playing hoop-la. Let puritans put on their blinkers, for here is innocent acceptance of the flesh.

This is an immense church, and its altars are reefs of coral islanded in a stormy sea. The sacred arena, the choir itself, is flanked by luxuriant choir stalls heavy with carved branch and blossom and pastoral scene, and the design is continued upward to embrace the great Baroque organs. At this eastern extremity each side of the choir rises in tiered ivory- and gilt-lacquered balconies like opera boxes. One waits for the fanfare of trumpets. But there is nothing more than the Gregorian—and the dinner bell.

In the refectory I sat next to a priest from Bremen, his biretta neatly folded on the table. The black-habited figures trooped in and took their places beneath the Rococo ceiling, the pilasters and flying cherubs. At the far end was an enormous enriched lead *ofen*, and at the other the abbot's table with the guests' table placed near it. The grace over, the lector began reading, and soon we were able to begin. Aproned brothers carried in bowls of steaming noodle soup, which we had barely eaten before the abbot stopped the reader and gave a further signal that all could talk. This was a privilege I had rarely encountered, and the priest from Bremen made the most of it. The buzz of conversation filled the refectory, accompanying the dish of curried meat and the final cup of peppermint tea, which rather startled me.

'It makes the monks sleep,' explained the priest.

The abbot, Dom Vitalis Maier, middle-aged, deep-chested and portly, came over to his guests for a few moments. Then we all filed out into the cloister and passed through the sacristy, with its massive elaborately carved vestment presses, and into the church choir.

I stood, with the others, in one of those elegant deep choir stalls, enthroned in the sacred forest, while Compline sighed like the wind, the responses flowing back and forth across the void. In the half-light the gilt gleamed like tinsel and the cherubs and *amorini* were ivory fleshed. The last praises. *Dormiam et requiescam*—'I will sleep and take my rest.'

We left the church and walked softly through the almost dark cloisters. The rustling of habits and the padding of feet. Otherwise silence. Fratre Ulrich came up behind me.

'*Hier ist es ruhig*,' he whispered, 'there is peace here, it is good to sleep in Benedictine peace.'

In my cell I heard only the wind in the trees. For a fleeting moment I remembered the woman who might even now be waiting at her hotel. . . . A bell tolled, chilling and purifying the hot blood, and a faint light glimmered upon the Crucified on the wall.

Morning breaks early in a monastery and at seven o'clock I was taking coffee and rolls in the refectory. The priest from Bremen was chatting to a brother, but there was little sign of the fifty monks. It was a solitary breakfast, as was the long day that followed it. There was plenty to see, however, from the picture galleries and museum to such treasures as the vestment worn by Martin Luther and the Romanesque chalice in the sacristy. I found pleasure in such details as the processional crosses, standards and staves topped with gilded

images, which stood against the walls near the circular abbatial
chapel. The ultimate joys were the library of 1725, with its Corinthian aisles supporting a balcony and its ceiling *trompe-l'oeil* and
delicate stucco by Johann Baptist Zimmermann, and the Kaisersaal,
its sixteen gilded life-size figures of the Hapsburgs a little in-
timidating.

On the following day I left Ottobeuren and made my way by
Kaufbeuren, still walled and towered on its western perimeter, and
Schongau, on its hill beside the Lech river, towards Oberammergau.
The sky was full of large Rococo clouds and deep patches of blue,
and southward it was held by the high wall of the Bavarian Alps.
White campaniles with black or green cupolas danced in the sunlight. The tiny village of Rottenbuch was entered through a vast
arch cut out of the buttress of a hoary white-limed barn, and the
heart of it was a quadrangle girdled with ancient buildings, some of
them perhaps relics of the ancient convent founded by St. Severinus.
The former convent church is small, grey and unobtrusive, but its
high altar is a Rococo theatre, and cherubs weaving garlands of fruit
hold back the curtains of the stage where the sacred mystery is
portrayed in sculpture.

Rottenbuch prepares one for the climax at nearby Wies, beyond
the glimpsed blue strip of the Walchensee and the chain of agonizing
calvaries. The church of Wies stands alone in the meadows, and
there is not even a hamlet to herald what is perhaps the most
beautiful church in the world, like a piece of Meissen porcelain.
And since we have used up all our superlatives we shall leave it at
that, except to point out that Wies, like Steinhausen (which is twenty
years earlier), is the work of Dominikus Zimmermann, the craftsman
who created Mozartian essays in architecture and decor. He lived in
the simple house near the church door and he died in 1766, the year
in which Johann Michael Fischer and Peter Thumb also died. The
Rococo virtually died with them, for the Asams and the Carlones
were already dead, François Cuvilliés died two years later and the
Feichtmeyrs lived only four or five years longer.

Since Oberammergau's Passion Play has become a fashionable
European artistic event, the town has acquired something of the
merits and faults of Stratford-on-Avon. The peasant art of wood-
carving has given way to exclusive ateliers and sophisticated dealers,
hotels vie with each other in the presentation of cabaret and cocktail,

jazz and the zither, and there is a hint of make-believe in such painted houses as the Hansel and Gretel Haus and the Red Riding Hood Haus. Yet Oberammergau has a satisfying quality and all is not yet lost. Earthy-smelling farms of noble proportions and cattle with the antiphony of their bells survive in the midst of cosmopolitan luxury. In the heart of the town a canal fringed with low white cottages seems strangely Flemish, and the nearby churchyard is a quiet oasis peppered with memorials to dynasties of local actors and woodcarvers.

The comfortable old posting-house kept by Anton Preisinger was my base for a few days. Preisinger played the Christ in the Passion Play of 1950, and his predecessor Alois Lang, the Christ of 1930, runs a rival hotel. Both retain the patriarchal beards which the actors normally begin to grow eighteen months before the play is performed. The Mary of 1950 has married the town tailor, and the Magdalen, Gabrielle Gropper, works in her father's hardware store.

From the oriel projecting from my room one could look down upon the little square, as animated as Piccadilly Circus. At dinner in the restaurant a German joined, uninvited, a not quite middle-aged English spinster at her table. He looked a typical Prussian, a giant with bald square head and cold pince-nez perched on the bridge of his nose. He was obviously insinuating himself into her favour, apparently with some success, when he leaned over and whispered to her. She suddenly turned carnation-pink, frowned angrily, shot up abruptly and went away without a word. . . . He remained, his sang-froid apparently undisturbed. Perhaps when Oberammergau had the Passion Play to itself there were no such seedy intruders.

In the bar of the big hotel in the square a man in traditional costume sat playing the zither, as he did night after night. His strong brown hairy hands moved quickly over the zither, but on his face was a look of unutterable boredom and despair, though he smiled faintly when the applause came and his glass of beer was replenished. The locals gathered here. The visitors were massed about the dance floor of the restaurant, where skirts flew and rumps swayed to alien rhythms. Around the corner the vast steel-girdled theatre lay dark and silent.

For various reasons it was necessary to change my lodgings, and I was now installed in a miniature castle on the edge of the town near the waters of the Ammer and the foot of the Kofel peak. This *gasthaus* was really a villa in Wagnerian Gothic, obviously built under the influence of Ludwig's castle of Neuchwanstein not far distant; it approximated to our own Victorian Gothic Revival and it reminded me of a house in Hereford's cathedral close. The villa was sheltered by thick fringes of pines, and a fountain played on the lawn where a girl exposed her Nordic limbs to the sun. In the bright green meadows there was a tangle of dark purple harebells, marsh violets, mauve primulas and pink lucerne, and all about were the far-flung pine forests rising to distant peaks.

But an hour's walk along the high road into Austria (though still in Bavaria) is the Benedictine abbey of Ettal, its great copper domes flashing against the dark climbing forests in the pass which seems blocked by the Zugspitze. This is another house of the Bavarian Congregation, founded by Duke Ludwig in 1330 in fulfilment of a vow he made when in difficulties in Italy. After its suppression with all German monasteries in 1803 it became a brewery, but it was restored to the monks at the beginning of this century. In the past it was at one time responsible for the survival of the Oberammergau Play, and the local art of woodcarving probably originated here. The community's present activities include the maintenance of a school and the production of jade- and amber-coloured liqueurs which are also put into chocolates. These liqueurs share the honours with the *bondieuserie* on the stall which stands in the outer court, presided over by a lame monk and his secular assistants.

The church is decidedly Italian in feeling, and it is not surprising to find that the architect was Enrico Zuccali (who, however, came from Munich), who began work in 1744. The plan, a circular body with a smaller oval choir, distinctly recalls Longhena's church of S. Maria della Salute in Venice. The façade, however, lacks the grand flight of steps and the three loggias over the three doorways originally planned for it, and the existing work was in fact completed only in 1899. Yet despite the Italian shell the decoration is of a mild Rococo, the figure sculpture with swirling draperies by Straub, father of Bavarian sculptors, and the stuccowork by Joseph Schmuzer, who designed Oberammergau's church and worked at several monasteries. The fresco in the dome is by the Tyrolean Jakob Zeiller, the work of two summers, and shows the Holy Trinity enthroned on clouds appearing to St. Benedict and to an angel with the wonder-working image of Ettal, joined by a host of monks and nuns, bishops and princes. The high altar largely follows the design of Franz Ignaz Günther, greatest of Rococo sculptors, though it was completed later and has a suggestion of the new classical style.

It was spring when I alighted at the station of Ebenhausen-Schäftlarn, the highest point of the little Isar-Tal railway between Kochel and Munich. Thick forest lay beyond the village, and pale golden strips of snow streaked the mountains southward. Just out of sight lay the valley of the Isar, where once had passed the Imperial procession, accompanied by the great bishops, on its way to Italy. The village with its wooden houses and farms straggled towards the edge of the forest. Almost the last house was that of the local cobbler. The road streaked downward, occasionally to be abandoned in favour of idyllic footpaths, and patterns of light played amid the cathedral of oaks, beeches on their straight boles and young firs. Here and there were patches of furtive coltsfoot and violets.

Kloster Schäftlarn lay in a clearing. The village was little more than the overflowing farm buildings of the monastery, and one of them now housed the inn. Here a family from Nuremberg—the man and his wife stolid and heavily built, and their twin elderly spinster daughters in ugly bright sweaters—held the dining-room with their chatter and laughter. The narrow road meandered through what had once been the abbey's formal gardens with their lost pavilions, and a simple fountain threw its single jet beside the highway.

The plain stuccoed buildings of the monastery, picked out in green and white, housed a boys' school under the care of the Benedictines of the Bavarian Congregation who have returned here, though not in great strength. One of the score of monks whom I met, along with a gangling thin companion, lifting his skirt out of the mud as he wended his way into the church, turned out to be Pater Bonifatius Rossmark, who had been a prisoner-of-war in England and then in Kansas. He was proud of his abbey church, the first I had encountered to designs by François Cuvilliés, the dwarf of Walloon descent who became first architect to the Elector of Bavaria. Not even the Neapolitan can outdo the Bavarian in his love of gilt and gaudy, and so here again were the flamboyant Rococo altars, the enriched painted ceilings and opera-box balconies and a heavenly host of sculptured figures by Straub. Round windows poured light into this serene church, and there was a steadying note of relief in the massed banks of ivy and fir trees, brought in, perhaps, for Easter.

Since the bombing of Cuvilliés' Reiche-Zimmer and theatre of the Residenz in Munich, little enough of this remarkable artist's work remains. The most interesting are the decorated apartments of Schloss Brühl near Cologne and the Amalienburg pavilion or hunting lodge in the park of Munich's Nymphenburg Palace. At the latter I duly arrived from Schäftlarn. Hemmed in by tree and shrub, the pavilion is thrust suddenly upon one so that there is little opportunity to appreciate it in perspective. It is a miracle that one accepts—or it is sheer heresy. Either way it has a quality of Grimms' fairy tales, and one waits for the princess to trip into a glass coach. The ceilings are yellow, the walls are blue, and all the stuccoed ornaments and doorcases and picture frames are silver. Returning through the wooded park to the white buildings of the Nymphenburg, where the celebrated porcelain is yet made in one of the wings, one may stand in Zimmermann's brilliant Festsaal and wonder why the palm is given to Cuvilliés' Amalienburg.

Munich, however, is rich in paradox and antithesis, and though bombing has erased some of the neo-Greek monuments set up under Ludwig I early last century it still offers some rare vistas and rarer experiences. D. H. Lawrence found it 'puffed under the eyes with beer and bohemianism'. The beer is still there but the bohemianism has wilted to a pallid spectre of its former self, though the tradition of hospitality survives, as do the delightful bookshops and the marionette theatre. There is intrigue all the way from the streamlined caravanserai that is the new railway station, where American servicemen in civilian dress straight out of *Guys and Dolls* prop up the hotel walls, to the river Isar at the other end of the town, its banks strange with the formidable buildings of the Deutsche Museum, the Maximilianeum and a bevy of ecclesiastical hybrids. In between lie riches both sacred and profane, from the Hofbrauhaus to the little Rococo church of the brothers Asam, with its Salomonic pillars and faded tinsel, and their own house adjoining it.

In the immense smoky halls of the Hofbrauhaus, the great Gothic beer palace, the people of Munich have gathered for the evening, massed about the tables and quaffing the brown Hofbrau beer from the litre pots of glazed earthenware individually known as a 'mass'. Plump waitresses in Bavarian costume peddle flowers and cigars. The Lenten fast is not yet over—it is Holy Saturday—and the special dark spring beer with a high wort content is available to sustain those abstaining from meat. Soon, at the beginning of May, the strong 'Bock' introduced at Einbeck in the sixteenth century will be served here. Yet there is no lack of viands and mounds of sausages festoon the tables (a waitress told me that some 15,000 sausages are eaten here on Shrove Tuesday). At the business end of each hall the great beer casks are enthroned, the central labelled in large capital letters HELL, though it contains nothing more sinister than 'light' or 'hell' beer.

'Politics spoil the character', runs a German proverb, and certainly the subject seems generally to be avoided in public. On this night of Holy Saturday, however, there was one table at which the laughter and banter did not ring out, and that was my own table. Here a small group were sorrowfully quiet and at times even muttered darkly of the Vaterland's changing fortunes and of humanity in general.

'We are fit only for suffering. We shall destroy ourselves, mark my words, and we shall have deserved it!'

There were other observations in this jaundiced Spenglerian vein, and gradually the reason for the leading speaker's vehemence seemed to be revealed. He was a cousin of a man shot down by his own countrymen at Altötting not far from Munich. It was towards the end of the war, when five men of Altötting—Martin Seidl, Josef Bruckmayer, Adam Wehnert, Hans Riehl and the priest of the Heilige Kapelle or Holy Chapel—obeyed an American order to keep the streets lit as a precaution against bombardment. They were then quickly taken by some Nazis behind the church in the market place and summarily shot.

Late that night the Hofbrauhaus resembled a bawdy Elizabethan tavern, but outside the streets were dark, silent and deserted. What light there was came from the stained-glass windows, like magic carpets flung across the sky, of the churches. It was midnight of Holy Saturday, and Gregorian chant floated on the Munich night. St. Peterkirche was packed to the doors. Priests in laced frocks and gorgeous vestments celebrated the holy mysteries before a golden altar blazing with light, and before the chancel stood a line of boys in scarlet capes bearing giant candles.

A few days later, in torrential rain, I arrived at Stock on the shores of the Chiemsee and boarded a little white steamer for the Herren-Insel. The largest of all the Bavarian lakes, exposed to heavy storms, the buff-coloured beds of reed about its banks give little hint of its awesome depth. The few passengers were islanders destined for the Frauen-Insel, but I sprang off at the little wooden jetty of the Herren-Insel, below the Altes Schloss, a seventeenth-century barrack-like cube which once housed monks but which now served as the quarters of the staff that administered the State-owned island, the hotel, farm and Neues Schloss of Ludwig II.

About the terraced Schloss Hotel flow the farm buildings, the great open shed with its wooden waggons and the byre where the hands sing chant-like folk songs to unheeding but superb red and white cows. On the edge of all this, near the shore, lies the little island chapel, glowing with a restrained Baroque and a sophisticated angel painted on the wooden ceiling.

Ludwig's palace lies at the end of a long glade shaded with beeches and firs and misty with wood anemones, violets, primroses and coltsfoot. It is, no doubt, sheer pastiche, a Wagnerian version of Versailles built in 1878-85 by Dollman and Hoffman, whose virtuosity may also be seen in Ludwig's palaces at Linderhof and Neuschwanstein not far away on what is called the Romantic Road. Yet it is enchanting enough, though its delights may be tempered by the tragic wraith of Ludwig, the recluse who lived there but twenty-three days in all and whose personality dominates the place and gives it a moody, distracting quality. The guides and interpreters live in the Altes Schloss, though one, a woman who learned excellent English in China, where her father managed a factory, and was widowed in the last war and then bombed out of Munich, now lives on the mainland. Under her guidance I embarked upon a self-obligatory tour, noting the enamelled peacocks in the vestibule, the grand staircase, the lilac antechamber and green salon, the pale blue Salle du Conseil and the Galerie des Glaces (lighted by 4,000 candles on summer evenings), the turquoise swimming bath, the vast almost-Rococo gilded bed and the dining-table which, like that of Louis XIV, was laid below and was hydraulically sent up through the floor for each course.

My mentor was one of the few who did not subscribe to the general verdict on Ludwig.

'*Er war nicht ganz beschränkt*—he was not so mad,' she said. Was she perhaps a Wagnerite, I ventured. She shrugged her shoulders; naturally, she liked Wagner's music, or some of it, but as to the Ludwig-Wagner relationship she knew little.

Back at the Schloss Hotel I sat in the multi-windowed terraced restaurant looking into the mist and rain of the storm-tossed lake. Since it was out of season the hotel itself was closed, upsetting my plans for the next few days. I intimated as much to the manager Hans Huber and his genial debonair son Max, ex-commander of a German two-man submarine and a prisoner-of-war in the Netherlands. Max deplored recent economic trends in Germany and he was enlightening on labour problems since he was himself suffering from labour shortage. He finally phoned a fisherman on the Frauen-Insel and arranged my stay there that night.

On the next and last storm-tossed boat I renewed acquaintance with the guide at the palace; who with other estate employees was returning home for the night. With others she disembarked at a village on the shores of the mainland. The Frauen-Insel now lay less than two miles away, riding low on the water like a reef (if it were not for the tell-tale onion-spire of the church). Much smaller than the Herren-Insel, it is inhabited by a larger permanent community of fortunate islanders who live off the fish in the lake, their fruit trees and their smallholdings. This is one of the most idyllic of islands, sandy-beached, gossammered with green willows and lime trees, an isle of content where little more is demanded than the few acres of rich soil and its enclosing waters can give. The summer hedonism of Munich and Salzburg peoples this island kingdom with bathers and yachtsmen, but out of season it returns to its normal life as a fishing village.

A tall slim flaxen-haired man in traditional Bavarian jacket and breeches strode slowly along the wooden jetty as the steamer hove to, and it was soon clear that this was Josef Lex, the fisherman who had arranged to meet me. '*Grüss Gott!*' he smiled warmly, and saying little more he shouldered my bag and set off with long strides across the little island.

Josef and his wife lived with his parents, and the family welcome was warm and courteous, perhaps mildly excitable since no other Englishman had ever received their hospitality. Much of the conversation floored me, and when Frau Lex asked '*Möchten Sie eine*

Wärmflasche haben?' it was some little time before I realized that
a *Wärmflasche* was a hot water bottle.

The house at the water's edge provided some measure of the
limited prosperity a well-conducted self-supporting island community can enjoy. Like the other well-designed homesteads of
natural wood, Josef's house was spacious, with a balcony over the
double front, and the amenities included electricity, running water
and modern bathroom, while the kitchen was fitted up with an
Aga-type cooker.

Josef had two good modern fishing boats, and the island could
muster some eighty vessels which drag the lake for pike, salmon and
other worthwhile fish. At Corpus Christi comes the gathering of the
island boats, when the fishermen wear traditional costume and the
maidens are dressed like brides. The boats are festively decorated,
and the long water-borne procession encircles the island, halting at
its four corners to sing the four Gospels, after which there is flag-
dipping and the shooting of guns.

Night fell quickly. After dinner Josef and his family and friends
congregated in the dining-room of the single hotel, the hotel itself
open only in season. It is a place of homely solid old-fashioned
comforts, rich in prints and antiques and having the inevitable tiled
stove and crucifix. And, unique gesture, it remembers its fallen
patrons, their photographs assembled on a wall of the dining-room,
which was after all their common meeting place. There they are,
eleven of them, all killed *im Russland*—Wilhelm Zeitter, Rudolph
Krammer, Karl Marx and the rest, all calm and thoughtful and no
doubt dedicated patriots. These names are to be found again on the
war memorial on the village green, with its fresco of an aged man
and woman mourning their lost sons against a background showing
the island set in the lake. It is a powerful and moving picture, full of
symbolism, since these might be Mary and Joseph against the Sea
of Galilee.

The next day brought a reluctant sun and relief from silver rain,
and the island lay fresh and fragrant upon its still waters. Great
linden trees, beloved of Schubert and Heine, gave a touch of seclusion to the Benedictine nunnery founded in 782. Attacked by the
Hungarians in the medieval wars, converted into a fortress and
destroyed several times by fire, it has been rebuilt again and again
by the nuns, who themselves did much of the work, carrying stones,

cultivating gardens and tilling the fields. In this cloister a nun wrote
the first religious-mystic poem in the German language.

Of a total population of about two hundred, seventy-four are
nuns, and the convent boarding school considerably swells the
population even further. The abbey church, where the nuns' choir
is hidden behind a gallery, is one in which the austere Romanesque
and Gothic mingles with the capricious Baroque, while the detached
octagonal tower with bulbous cap contributes a note of whimsy.
There are riches here of painting and sculpture, but for the islanders
none so rich as the shrine of St. Irmengard. The treasures of the
nunnery itself may be beholden only by feminine eyes, and Frau
Lex told of the immense, almost hierarchical portrait gallery of
abbesses in the cloister. There is, however, no sex bar to the purchase of the amber-coloured Kloster Likor and the stomach bitters
distilled by the nuns.

It was not surprising to find celebrities at rest in the beautiful
churchyard, and among them lies Jodl, one of Hitler's more influential generals. Writers and artists have long been attracted to the
Frauen-Insel, which has figured not a little in their work, notably
in that of Josef Viktor von Scheffel, the problematic poet of donnish
humour and fantasy, and in that of the prolific popular novelist
Wilhelm Jensen, who also lies here.

In early summer the cherries hang blood-red on their boughs.
The last *schneeglockche*, that ubiquitous snowdrop-like flower, lies
withered on its stalk. The last snow is melting from the peaks on the
mainland, from those Bavarian peaks which gave D. H. Lawrence
claustrophobia ('mountains *never* move—they are *always* there').
Boatbuilders are busy on the shingle, and fishing nets are drying on
racks in the sun. Over in his workshop-studio Georg Klampfleuthner, the potter, is at work.

9

SPANISH EARTH

THE flower stalls were already out beneath the plane trees on Barcelona's Rambla, and a sharp shower made the crowd in the Plaza de Cataluña break for cover as I left for the Grand Canyon country of Montserrat. Out in the countryside an interminable drought had left dry river beds and parched red earth, and shrubs and terraced vines were languishing. The 'bus made its way round through bluffs covered with birch and honeysuckle, holly and eucalyptus, and above the valley rose the fantastic mountain of Montserrat, the Sacred Mountain, perhaps the Montsalvat of Parsifal, the inaccessible and mysterious resting-place of the Holy Grail, its pale rocks shaped into incredible fingers, flutes, domes and sphinxes. In this eyrie high up in the cold bright air between heaven and earth lie the yellow stone cubes of the monastery.

Montserrat, from below, a swallow's nest perched precariously on the cliff, proved on arrival to be a self-contained village, with hotel, streamlined bar, restaurant, shops and a post office where a monk actually handed over one's stamps. These Benedictines will provide in a hostel bed and blankets, a frying pan and cutlery and leave you to your own resources. It was, however, more satisfactory to be accommodated within the monastery, in the splendid *Cella Hospitum*, where my tastefully furnished cell looked over the outer court towards the Meteora-like mountain.

The first monk I encountered was young Fray Basilio, who introduced me to Padre Michael. With Padre Michael, who hailed from Tarragona, I had a deal of conversation in the monastic parlours. The large community of some hundred and fifty monks uses the Catalan tongue for all administrative purposes, though it appears that Catalan in Spain is officially under much the same ban as is Breton in France. Montserrat now belongs to the Cassinese Congregation of Subiaco, as do the monasteries of San Clodio, Vilvaneyra, Samos and Pueyo, where during the Civil War the monks were martyred to a man. Here they were more fortunate, escaping to monasteries all over Europe, though twenty-two of them were hunted out and murdered by the Communists, who turned Montserrat into a hospital and held their 'parliament' in the refectory. This recalled the misfortunes of the Peninsular War, when the monks here were 'hunted like chamois along the cliffs' by General Suchet's men when the French took over the monastery as a garrison fort.

Meanwhile Montserrat was alive with pilgrims, entire families combining a day's outing with a pilgrimage to Nuestra Señora de Montserrat, the Black Virgin. They climbed even higher by the little aerial railway to the hermitages of San Giovanni and San Juan, where, ignoring the restaurant built into the living rock and planted with geraniums and bougainvilia, they cooked on camp fires and strummed guitars.

From the monastery terrace set with sculptured figures one could see the plain of Catalonia far below. Passing through an arcaded forecourt, with remains of the Romanesque buildings, one enters the church, a dim cavern fretted with gold, with rows of hanging lamps as in an oriental bazaar. At the end of it, high above the altar, is the tiny *camarin* of the Virgin. Peasant girls climbed the little staircase to the shrine, where they knelt in the golden brilliance before the smoke-tarnished Madonna, like a gypsy queen in her finery, darkly smiling and at peace. Well she knows the secrets of the human heart, as she knows the miseries of human travail, for her memory is long. Pedro III of Aragon sat at her feet throughout one long night. His successor came to beg her support for his invasion of Majorca and borrowed one of her rings to take with him. Queen Violante climbed the mountain barefoot and fell exhausted before her. Carlos V held a candle from her shrine as he lay dying, and Don Juan of Austria asked to be buried near her. And still they come.

Workmen were busy reconstructing the choir, and there was the clanging of hammers and the scraping of chisels digging into the stone floors. I found my way through a series of brilliant marble chapels into the labyrinthine corridors of the monastery, into the library and the picture gallery established by the late abbot, Dom Antonius Marcet, who had entered Montserrat at the age of eight.

The cloister was a well of light, neo-Romanesque, and filled with sweet-smelling magnolias and potted geraniums.

At Vespers the few guests sat in a tribune high at the side of the basilica. The monks used the *alto coro* over the west end, and the chanting was disturbed by the building operations still in progress, for all had to be completed by Easter, then only a fortnight ahead. The monks remained in their stalls, but out in front there stood the choirboys of the Escoliana, the celebrated and ancient school of plainsong, under their conductor Dom Ireneo Segarra. The soloist among these white-surpliced angels was the boy wonder Buenaventura Bajet, a voice preserved in thousands of wax discs. Involuntarily we rose and crowded to the rail at the end of the tribune as the choir sang the *Salve Regina*. A monk of Montserrat, Dom Bernard Boil, accompanied Columbus in 1493 as vicar to the newly discovered Central America, and Columbus himself has told us how the *Salve Regina* was sung each night on the voyage. And now, softly and sweetly, there came the *Virolai*, the Catalan hymn written by a monk of the abbey.

> *Rosa d'abril, Morena de la serra,*
> *de Montserrat estel :*
> *illuminau la catalana terra,*
> *quiau-nos cap al cel . . .*[1]

Padre Michael collected us and we went through the labyrinth again and into the enormous refectory, which quickly filled with the immense community, though the table of the abbot, Dom Aurelius Escarré, was vacant for he was in bed with heart trouble. The lector had now begun reading, and soon the aproned servers wheeled in the supper on double-decker trolleys. This was decidedly palatable, first onion soup, then boiled potatoes and cabbage, followed by fish with salad and ending with apricot purée. There was white wine throughout and, strangely, a glass of white milk to hand.

Afterwards, in the fading light, we stood talking to Padre Michael and Fray Basilio in the cloister. One young guest had studied at Georgetown in the United States and also in Mexico, and he was now reading law in the University of Madrid. He it was who

[1] Rose of April, Dark one of the Mountain,
Star of Montserrat;
Shed light over Catalonia,
Lead us up to heaven . . .

informed me that the best Spanish is spoken in Valladolid and Vittoria, to which I remarked that the best French was said to be spoken in Tours and the best German in Hamburg and Hanover. He, however, had the last word, which rather shook me.

'Yes, and the best English is spoken in Dublin!'

There was a faint pattering in the cloister garth which quickly reached a crescendo. We all turned towards it.

'Rain,' murmured Padre Michael. 'For days we have prayed for it, the people too.' And, at last, after months of drought, here it was, the precious water which we in the north squander with prodigality. When I reached my room heavy rain was beating like a drum-roll on an adjoining patio roof, and eventually it lulled me to sleep in an antique-styled bed beneath the mural inscription *Signatum est super nos lumen vultus tui Domine*.

With morning the sacred mountain was enveloped in thick billowing mist, and through the breaks a powdering of snow could be seen on the ultimate heights. I breakfasted alone on a cup of thick chocolate and a large bowl, without handles, of milk slightly stained with coffee. There were but two monks in the refectory, their powerful granite-like heads reminding me of a painting by Pascual de Lara. Montserrat was now deserted, and I spent the day loitering about the village and following tracks among the Surrealistic rock formations. Towards midday next morning Padre Michael kindly arranged an early solitary lunch consisting mainly of rice and noodles and *tortilla*. Had I remained for the community meal I would have seen not only the abbot but also the Abbot-General of the Cistercian Order and the Cistercian Abbot of Poblet. At the abbot's table these three places were now laid, each with three wine glasses (as against the two tumblers provided for each monk). The last I saw of the sacred mountain was from an air lift swinging through space to the caramel-coloured river far below in the plain.

On the train that crawled through the night from Barcelona I had for company a morose peasant and his crate of twittering parakeets, but even they had departed by the time I was stranded in darkness in the village of Espluga de Francoli. I had hoped to reach the abbey of Poblet, but this lay nearly four kilometres away in unfamiliar country and it was already after ten o'clock. It was obviously unthinkable to tramp on and arrive, unexpected and unannounced, at such an hour. In the deserted narrow streets the balconies

festooned with flowerpots could just be discerned, but I came at
length to a well of light in a small plaza. It was a *fonda*. Here the
Garrell family dispensed hospitality and displayed much curiosity.

The son of the house told me that Poblet had robbed Espluga of
its glories. For many years the parish church had contained the
remains of eight kings, nine queens and ten princes of the ancient
kingdom of Aragon, hidden here for safe keeping at the sacking of
Poblet in 1835. Then one night, only three years ago, soldiers with
fixed bayonets stood guard over these remains. The next day the
Generalissimo Franco himself passed through the village, and the
kings and queens and princes were taken from Espluga on three
horse-drawn carriages, back to Poblet to be re-buried in restored
tombs. But we still have the radioactive waters—why does nobody
come? he concluded.

Morning proved Espluga to be not unattractive. Outside, the
fonda girls were filling pitchers at an elaborate fountain, and another
square, the Plaza del Generalissimo, was hemmed in on two sides
with churches and set about with box hedges and memorials to local
worthies.

I took the road to Poblet. Southward stretched sage-green
shrublands, above them tracts of cultivated land with red and green
stripes like awnings rising to a plateau of red soil, itself backed by
distant mountains. Peasants had drawn up their two-wheeled carts
beside the road and put their horses to graze and were breakfasting
over a wood fire. Another man trudging beside a heavily-laden mule
called out '*Buenos dias!*' A calvary fell behind me, and then another,
and soon the vineyards and wooded hills immediately to the north
were screened by the long battlemented wall of the monastery, in
which dark blue flowers like giant blackberries had found a foothold.

Soon I was passing through the outer gatehouse and into the
first of the three walled precincts. The doors of a big stone barn lay
open, and within it was heavy with giant wine casks—was this the
El Priorato wine which was once so celebrated and which emanated
from Poblet? Beyond flowed the honey-coloured monastery in a
golden light, girdled by its fortified wall broken by towers and a
strong gatehouse and the richly sculptured entrance to the church.
Poblet was a daughter-house of Clairvaux via Grandselve and Fontfroide, both in Languedoc, so that here the Cistercian Burgundian
style is modified by the Languedocien. The austere church, how-

ever, is virtually Romanesque, with a more sophisticated treatment in the eastern chevet of chapels. Abandoned until 1939, some measure of restoration was now in progress, and workmen were busy installing new side-chapels.

The porter admitted me through the fortified gatehouse begun in 1309 under Pedro the Ceremonious and showed me into a long vaulted apartment in the medieval palace of Don Martin, for the medieval prelates often had suites in these monasteries, or at any rate there was provision for such a visit as that, in 1493, of Ferdinand and Isabella with their three children (one of whom was our Catherine of Aragon), who came here in thanksgiving for the capture of Granada from the Moors, bringing a retinue of three hundred ladies and five hundred serving-men. At that time Poblet was an exclusive and wealthy house, and it is said that each monk had two personal servants and rode a white mule, while postulants had to prove their armorial quarterings to the satisfaction of the Chapter. In the political troubles early last century the monks were divided, some espousing the Liberal, some the Absolutist, cause. I had no doubt when Padre Agustin introduced himself that the present struggling community, the only one of the Cistercian Common Observance in Spain, led saner and holier lives. He hailed from Barcelona—the forty monks were all Spanish—though he had spent four years at Hauterive in Switzerland, and he was lean, tall and bespectacled, with an obvious zest for life unquenched by discipline and abstinence.

We entered a beautiful cloister, a near-reproduction of that at Fontfroide, though this has a small pavilion containing a fountain or lavabo jutting out into the garth massed with cypress, laurel and rose. We saw the splendid chapter house, its pavement overlaid with a row of tombstones with abbatial effigies in low relief, and entered the church. Behind the purple Lenten veil concealing the high altar a towering snow-white *retablo* was now revealed, a Renaissance work in alabaster with sculpture by Damian Forment, a work of art which, strangely, provoked a revolt of the monks and led to the confinement for life of the abbot responsible. Padre Agustin pointed out that Poblet was today one of three Cistercian houses working towards a revival of the ancient and traditional Cistercian rite (the others being Boquen in Brittany and Hauterive), and that at the moment the original Mass could be said by only one monk.

The unique features of the church, however, are the low stone arches like bridges that span the crossing, covered with the gleaming tombs and royal effigies of alabaster which were once surmounted with carved and painted wooden canopies. These have recently been restored from numerous fragments by the Catalan sculptor Frederico Mares, with such thoroughness and research that the material used is from the very quarry in the Pyrenees that had supplied the original alabaster. From the church we climbed the stone staircase out of the north transept into the dormitory, one of the largest and most impressive ever built anywhere by the Cistercians, the way the medieval monks went to the night-office, as they do today.

The monks were now filing into the Romanesque refectory, where from the original stone fountain in the centre water is still drawn and taken to table, and Padre Agustin settled me in an adjoining chamber with tapestry-hung walls. Here Fray Juan quietly and discreetly served me with a lunch of *sopa de pane*, potatoes and peas, *tortilla* and pimentoes, bottled pears and cheese. The wine and the whole of the food was of local provenance, with the exception of the American cheese.

The monks in a single flowering white line came chanting out of the refectory, one postulant in civilian clothes tagging on at the end. A freezing wind blew through the cloister, and there was no form of central heating anywhere. My friend now took me to the library, which, if it no longer contained such treasures as the rich library of Pedro I, bound in red leather, was well stocked. Padre Agustin was a great lover of English literature (which he had read in Spanish and French), and he proudly indicated volumes of Shakespeare and Milton and anthologies of English poets. We visited the calefactory, locutory, infirmary, dispensary, kitchen and wine cellars, and deep in the hinterland of the monastery we paced the little cloisters and courts, violet-scented and loud with bees. A building that was a mere shell was to be the printing shop, where the machines would be German, all except the linotype which of course was to be English. Nearby a beautiful purple lilac was in bloom, and Padre Agustin recalled the opening passage of Oscar Wilde's *Picture of Dorian Gray*: '*The studio was filled with the rich odour of roses, and when the light summer wind stirred amidst the trees of the garden, there came through the open door the heavy scent of the lilac. . . .*'

Reluctantly I was compelled to refuse an invitation to stay for a few days (explaining my thwarted plans of the previous evening), and Padre Agustin stood below the frowning gatehouse and waved me off along the hot white road to Espluga de Francoli.

A couple of hours after dining in the Escudillers of Barcelona I was in Madrid, dropped from the sky in an aluminium shell and finally deposited near the Puerta del Sol. The next day I went to pay my respects to Fray Justo Pérez de Urbel at the little Benedictine priory in the Calle San Bernardo, once a flourishing community founded under the protection of Philip IV when the monks of Montserrat in Catalonia were expelled in 1641. The Baroque church fronting the street was designed by no less an architect than Pedro de Ribera, that master of the drunken Churriguerresque, though this is mildly festive. The more recent history of this miniature second Montserrat is a melancholy one. In 1834 during an outbreak of cholera in Madrid it was rumoured that the monks were poisoning the water, and on 17 July the mob broke loose and massacred most of the community. Almost exactly a century later history repeated itself, after the monks had been accused of distributing poisoned sweets to children in the poorer quarters of the city. On 18 July 1936, the military rising under General Franco began. That same night the Republican Government distributed arms to the workers, and within a few hours the revolution was under way. On the following day, Sunday, Mass was said as usual in the parish churches, but within twenty-four hours all monasteries and convents were closed and the religious were either prisoners or fugitives.

On that fateful Sunday the prior, Dom José Anton Gómez, dissolved the little community of six monks, a laybrother and two servants. The monks dispersed to find lodgings with friendly local families. On the Monday morning five of them returned to say Mass. That afternoon women broke in and looted the monastery. Soon the church treasures were also looted, and the Communists turned the church into a dance hall and the monastery into a prison. The prior, after having endangered several of his friends by accepting their hospitality, finally went to live under false papers at a small hotel. In September he was discovered by the 'People's Police' and taken into custody, and a few days later his corpse was found on the road to Andalucia.

Dom Antolin Pablos Villanueva had taken refuge with a deaf old lady whom he used to confess, but one day he was recognized in the National Library and put in prison. In 1939 his body was found in the common fosse, probably one of the four hundred prisoners who had been shot on the edge of a ditch outside the town three years earlier.

Dom Rafael Alcocer Martinez had taken refuge with his cousin and together they lived in a boarding-house where the monk posed as a coal merchant. Upon hearing that the house was about to be raided Dom Rafael found employment with a friendly bookseller, where he was given a bed and a stove for cooking at the back of the shop. Showing little discretion, however, he went about the town, mixing with people and visiting public places. When Toledo was relieved by the Nationalists these people celebrated the event by a dinner party at which the monk was present. A girl who was among the guests talked about it and was arrested by the police, who wrung a confession from her and ultimately shot her. Dom Rafael was then apprehended and also shot.

The remaining three monks were also arrested in houses of friends. Padres Luis Vidaurrazaga Gonzalez and Emilio Santamaria were sent to the Ventas Prison, but Padre Luis strove for freedom and having obtained it was shot by militiamen. Dom Emilio survived and was prior when he died a few years ago. Dom Daniel Palomero was released from prison on account of his age and sent to Alicante where he found refuge with a poor peasant. Today, over eighty years of age, he is the sole survivor of that little community.

The prior of the present community, called here in recent years from the abbey of Silos, is Dom Justo Pérez de Urbel, Professor of Medieval History in the University of Madrid, poet and author of over a score of books. I found him to be short, bespectacled and balding, fluent in French, hesitant in English, bustling with nervous energy and at the call of everyone. It was a busy day, for the abbot of Silos in Old Castile, Dom Toribio Ramos, was an honoured guest. Today was the jubilee of the abbot's ordination, and at lunch in the refectory, like the dining-room of a simple house, he sat at the superior's table, especially laid with a white cloth and two large silver-plated ewers filled with flowers. After a short reading conversation was allowed over the prawns and tomatoes, the mixed vegetables, the fried fish, fruit and white wine.

The abbot is the head of a powerful group of monasteries comprising Santo Domingo de Silos itself, where is a celebrated Romanesque cloister, and its daughter-houses here in Madrid, in Navarre and in Buenos Aires. All belong to the French Benedictine Congregation, for Silos was restored late last century by monks from Solesmes and Ligugé. Dom Toribio extended an invitation to Silos, though he thought that might not be possible during the next fortnight because of the heavy reservations for the Holy Week ceremonies. It was late in the afternoon when I stepped into the nineteenth-century Madrid of Pérez Galdós and entered a bodega of the people noted for its *tapas*.

I was not in the mood for Madrid and quickly left for Toledo, that place where the Devil was first officially declared to exist as a personified being. Naked and scorched upon its high rock, this ochre-coloured town is almost encircled by the sluggish Tagus, spanned eastward with silver poplars, and still towered and gated against the Castilian plain. Its community has been blooded by Christians, Jews, Mozarabs, Moors and pure Arabs, it is an epitome of Mudéjar art, and it is the town of El Greco. It was Toledo that made the Cretan Domenico Theotocopuli more Spanish than the Spaniards, and one returns again and again to the magnificence of *The Burial of Count Orgaz* and *The Ascension of the Virgin*. These are such moments of incredulity as are frequently to be experienced in Spain, matched at the other end of the scale by a glimpse of Ribera's astonishing and horrific *The Bearded Lady of Naples*, which is also in Toledo.

After resting for a few days in Toledo I left for Guadalupe in Estramadura, passing through prairie-like country and sage-green olive groves until, beyond Talavera de la Reina, a centre of pottery and horse breeding, the peaks of the Sierra de Guadalupe twisted the horizon. For a brief moment the great monastery of Guadalupe on its hillside became visible, only to disappear again, but the 'bus shuddered and shot over a knoll and suddenly we were there, in the heart of a medieval village. On one side of the tiny plaza the fortified monastery towered up above the flight of steps to the church, on which old men sat in the sun, and on the other a decrepit village flowed away into obscurity. Girls were filling pitchers of Talavera ware at a fountain, and hawks wheeled high in the sunlight.

I rang the monastery bell, and a Franciscan friar, grey-habited with sandalled feet, admitted me. *Sí, sí,* I could certainly have a room, he said, and he put me into a parlour dark and heavy with antique furniture and hangings, where, despite the hot day, a *braseiro,* a large copper bowl filled with hot ashes, stood in the centre of the floor. And now others who had been on the 'bus came trooping in, for the Franciscans of Guadalupe maintain a guesthouse almost amounting to an hotel, admitting both sexes. There were two priests from Madrid, a honeymoon couple and a woman from Saragossa who had come here for the ceremonies of the *Semana Santa.* In a few moments Padre Julio, the superior, a slight ascetic-looking friar, came in to welcome us, and he then deputed a serving woman to show us to our rooms.

We were taken through a small courtyard with a palm tree and a little fountain peacock-bright with azulejo tiles into another wing, and then into a Gothic double-storeyed cloister with painted ceilings and doors and windows with *laceria* ornament. My own room, off this cloister, was vast and contained four iron bedsteads, all with respective washing basins and stands. Since there were no other occupants I could take my choice. A window looked over a patch of earth where chickens scratched and into the patio of a house on the edge of the monastery, where a woman was hanging out her washing, which, since this included some unmentionable articles of underwear, seemed a little hard on Franciscan friars dedicated to celibacy.

We were all conveniently in time for lunch in the pleasant dining-room, hung with delightful Talavera plates and dishes, which was surprisingly full. The newcomers were seated at one long table at which Padre Julio joined us, and I was sandwiched between the woman from Saragossa and one of the priests. The latter, Don Antonio Luengo, was the librarian of Madrid's Biblioteca Ateneo. He was shortly going to the United States and was worried about his as yet imperfect English. Most Spaniards will not speak a foreign language until they are fluent, even though they may probably understand it well, for fear of losing face, but Don Antonio was happy to practise on me, to our mutual advantage. It was a long drawn out noisy lunch with many jugs of wine accompanying the *entremeses* or hors d'oeuvres, the poached eggs *flamenco,* the stewed lamb and fried potatoes.

In the afternoon I was able to wander about the monastery, where some restoration was in progress. It was founded by Alfonso XI, in 1340, after the victorious battle of El Salado against the Moors, for the powerful Hieronymite Order (best noticed at Segovia), and its first prior was a Cardinal of Rome. Suppressed with most Spanish monasteries early last century, it was given into the charge of the Franciscans in 1851, when a specific number of religious Orders were allowed to return to Spain but at which time the Hieronymites were extinct.

The principal cloister is one of the finest Mudéjar monuments in the country, double-storeyed in mellow brick, with tiered pointed horseshoe arches of great beauty, and in the centre, like the lavabo of Poblet, is the Glorietta or Templete, a pavilion-like fountain with massive gabled octagonal crown rising to a spire. The cloister garden is enclosed with Renaissance iron gates, an oasis of sweet-smelling orange and lemon trees. This is a well of blinding sunlight which plays on glaring African white plastered walls, and snow-white too are the beak-clacking storks perched statue-like on the enclosing towers.

The dark church with its *coro* in the centre has rich Churri-guerresque stalls and Gothic aisles closed by iron screens, but the true glory of the church has overflown into the ancillary chapels, the *relicario* with its Etruscan-like ledges and niches filled with relics, and the sacristy. The last is one of the triumphs of Spanish Baroque, where the vestment presses and mirrors, the identically framed paintings and windows, are part of the decorative scheme. And these paintings are by no less an artist than Zurbaran, who spent a year working here. Zurbaran was the painter of monks, in particular of Carthusian monks, though here they are the Hieronymite priors of Guadalupe (and, in the adjoining *capilla de San Jeronime*, studies in the life of St. Jerome himself). Yet there is little emotion in these life-like portraits, though here and there the painter has attempted a kind of desperate religious ecstasy which does not quite come off.

And now the pilgrims were climbing the staircase behind the church into the *camarín* or Chamber of the Virgin. It is a festive apartment, covered with gilt and jasper and marble, with walnut and cypress wood, having statues and faded paintings by Luca Giordano. In a little glass-cased throne sits the Virgin of Guadalupe, so arranged that she is revealed above the high altar in the church below and yet is able to swing round into the *camarín* and be taken out for her clothing ceremonies. One by one the pilgrims knelt and kissed the hem of her rich garment, and the friar in charge looked on approvingly. Then we were shepherded into the Virgin's jewel room adjoining, filled with seventeenth-century furniture and its walls lined with crimson silk. The friar was an enthusiast and gently handled the rich brocades and flashing gala dresses of this Queen of Heaven, a wardrobe not lacking in diamonds and pearls and in the woven silks and embroidery, the gold and silver ornaments, which were made here when Guadalupe was a celebrated school of ecclesiastical art. But perhaps the cult of the Virgin of Guadalupe is unique, for devotion to her spread through the entire Hispanic world and she became the Patroness of Mexico.

The day had quickly passed. Late arrivals were garaging their car in the disused Renaissance church at the back of the monastery. They were a Dutch married couple, and they were obviously mystified when the friar at the door asked if they wanted a *matrimonio*, a room with a double bed. Friars were strolling in the courtyard. Bats flew in the dusk about the Gothic cloister. In the church the guests gathered for the nightly ceremony of the *Via Crucis*, the officiating priest standing before each Station of the Cross, accompanied by two acolytes and a cross-bearer in red and white capes, young boys with Murillo-like faces, the people kneeling before each *statio*, and finally the friars high in the *alto coro* joining in the praises.

We waited in the parlour for dinner, grouped around the *braseiro*, which Don Antonio constantly stirred with the giant spoon provided for that purpose. For dinner there was noodle soup, hard-boiled eggs in a thick sauce, cold ham with crisps, and tinned strawberries. Padre Julio was in good form, and it seemed strange shortly afterwards to be lying in the darkness of the Gothic cloister where the bats eddied.

Next morning I went into the village. On the edge of the little plaza an improvised ramshackle cinema advertised the showing of *El Talisman* during Holy Week, which it billed as 'the fight for possession of the Holy Sepulchre'. That appeared, however, to be the sole amenity in the village of Guadalupe, which is primitive to the core, without light, heating, water or anything at all. The principal street is narrow and tortuous and roughly cobbled, with houses jettied over a long continuous wooden arcade like a hacienda, which all but shuts out the light from the street. Most of these houses have workrooms on the ground floor, with heavily studded wooden gates. Balconies are festooned with potted flowers, and here and there are iron crosses affixed to the walls. Coppersmiths were at work, and there was the beating of iron, and several girls sat outside their houses making lace on circular frames. Hens, chickens and dark pigs roamed freely, and a train of heavily laden mules all but grazed the walls with their panniers. Here was poverty and squalor, not, on the face of it, entirely unromantic, and a life perhaps in close touch with elementals, unhampered by what elsewhere passes for progress.

It has been said that the Spanish are very badly adapted to the twentieth century. It has also been said that opportunity is a fine thing.

Two days later I crossed the parched lands to Avila, over austere biscuit-coloured country that recalled Benjamin Palencia's dramatic landscapes. Palencia, who lives in a deserted windmill near Avila, is a painter who, abandoning the schools of Paris, adopted Giotto as his master and all but transferred the hills of Umbria to the baked golden plains of Castile. He is a poet and a romantic, and he prepares his own colours, unmixed with oil, which he applies with home-made tools. That night was decidedly crisp, and with morning thick snow lay like cotton-wool on the tiled roofs and on the manes of the chained petrified lions before the cathedral. Winds howled through this mountain town, the highest in Spain and said to be the nearest to heaven in more than one sense. I breakfasted on coffee and *churros* in a café, where the men were already playing chess, in the Plaza Santa Teresa, arcaded on one side and presided over by a statue of Avila's own saint, though she belongs to the world. 'Oh, 'tis not Spanish but 'tis Heaven she speaks!' wrote Crashaw.

I found my way to the Convento de la Santa Teresa, high on the city walls, where the site of her birthplace is now covered by an indifferent Baroque church. Here brown-habited Carmelite friars show some of her relics as though they were trinkets, her rosary, the sole of a sandal, and, horribly, one of her once fastidious fingers enclosed in a crystal reliquary. There seems little here to speak for her, and one feels more her presence in the Convento de la Encarnación outside the walls, those vast tawny granite walls and towers that tightly bracelet Avila and which are far more perfect than the much-lauded Carcassonne or even Jerusalem itself. The unpaved roads were now muddy streams, for the snow had turned to rain, the first here for five months, but the mountains were still snowy white coverlets stretching away to the Sierra de Guadarrama on the one hand and, on the other, the Sierra de Gredos, where the ibex hides behind the rocks and the wolves in winter come out to howl near the city walls.

The pale rosy-brown convent of the Encarnación with its flat tiled roofs and its walled garden stands away from human traffic, as do the cells of all enclosed Carmelite nuns. Here St. Teresa spent twenty-nine years of her life, becoming prioress before she left to embark upon the far-reaching reform of her Order. Her cell has been thrown into the enlarged Baroque church with its golden altars and its grille through which flows the singing of the invisible nuns. In what remains of the original convent are the monastic parlours and the grilles behind which she talked to St. Peter of Alcantara and St. John of the Cross. The affinities and differences between those spiritual *conquistadores* Teresa and Juan de la Cruz have been often remarked. Both were poets and reformers, but Juan lived habitually in an abstract world, while Teresa (who even used *eau-de-Cologne*) was as practical and alert as the matron of a modern hospital. 'God deliver me from sullen saints,' she once said. Both became Carmelites at the age of twenty-one, both preached solitude with God and manual labour, and both encountered strong resistance. Juan indeed came under the lash of his superiors and was banished to a 'desert house' in Andalucia, one of the hermitages founded for the brethren to retire 'according to the custom of our holy fathers'. These 'deserts' were once numerous in Spain, but they were all suppressed with the exception of Las Batuecas near Salamanca, though it would appear that others have been reopened in recent years. Life in a modern Carmelite 'desert' is little different from that of former years. Each settlement of cells is enclosed by a wall, rather like the Sacro Eremo of Camaldoli. There are fasts on bread and water, and on Fridays the meal consists of beans cooked in water without seasoning. For breakfast onion soup is allowed, but there is never coffee or sugar. At the Encarnación we have drawn close to an intriguing and inspiring phase of European history, though these melancholy relics, Teresa's wooden pillow and bits of her embroidery, seem as unreal as a dream.

There are still other landmarks in this Teresian saga, including the little convent of San José, known as '*les madres*', which was the first of her seventeen foundations. When Juan de la Cruz joined Teresa's crusade he became spiritual director of this convent, and her *Way of Perfection* was written as a guide for these nuns, who today, strictly enclosed, see only a tiny fragment of the vast Castilian sky. In the little anteroom I rapped and was answered by an invisible nun behind a revolving hatch. The turntable twirled, and there floated round to me a note scrawled in what appeared to be a mixture of Spanish and French telling me to call later. Alas, I never did, and I did not see the chapel where the first nuns made their vows, nor did I see St. Teresa's little drums and pipes, said to be kept there.

In the grey wet cobbled byways just inside the walls there came ox waggons and covered carts. A girl with tresses of black hair carried a pitcher on her hip Roman fashion. Here and there were plain granite calvaries and abandoned belfried chapels. Melting snow still dripped from roofs, and I waded through a miniature lake to enter the Dominican monastery of Santo Tomé, its church façade in rich late Gothic like a *retablo*. Here the high altar is raised in mid-air, high on an ornate bridge-like arc of stone, perhaps almost unique in Spanish churches, and before it lies the tomb of Don Juan, the only son of Ferdinand and Isabel and heir to the throne, dead at the age of twenty, his handsome effigy beautifully carved in white marble by a Florentine sculptor.

Entering the convent itself, a wide marble staircase led me to the study of Padre Vacilio, who offered me a glass of white wine. Including professors and students there was here a community of about one hundred and fifty, for this was and is one of the chief Dominican powerhouses, supplying the mission fields in China, Japan, Indonesia and the Philippines, while one friar was then studying at Oxford. Since Avila lay in Franco's country during the Civil War there was no local rising against the monasteries, but most of the friars and students went to Hong-Kong and Manila—Padre Vacilio remained here—and part of the convent was garrisoned. The Reds attacked the town and bombed it a little and two friars were killed.

It seemed strange to see Padre Vacilio, short and rotund, smoking a cigarette as we passed through the convent, though, of course, Dominicans are not monks; they combine the contemplative and the active and are indeed Friars Preachers. He continued to smoke as we paced the three cloisters, one called the Cloister of Kings, since it once housed visiting monarchs, and another called the Cloister of Death, since its garth once contained the burial ground. Spaniards have a penchant for this brand of terminology, and there is in Avila a Street of Death and Life (not, be it noted in this area of Christian mysticism, Life and Death).

Beyond Avila on the road to Segovia few villages rise out of the tableland of rock and scrub, and these are little more than small settlements of stone dwellings huddled about an arcaded plaza. Beside the road were threshing-floors where soon the mule- or ox-drawn *trillos* would make their slow timeless circles, revolving from dawn to dusk. Not that there would be much corn to thresh in this area, nor do many cattle graze here. The only real pasturelands are in the north, though the best soil is probably that of Murcia far to the south-east. Spaniards say that if you want a load of manure get a load of Murcia soil. Spanish farmers tenaciously resist change and continue to employ methods which are centuries old. For all that the success of the Spanish Government often depends upon the harvest and thus, most illogically, upon the weather.

Segovia was heralded from afar by the tower and cupola of its cathedral, and soon I was walking beneath the great Roman aqueduct in the lower town, so familiar from the watercolours of my friend Sidney Causer. A giant striding across the road, cutting into the sky and framing it in numerous arches, it is no museum-piece for it yet carries Segovia's water, even though it be in a covered pipe. Skirting the town by the low road banked up above the river Eresema, I passed along the Roman walls, where snow still lay in the shade beneath the rockface, until a bridge carried me across the river. On the far bank lay the Hieronymite monastery of El Parral, a vast huddle of mellowed buildings, and I rested in a bed of wild mint made even more aromatic by the hot sun. The valley was densely wooded. Above the high fortified walls of the town on its rock there peered belfries and a dome, and where the rock plunged into the plain, right on the last spur, the Alcazar thrust its fairy-tale towers into the clear sky.

The church of the monastery was penned against a bastion of rock. The place seemed abandoned and derelict, and the interior of the church was gaunt and empty, with half-ruined chapels to which there yet clung some noble medieval sculpture. The choir alone seemed to have been taken care of, and flanking its towering gilded *retablo* were the Plateresque tombs of the Marqués and Marquésa de Villena, the founders of the monastery under the patronage of Enrique IV. Yet a beginning had been made, and this was now the only Hieronymite monastery in Spain and indeed, with the exception of a few houses of another Congregation in Italy, in the world. I sat on the choir steps and recalled the strange history of this Order.

The origin of the Hieronymites or Jerónimites, hermits who took St. Jerome as their patron, is almost as obscure as that of the Carmelites, but it probably began with the foundations of Jerome himself in Palestine. The medieval revival in a slightly different form began early in the fourteenth century, and in 1370 the hermits took possession of the Spanish sanctuary of San Bartolomé di Lupiana, but shortly afterwards they abandoned the eremitical life for the cenobitic, adhering to a modified form of the Augustinian rule. From the mother-house of San Bartolomé the Order spread throughout the Peninsula, and in 1415 the priors of twenty-five Hieronymite houses met at Guadalupe to revise the rule. Enrique IV himself built Guadalupe, where is his tomb, El Parral at Segovia and San Jerónimo at Madrid. When Carlos V abdicated he retired to the Hieronymite monastery of Yuste in the Sierra de Gredos, and his son Philip II handed over the Escorial to the same Order. In Portugal King Emanuel the Fortunate installed the Hieronymites at royal Belem on the Tagus. Eventually, however, the great Order crumbled and was lost, for the second time.

In 1925, in a little church hard by the Prado of Madrid, once Los Jerónimos but now a parish church, a small community gathered to whom General Primo de Rivera, the Dictator of the day, gave possession of the ruins of El Parral. Shortly afterwards the fall of Primo de Rivera was followed by that of the Monarchy, and soon there was the chaos of Civil War. Through it all the Hieronymites survived, struggling for existence in these ruins above the Eresema.

I rang at the simple wooden gate. A young brother in white woollen habit with a brown scapular admitted me and took me through a small cloister into a parlour which was almost bare, the floor tiles loose and broken. Here a few minutes later Fray Luis de

Cordoba greeted me. He was fairly young, with a smiling lined face like a Zurbaran. He was as happy as a child and he seemed to have a capacity for humour and friendship. I took to him at once. He told me how during the Civil War there was but a handful of monks here. The younger men had gone away to support the Republic, leaving four ancient brothers who existed as best they could, so poor that they went barefoot. Then, suddenly, there was a new flowering. Young men with religious vocations were inspired by the possibilities of the newly awakened Hieronymite Order, and so they came to El Parral. Now there were twenty monks, and already a foundation had been made at Santiponce outside Seville, an old Hieronymite monastery with a beautiful little Baroque church in which life-size gilded angels hung from the roof, and in which the body of Cortés had rested before it was removed to Mexico.

'You must go to Santiponce,' smiled Fray Luis, 'and you must meet our porter, José Bazán—he is a character. Before we went there he was the caretaker, unpaid, but he loved it so much and guarded it so well that three times every night he would go around the monastery with a revolver, just to see that all was well. He even cleaned the frescoes by rubbing whites of eggs into them. And you must meet my friend, Padre Maria de Madrid—he is now the prior there.'

Fray Luis disappeared for a *momentito* and returned with an invitation from the prior, Padre Antonio de Lugo, to stay for a few days. He shouldered my bag and conducted me through the great cloister with its Plateresque arches, up to its arcaded second storey and into a large cell. It was a forbidding room, completely bare but for a single plain table and chair lost in the centre. Off it ran a tiny room like a cubby-hole containing bed and washstand and nothing more. At the end of the larger room there was a French window which, had I opened it, would have precipitated me to the ground far below—for the balcony was missing. Beyond lay the valley and, flowing in the distance, the snow-covered Sierra de Guadarrama.

Since it was now early evening I decided to have a couple of hours in the town, and I warned Fray Luis that I would probably dine out. Soon I was crossing the Eresema and climbing through a medieval gate in the town walls, following narrow alleys until they brought me into the Plaza Mayor, where Isabel was first proclaimed queen. The honey-coloured cathedral stood lonely and silent. The *paseo* was already in progress, moving tightly and chattering down the narrow Calle de Juan Bravo, past the Romanesque church of San Martin and into the Plaza Azogeujo, where the aqueduct was now in the gathering darkness a tyrant thrusting its will upon the town. Here I dined on *paella* in an arty restaurant filled with traditional bric-a-brac and dubious if well groomed characters. Then I walked back through the valley.

In the morning I breakfasted on a bowl of coffee and stale bread in the refectory. The monks had breakfasted long ago. They rise at 1 a.m. for the night-office, retire to bed again at 3, and rise for the day at 5. Eight hours in every twenty-four are spent in praise of their Creator. I noticed, however, that more speech was allowed than in many monasteries, and for recreation the monks sometimes played croquet in the tangled gardens behind the monastery. Such is their life, however, that once a week they are compelled to discipline themselves by flagellation for half and hour in their cells—a strange balance that may well keep the psychoanalysts guessing.

In the gardens, smoking a cigarette and gazing vacantly at the clumps of willow falling towards the river, I encountered young Don Manuel, who was reading philosophy at Madrid. He knew the community well.

'They are very poor here,' he said, 'and in midwinter the cold is formidable. There is no heating and it is almost impossible even to wash, for the water turns to ice.'

I asked him about cattle.

'Cattle? Well, see for yourself,' and he led me behind the meagre pear and other fruit trees and the beds of lettuce and potatoes to the swinery.

'Three pigs,' he said. Then he pointed vaguely. 'Three cows, three sheep.'

He assured me that there was no religious symbolism in these numbers.

It was now Jueves Santo, in England Maundy Thursday, and I wanted to see the evening procession in the town. Fray Luis thought the special Mass in the monastery church would be more impressive, but I assured him that I could be at both providing that I missed supper. Consequently I gave up a seat in the choir and stood that night with the people in the bare nave. They had come from all over the town, in their best clothes, many of the women wearing rich silky mantillas, and a few had brought chairs, since there were none in the church. The choir chandeliers and candles were now lighted, and the monks came in procession. Soon the haunting *Kyrie Eleison* filled the church, and at an opportune moment I slipped out and climbed into the town. . . .

When I returned I was compelled to hurry back through the dark alleys, under the old gate where a solitary lamp glimmered, and across the bridged silent river. Fray Luis had arranged to meet me in the church, since the gate would be locked, but I was unprepared for the scene, as startling as a vision, that I encountered. Before a specially constructed chapel massed with lights and flowers all the white-habited monks were kneeling in silent adoration. I too could do no other, waiting there until Fray Luis rose up and took me into the monastery.

The next day, Good Friday, I was on my way to Valladolid. Since it was a public holiday the morning train had been cancelled, and I had been compelled to cool my heels all day in Segovia waiting for the early evening train. This had upset my plans, for I was expected at the English College at Valladolid and I had arranged to see the great procession, greater perhaps in its length and its religious solemnity than that of Seville. Now, resigning myself to having missed both the procession and, probably, dinner at the college, I was train-bound across a biscuit-coloured country planted with forests of pine. Yes, I thought, the Viernes Santo procession would certainly be over, since it was scheduled to begin at 8 o'clock, and here I was rolling into Valladolid station well over two hours later. Quite miserable and frustrated, I walked in the direction of the *Colegio y Ingleses*. The streets were quite deserted.

I turned a corner and suddenly found myself up against a solid black wall of people, and then I could see this wall stretching away in all directions. Balconies were crowded to the top storeys. It meant only one thing—the procession had not yet passed. But I was only just in time. Mounted Civil Guards with drawn sabres cleared the way. There was the throbbing of hundreds of drums, and then came the first of the *pasos*, those life-size groups of sculptured biblical figures mounted on wheeled platforms, draped in rich hangings and massed with flowers, and lighted by ornate lamps and myriads of candles. They were magnificent, some of them by Juan de Juni and others by Gregorio Hernández, who ranks with Salzillo as the greatest

of the *paso* sculptors. The entire story of the Passion was here in
scenes that resembled El Greco and Murillo come to life. The crowd
was silent, for these Christs were truly agonized and seemed to drip
real blood, and these Marys were truly stricken with grief and cried
real pearl-like tears. And walking slowly beside and behind them
came the penitents of the *cofradías*, each in his medieval gown or
tunica, a long cloak or *capa* reaching to the ground, and a *capirota*,
that lofty pointed conical hood covering the entire head and shoulders, with narrow slits for the eyes. Each wore the colours of his
particular *cofradía*, some with white hoods on green capes, and yet
others in violet, maroon, scarlet and pale blue, some gorgeous, others
terrifying. Each, too, carried a torch or an illuminated cross of
cunning design, and some dragged chains or shouldered heavy
wooden crosses. At times this might almost have been the *auto-de-fe*
of the Holy Inquisition, except that now, on this day, some prisoners
are released from Spanish gaols. And behind the penitents came
clergy, civic dignitaries and high-ranking soldiers with reversed
arms, for this was after all a funeral march. Now the trumpets rang
out again, and there were more drummers, and then a military band,
and, at another interval, a pipe band, with the *gaita* or bagpipes of
León and Galicia.

At this moment the processions would be wending their melancholy ways through all the Spanish towns, while the *Caladiños*
would be pacing through the cathedral of Santiago, and the
Brotherhood of the Buena Muerte, with coffins and skulls and
torches, would be crossing the oldest streets of Barcelona. But here
in Valladolid the long interminable procession was continuing late
into the night. For over an hour and a half I stood in that wall of
silent people, while some two thousand penitents alone and twenty-
two *pasos* went by. At intervals the glittering cavalcade would halt,
and minutes later go on again. Rattles were used to guide the unseen
hefty men who, beneath the rich hangings, dragged the *pasos* along.

It was nearly midnight when I reached the English College in a
dark deserted street, though I could make out the pink brickwork
of its Baroque church and the iron grilles on the windows of its
plain barrack-like walls. My embarrassment turned to relief when
the *señora* who answered the bell informed me that everyone was out
seeing the procession, except the Rector, who was in bed. She was
obviously puzzled and flustered by a stranger's appearance, but she

showed me into a parlour where I waited in an atmosphere recalling such English colleges as Oscott and Stonyhurst. This was one of the colleges, like Douai and St. Omer in Flanders, founded at the counter-reformation to train English priests for the dangerous English mission field, where twenty-four of its fellows were to die as martyrs. It owes its inception to the Jesuit Robert Parsons in 1589, and it is maintained for no other reasons than sentiment, tradition and a happy sense of continuity, reasons which are valid enough. Among the first seminarists were a scion of the Cecils and two descendants of the great Chancellor, Sir Thomas More, and it was one of the latter who delivered the Hebrew address to Philip II on his visit to the college, when the students made twelve speeches in ten languages, including Welsh and Gaelic.

When the bell rang again the *señora* scurried down the long tiled corridors. In a flurry of black soutanes in stalked two of the professors. Immediately upon seeing me they smiled and advanced with outstretched hands.

'So—we expected you hours ago; you are a naughty boy,' said 'Don Bernado'. 'Have you seen the procession? You have—good. We had a place for you on a balcony, with the Embassy staff, but never mind. Have you dined? No? Come along then.'

'Don Bernado' had a store of energy. He and his colleague led me to the professors' refectory, explaining on the way that the *señora* had not recognized in me the expected guest. Perhaps, they suggested, she had expected me to be disgorged from a Rolls-Royce.

The refectory with its oil portraits of ecclesiastics again reminded me of Oscott. My friends had dined, but they were kind enough to sit down with me as I relished a splendid dinner of prawns, omelette, cheese, fruit and wine. It was long after midnight but we sat talking in a haze of cigarette smoke. After all it was now Sábado Santo or Holy Saturday and there would be no early Mass. It was nearly two o'clock when I was shown to my room, which turned out to be the bishop's suite, as rich and heavy as plum cake in its Victorian furnishing and *objets d'art*.

At breakfast I met Dr. David Greenstock, the Vice-Rector, whose chief occupation outside his scholastic duties was experimenting on the college farm on the edge of the town. With him I went over the college—the mildly Baroque chapel with its curious red latticed screens enclosing the gallery, like the hidden choir of a nunnery in Naples, and its mutilated figure of the *Vulnerata*, the Madonna mutilated by Drake's men in the siege of Cadiz, the excellent library, and the refectory and classrooms of the students. There were now some thirty-five students, who would return ordained to England, having learned another language and another culture.

With David Greenstock I saw something of Valladolid, where he called upon a carpenter and also bought Easter eggs for some children. Children and fishing were his main interests apart from a wish to retire to the Cotswolds. We passed the house of Cervantes, entered several churches and saw a new *paso* being assembled in Juan de Herrera's unfinished cathedral. Near the University we sat in the sun and then explored the college of Santa Cruz, one of the earliest buildings of the Spanish Renaissance. In its museum my friend pointed out a statue which had once belonged to the English College. Many of the college treasures were lost in the Spanish War of Independence. It was at that time that gold and jewels were left in a strongbox with the college butcher, but the butcher was found dead and his sons and the strongbox missing.

On our return I went up to the room of the Rector, Monsignor Henson, who had published the college register and knew his archives inside out, to thank him for his hospitality, and he was able to join us for lunch.

Burgos has some Gallic touches. There is a suggestion of the Paris Left Bank in the Espolón which fringes the river, with its topiary gardens mixed up with a few timid palms and statues of Spanish monarchs, as there is more than a hint of Aix-en-Provence in the little squares with plashing fountains. Yet it is an essentially Spanish town, perhaps the first real Spanish town to be encountered coming from the north, as one feels it should be for it was the home of the Cid, the hero of the most celebrated Spanish *chansons de geste*. His magnificent bronze figure mounted upon his charger Babieca, his cloak flying in the wind and his sword outthrust, stands before the bridge of San Pablo, attended, on the bridge itself, by the granite figures of medieval mailed knights and their ladies. It is strange that Burgos should let the centuries slip by and postpone such a tribute until 1952, when the sculptor Juan Cristóbal was called in. El Cid now lies beneath a red marble slab in the cathedral, that most elaborate and whimsical of all Spanish cathedrals, with its extravagant chapel of the Condestable, its *escalera dorada*, that gilded grand staircase that might have come from an opera house, its *retablos* that outdo the Neapolitan in their love of gold, and its Santo Christo, that awesome, almost terrifying crucified figure said to be covered with human skin and to possess human hair and nails.

One day I crossed the Bridge of the Lepers and walked along the tree-lined road still called 'the path of the dead' to the Cistercian nunnery of Las Huelgas. There are many Cistercian convents in Spain but this is the aristocrat among them, founded by that Queen Eleanor who was the daughter of our own Henry II and sister to Richard Cœur de Lion, and who became the wife of Alfonso VIII. Its abbesses were once princesses-palatine, so powerful that it was said 'If the Pope were to take a wife, he could not find a fitter one than the Abbess of Las Huelgas.' These temporal glories have departed, and it may well be that the Las Huelgas of our own time is nearer in spirit to St. Bernard than ever it was in the past. Today there are some forty nuns, still called *señoras doñas* and aristocratic virgins yet, though they are bound to the ancient rule of strict enclosure and perpetual silence (save for one chattering relaxing hour of the day) and abstinence from fish, eggs and meat, rising from their solitary palliasses at two-thirty each morning.

I passed through a gateway into what was once the outer court, its offices now a huddle of slum dwellings, and into a smaller court closed by a colonnaded portico hung with the coats of arms of former abbesses. An ancient crone told me I could not enter that way, and I had to go back across the open *compás* to the fortified Romanesque church. From the nave, running across the front of the choir, I could see through the grille the white-robed nuns in their medieval coifs just disappearing through little doors. There was a fog of incense. The Office had just ended. Later I was able to enter both monastic choir and monastery, for these have in recent years been thrown open to the public.

What is remarkable about Las Huelgas, even more so than its riches of architecture and decoration, or the splendid embroidered tapestries of green silk shot with gold, is its collection of royal tombs, for here were buried six kings and queens and some thirty princes and princesses. Alfonso and his queen lie in a huge double sarcophagus, gilded with the royal emblems, in the centre of the choir, and spreadeagled along the aisles lie the coffers of the Infantes and Infantas. These tombs were opened by a Government Commission shortly after the Civil War, and their contents are now displayed in rows of glass cases. It is a revelation. In a few moments the centuries have slipped by, and one is looking at the very garments in which these illustrious dead were buried—long trains of cloth-of-gold and Arabian brocades, coronets and jewels, the three striped head cushions of Queen Eleanor, her enormous headdress striped in red, gold and black, and her sandals of Arabian design, the light green surcoat and silk garments embroidered with armorial shields of Ferdinand, eldest son of Alfonso X, together with his cap embroidered with the arms of Castile and León in coral, gold and mother-of-pearl, his mighty broadsword and his elegant ring, the coffin itself lined with Arabian silk and overlaid with Persian brocades, medallions of gold and a cross of silver. It is all as magnificent as it is pathetic.

Now we had passed through the great cloister with its perfect Gothic chapter house and into the original Romanesque cloister and a maze of barrel-vaulted passages with Mudéjar ornament, to arrive in the monastery garden. There, standing quite alone, was a chapel of Moorish design housing a great converted altar of Byzantine magnificence. And on the altar was the seated figure of St. James, the celebrated articulated statue with movable arms, the right hand grasping the sword which had bestowed the accolade on St. Ferdinand and other kings of Castile.

That afternoon I wandered through small pine forests where young seminarists with blue sashes at their waists were making sport, on my way to Miraflores, the first of the Spanish Carthusian monasteries to be restored after the wholesale suppression of 1835. It stands on a gentle rise in the Castilian plain, and beyond a calvary a patio leads on to a little cloister where an aged monk was now filling a pitcher at a fountain. From here one enters the honey-coloured Gothic church, where the traditional screen divides the choirs of the fathers and the laybrothers. The entire background, behind the high altar, is filled with the vast golden *retablo*, crowded with imagery and its crucifix set in an enormous wreath-like circle. Before this, in the centre of the floor, is the tomb of Juan II, the poet-king who founded the monastery in 1441, and his wife Isabella of Portugal, grand-daughter of John of Gaunt.

This marble tomb is star-shaped, a design which in origin may be Moorish, and upon it lie the royal effigies, crowned and in ceremonial robes, and laid about with richly sculptured allegories. It is a masterpiece of Late Gothic sculpture from the hand of Gil de Sílóee, a considerable artist of German-Jewish blood, who was also responsible for the tomb of the Infante Alfonso here and for the *retablo*, as his father was responsible for the *escalera dorada* in the cathedral. Strangely, though there must be some link, both this *cartuja* and much of the cathedral were also designed by German craftsmen, Hans and Simon of Cologne. There are here riches of choir stalls and painting, and, in one of the chapels, an impressive painted wood figure of St. Bruno, the founder of the Carthusian Order, by the seventeenth-century Portuguese artist Manuel Pereira.

Miraflores has attracted some remarkable men, and the Portuguese Manuel Ribeiro, formerly a Communist, has described in his novel *El Desierto* the experiences at Miraflores that led to his conversion. In this second phase of Miraflores' history we encounter an outstanding English prior, Dom Edmund Gurdon, who ruled from 1920 for fourteen years. He seems to have taken more part in external activities than his Order allowed, and he was finally removed from office and died a simple monk at Pavia in Italy. Burgos, however, did not forget the charitable works he had promoted in the town, and the Town Council put up a bronze tablet to his memory.

An American Carthusian, Dom Pablo Maria Moore, formerly a Benedictine psychologist and psychiatrist in an American university, was here for many years until he recently returned to the United States, to the new Carthusian foundation in Vermont, in the founding of which he had been instrumental. From Dom Pablo Maria I had an introduction to the procurator of Miraflores, Dom Pedro de Soto y Domecq. In private life he was the Conde de Puerto Hermoro, and before becoming a Carthusian he had served with the Spanish diplomatic service in England and America. The cowled white woollen habit could not hide his fine physique, nor had the cloister blunted his soft speech or diminished his courtly bearing. He was an Anglophile, he had subscribed to *The Times* long after he had left London, and he was anxious to know of any new English books on mysticism. He remembered the buttercups and daisies that strew our English heaths, and here in the cloister garth he pointed to the same wild flowers growing in the same profusion.

This cloister garth was empty and desolate save for a few pines, whose cones littered the ground, and a few rose trees, from the wood of which the monks make rosaries. In one corner of it was the burial ground with nameless black crosses about a calvary. We hovered on the edge of it and Dom Pedro indicated the latest interment, for there was no clue. The monks are buried in nothing but their habits, twelve feet deep, and in another three or four years the bones are shovelled together to make way for another corpse. It seemed strange to me, though not to Dom Pedro, to be talking in almost the same breath of receptions and balls in the London mansions of the nineteen-twenties and early 'thirties. The inevitable end was the same for all, and this melancholy plot was both a symbol and a reminder.

There was an utter silence, for St. Bruno, like St. Bernard, had set a clamp upon the tongue. Yet there have always been ways of communication. A facile method of getting over the Silence, before the days of sign language, was to spell out messages with pegs placed in alphabetically marked holes on a wooden board. Such a board was used at the Carthusian monastery of Valldemosa in Majorca, where it has survived. Noting the cloister vaults painted late last century, another Gothic Revival, we passed the cells of silence, again very little different from those of the *chartreux* of France and the *certose* of Italy. All but one were inhabited. There were twenty-five fathers and thirty-seven brothers, including one American who, presumably, would eventually go to Vermont.

In some of the corridors there were many paintings, mostly modern portraits of laybrothers by a Portuguese monk who was sent from here to the newly restored *cartuja* at Jerez in the deep south. One portrait, however, is of John Houghton, the prior of the London Charterhouse, martyred at the Reformation and since beatified. It is a powerful portrait recalling Zurbaran, and indeed Dom Pedro attributes it to that master, though on stylistic grounds only and without documentary evidence. But if it be by Zurbaran from where did he get the likeness, for John Houghton had been dead nearly a century when Zurbaran was in his prime?

There is indeed an entire Carthusian province of painting. Most of Zurbaran's Carthusians are now in museums, like his painting of the brethren in the refectory of Jerez. Then there was the Carthusian Fray Joaquin Juncosa of Scala Dei near Tarragona, where he painted portraits of priors for the chapter house and other subjects for the church, as he also worked at Montalegre near Barcelona, later coming into conflict with his superiors and abandoning the Order, though he died, absolved from his offence, in an Italian hermitage. Goya painted an entire decorative scheme for the vast *cartuja* of Aula Dei near Saragossa, and Francisco Ribalta decorated that of Porta Coeli near Valencia. Today the Carthusians are returning to Spain, and they now hold Miraflores, Montalegre, Aula Dei, Porta Coeli and Jerez.

As I left Miraflores I reflected upon this monastic revival. Only a few miles away at Cardeña the Trappists had restored the old Benedictine abbey associated with the Cid. Not far distant was Silos, and in Navarre there was the royal monastery of San Salvador de Leyre, recently restored by Silos. And southward, above Segovia, there was El Paular, another old Carthusian monastery now rejuvenated by the Benedictines. All these, with others, are once more centres of spiritual life. Is this ancient patriarchal way of life an anomaly in our atomic age, or is it the solution to our dilemma?

Miguel de Unamuno, who well knew the impossibility and the consequent agony of reconciling the human desire for eternal life with scientific knowledge, once said, 'I feel that my soul is medieval, and that the soul of my country is medieval.'

10

HOME GROUND

THE first monk I ever saw was a Trappist of Mount St. Bernard in Leicestershire. In an almost Triassic landscape, the turf sprigged with the last surviving trees of the Charnwood Forest and upthrusting granite crags polished by sun and wind, I came upon the rough grey granite buildings of the monastery. And there he was, bending over a young rose tree, his medieval white habit touching the ground. The timidity of youth prevented me speaking to him, but he hailed me heartily and gave me tea before I left. And when I did leave I realized that monks—and this seemed strange—were men.

Today a great tower shot with light rises from the new church, and, a little nostalgically perhaps, one remembers the humble little chapel of yesteryear, though its restrictions in the celebrating of the *Opus Dei* were severe. Certainly Pugin had always hoped to build a church designed in accordance with the Cistercian liturgy, but it is equally certain that he did not envisage a church on the present scale with its central double-sided high altar and its choir stalls largely designed by Eric Gill, that remarkable sculptor, who advised the community on several aesthetic matters.

With Pugin, however, we are back at the beginning. The heroic Odyssey of the Trappists in Europe, with more elements of drama and human endeavour than Hollywood could ever imagine, has already been noticed. Suffice it to remember that out of that bitter crucible was born, in 1835, the first monastery in England since the Reformation (since Lulworth was but a brief candle extinguished for ever).

The monastery may be regarded as the joint product of Ambrose Phillips de Lisle, Augustus Welby Pugin and the Earl of Shrewsbury. The buildings were begun in 1842. Here for the first time since the Reformation stood a monastery on the traditional model, with church, cloisters, chapter house, refectory, dormitory, guest-house and all the ancillary buildings, all in grey rubble granite. Then, as now, one entered through the gatehouse with its trinity of gables into the quadrangle bright with flowers. Here are the guest-quarters, where the chimney-piece of the reception room is decorated with the arms of de Lisle, the Earl of Shrewsbury and the abbey, and where the dining-room above the gateway is enriched by a *Crucifixion* after Van Dyck and a *Veronica* attributed to Albrecht Dürer. A writer visiting the monastery in the middle of last century described the guestmaster Father Lawrence as a man in whom he had 'never seen a sweeter expression of face; slightly worn, slightly ascetic, but when he smiles his grey eyes light up, his white teeth gleam and he is the embodiment of good humour'. How well we know him, for there is always a Father Lawrence wherever Trappists pray and till the soil.

Dickens has described the reformatory which existed under the monastic wing last century, when he encountered 'the cleverest pickpocket in England', and it was during this period that the monastery had a celebrated medievalist in the person of Brother Anselm Baker, who became known as 'the herald monk'. Entering the community in 1856, he received instructions in heraldry from Francis Baigent, a Winchester antiquary who was a friend of the de Lisles and, later, of Cardinal Gasquet. Anselm Baker's work as an illuminator earned the praise of the College of Arms in London, where most of his later work now is.

When I was last at Mount St. Bernard, to which a chance acquaintance *en route* referred as the 'consecration camp', both dormitory and refectory had overflowed into the farm buildings, recalling the expedient adopted at Mount Melleray in Ireland where the dormitory has a double-decker arrangement of cubicles which is perhaps unique in monasteries. Another Irish Cistercian house has in recent years made a foundation in Scotland in the former baronial castle of Nunraw. This leaves but one other Trappist house in Britain, and that is on Caldey Island off the coast of Pembroke, founded early this century by Anglican monks who later became Catholics. The monastery was taken over by Cistercians in 1929.

Caldey is a self-contained manor of which the Cistercian abbot of Chimay in Belgium is lord, the prior of the Caldey monastery being his representative, and the old seigneurial laws are still maintained. Caldey is thus a kind of *imperium in imperio*. The crossing is perhaps best made by the island boat navigated by a laybrother. Beyond the tiny quay and the brow of the hill with its calvary is a landscape which has a Mediterranean flavour, the red-tiled white-washed villas clustered about a monastery of white roughcast walls and red-tiled roofs broken up by towers and turrets and Roman-esque windows, an Edwardian fantasy. Certainly it is dramatic. There may be in it a suggestion of Hollywood and one's local Odeon but at least it is original and exciting, and if one must tie it down to some particular milieu it is probably that of Lombardy. Yet there is little of the theatre, indeed none, in the Cistercian life which goes on, *mutatis mutandis*, as it did at Margam, Strata Florida and Valle Crucis before the Reformation. The Spartan rule of *Laborare est orare*, work is prayer, remains, and in the early morning the prior will be found at the head of his flock working in the fields.

In the hamlet is the lily pond with its balconied bridge, the village *rialto* on which the gossips meet. Here, too, the *familiars* or workers employed by the monastery angle for carp. Beyond rock garden and shrine is the village church of St. David, with screened chancel and Oberammergau woodcarvings. Roses blush in the pergolas of the terraced gardens, and in Anglican days peacocks strutted here. Beyond the monastic gatehouse strangers are normally forbidden to go, but I recall the cream-walled cloisters, the oak-panelled refectory with open timber roof, the octagonal kitchen inspired by the Abbot's Kitchen at Glastonbury, and the abbatial house. The latter with its minaret-like tower is pre-Reformation in majesty of conception, with an unusual private chapel exhibiting marked Italian influence and containing a marble pavement and an altar of pink alabaster.

South-westward is the original priory of the Tironesian reform, with fortified gatehouse, church, refectory and prior's house grouped about a cobbled court. These rude buildings of twelfth- and thirteenth-century date represent one of the early cradles of Celtic Christianity, for they are the successors to the seventh-century *clas* founded by St. Samson. St. Iltyd was here and St. Gildas and St. Dubricius (Tennyson's 'Dubric the High Saint') and SS. David, Malo and Paul of Leon. This early monastery may have been a school of learning on the model of Lérins. Nothing could be more eloquent than this hoary church with its crooked stump of a

tower, its cobbled floor and archaic barrel vaulting, its Ogham stone
and its sanctuary-lamp yet lighted by the presbyter's assistant. Yet
though the monastic life dominates Caldey, there is the music of the
sea as well as of Gregorian plainchant. There are blood-splashed
hedges of fuschia. Golden gorse blooms for ever. The cliff tops are
mantled with gilded samphire, purple orchids and pink thrift like
coral. Goldfinches and bullfinches dart about poplars, pines and
rhododendrons. Above the grape-coloured sea wheel the oyster
catchers and an occasional puffin with brilliantly coloured parrot-like
beak.

During the last war Caldey had a succession of misfortunes. The
church had been burned out, cattle had been lost over the cliffs,
the submarine cable to the mainland had broken and there was no
telephonic communication (nor was there for eleven years). Early in
1942 two superiors died in successive months, and eight monks had
been called to the Belgian colours. That was the situation when
Père Jerome was elected prior. In the winter of 1949 I was back,
with Brother Thomas, the monastery steward, waiting for me in
Tenby's harbour, his motor boat packed with mail and stores. The
monastery had just been linked to the mainland by a short-wave
radio telephone, and when the bell rang in the island's exchange
underneath a chapel it was usually answered by Richard Cummings,
sub-postmaster and lighthouse keeper, who had brought up seven
children on the island, better behaved, perhaps, than the Tenby
schoolboy who was once heard to mumble in church '*Ora proboscis*'.

Dom Jerome had earlier told me of the wartime misfortunes of
his mother-house at Chimay, which I knew as Forges, the scene of
Verhaeren's poems *Les Moines*. It was occupied by the Germans
while the monks lived in neighbouring cottages. I recalled other
Belgian monasteries, notably Clervaux (Luxemburg), Orval and St.
André outside Bruges, where during the war the colours of all the
Belgian regiments were hidden for safe keeping. I was reminded
again of St. André when Sir Frank Brangwyn, the painter, asked me
about the Chinese monk, now dead, who was there. Certainly Dom
Celestin Lou Tseng-Tsiang was a remarkable monk. Three times
Foreign Minister of China and ambassador to a number of countries, he equated the faith of Confucius with that of Christ. When
ambassador to St. Petersburg he married a Belgian woman who was
lady in waiting to the Empress. They finally moved to Belgium, and

when his wife died he paid tribute to her by becoming a Benedictine of St. André where he lived as a simple monk. King Albert was deeply moved by this gesture and wrote him an inspiring letter.

England, Wales and Scotland each possess but one Cistercian monastery. An even rarer community, however, is that of St. Hugh's Charterhouse deep in Sussex, and rare too is the glimpse of these Carthusians in straw-brimmed hats taking their weekly walk or *spatiamentum* along the Sussex lanes. There are but a score of Carthusian monasteries in the world today, and this is the only place in Britain where the organized eremitic life is lived. It was founded in 1873 when two monks of the Grande Chartreuse, one French and the other a former Russian general, came over to sign the agreement for the purchase of the land. For the next ten years an army of builders and labourers of all nationalities worked on the vast project, and at one time police had to live on the site in order to keep the peace. Designed by Normand *et fils* of Calais, this walled yellow ochre-coloured town is of Romanesque design with Renaissance embellishments. The woodcarvings were by Buisine of Lille and the oil paintings by Sublet, both of whom are to be encountered in other monasteries of the Order. It is pastiche of the better kind, rich in furnishing and ornament, with splendid inlaid oak floors, though this note of luxury is not extended to the cells, which are on the same plan and scale as Carthusian cells elsewhere.

The last French prior of Parkminster was Dom Marie Pépin, and the first English prior of what had always been a French house was the late Dom Hugh Weld. I had met both of them, but I retain clearer memories of Dom Hugh, the son of a Governor of Tasmania, a member of an ancient family, a gentle scholar and a true contemplative.

The scale of Parkminster with its half-mile of cloisters seems more oppressive than that of other Carthusian monasteries, and the silence of its cells and enclosed high-walled gardens is almost disturbing. Even those monks who may pass by on some secret errand make no noise, for the thick soles of their boots are made of cork to withstand the cold in the unheated church. Many have tried their vocation here, few have stayed, and it has even been whispered that some who left began to show signs of mental instability. The chapter house is frescoed with flamboyant rather gruesome pictures of the execution of the London Carthusians at the Reformation. A white-habited figure kneels against the block and the executioner stands with his axe poised ready to strike the fatal blow. One novice said that if the axe did not fall he would have to go. He went. Those who stay live on little more than one meal a day, without meat, and they still make their way to the night-office bearing their little lanthorns along the dark cloister, for there is no electric light. And, at last, known only unto God, they lie beneath those nameless wooden crosses.

There are Benedictine monasteries of French origin at Farnborough and Quarr. The former, girdled by Hampshire pines, was founded late last century for Premonstratensians under the patronage of the Empress Eugénie, but Benedictines of Solesmes shortly took over. The abbey church is of flamboyant Gothic and was inspired by the church of Ferté-Bernard in Sarthe. It was the work of Destailleur, the architect of several Paris Government offices, and it contains the tombs of the Empress, Napoleon III and the Prince Imperial. At one time it could show busts of these royal figures by Jean-Baptiste Carpeaux, the foremost French sculptor of his time, but these were apparently taken to Malmaison. Farnborough seems still to be dominated by the personality of the Empress, and one recalls her dark stamp of Spanish beauty in the paintings of Winterhalter. Tutored by Stendhal, praised by Merimée ('every hair of her a lioness') and loved by Queen Victoria, this pious sovereign who foresaw the threat of Prussia lived in a Victorian villa near the abbey. And at her funeral in 1920 the Kings and Queens of England, Spain and Portugal stood in the sanctuary, while a Daudet represented French letters and a Murat the memory of the Grand Army.

There in the crypt stands her plain sarcophagus and with it those of the effete Napoleon III and the young Prince Imperial, the fêted heir to the Second Empire and the last serious claimant to a lost throne, ambushed and killed in Zululand in an Imperialist adventure. The tombs are of cold, dull Corsican marble, and all about are the Napoleonic emblems, the eagles, the bees and the Emperor's coronation robe.

The French monks of Farnborough have recently returned to Solesmes, though some have gone to Quarr, and the abbey now belongs to another Congregation. Quarr Abbey on the Isle of Wight thus remains the only French Benedictine monastery this side of the

Channel. Founded at the beginning of this century for monks of Solesmes, it was not until the eve of the Great War that the present monastery was built beside the site of a medieval monastic ruin. Architecturally it is perhaps the most significant of them all for it was designed by Dom Paul Bellot, himself a Benedictine monk. Bellot, who died in 1944, was designing revolutionary buildings in brick or reinforced concrete at a time when Art Nouveau was still in full swing. In his use of functional forms he anticipated by a few years such men as Auguste Perret, Walter Gropius and Le Corbusier, and he revived the Moorish parabolic arch. His buildings are to be found in France, where they include the cloisters of Solesmes; Holland, notably the choir of Ousterhout; Africa and Canada. Quarr with its golden-orange brickwork rising above the Solent is among the most remarkable and beautiful of them, eminently suited to the plainchant for which the French Benedictines are noted. When it was built it was as revolutionary as is today the Benedictine abbey of Collegeville in Minnesota, where those monks who work among the Chippewa Indians of Red Lake have commissioned Marcel Breuer, one of the architects of the new Unesco building in Paris, to design a church that is virtually a folded concrete shell.

When I first knew Quarr it had not been raised to the dignity of an abbey, and the prior, Dom Emile Bouvet, was a shrewd Norman, as the first abbot of Farnborough, Dom Fernand Cabrol, whom I also knew, was a native of Marseilles. The community then included Dom Pedro Subercaseaux, a member of a Chilean family distinguished for its ambassadors and a leading painter of Chilean historical subjects. Much of his work enriches the abbey church, but his best work is to be seen in the public buildings of his own country. Dom Pedro's profession as a monk was singular for he was a married man, but both he and his wife decided to take religious vows, for which Papal permission was obtained, and the latter became a nun in Spain. Later Dom Pedro went out to a monastery in Chile where he recently died.

Benedictine monasteries far outnumber others in this country, though there are but two in Ireland, probably, it has been suggested, because the Benedictine motto is *Pax*. All the houses of the historic English Congregation maintain public schools, so that the life there, though still in the spirit of St. Benedict, resembles the life of an Oxford college. There is Belmont in the Wye valley, a Gothic

Revival period-piece—where I once saw in pouring rain the coffin of an early Australian Benedictine archbishop exhumed for shipment to his native country—Douai on the Berkshire downs, Fort Augustus on the Caledonian Canal, Ampleforth on the edge of the Yorkshire moors, and Downside, that vast abbey on the Mendips. During the war years the guesthouses were filled with Old Boys, many of them high-ranking officers, many of them never to be seen again. After lunch there was good talk over the port, and one, less inhibited than most, spoke with startling candour of the loss and recovery of his faith. 'One night in Toronto, when I wore the King's uniform, I spruced myself up and went onto the streets prepared to sin as fully as possible. I could have murdered that night. . . .'

The early history of some of these monasteries has already been noted, and, as we have seen, Ampleforth is the lineal descendant of Westminster Abbey. One of its abbots, Dom Edmund Matthews, who died in 1939, was the first English Benedictine monk to take a degree at Oxford since the Reformation. He was himself prominent in establishing Ampleforth's humanitarian and classical tradition, as was the headmaster who succeeded him, Dom Paul Nevill. When the latter's opposite number of another school said 'At Blank we educate our boys for life,' Dom Paul retorted 'At Ampleforth we educate them for death'. There too one met Josef Heu, the Austrian sculptor and artist, a refugee from the Nazis, and Hugh Montgomery, the diplomat who became an Ampleforth schoolmaster for a brief space and has since become a priest of the Oratory.

The new church of Ampleforth was designed by Sir Giles Scott, though it is not yet completed, and the Victorian Gothic plasterwork of the Hansoms looks gimcrack beside the magnificent new altars and chapels inspired by a church in Perigeux. This measure of transformation is steadily sweeping through both abbey and school, where most of the woodwork bears the carved mouse that is the signature of Robert Thompson, the craftsman of Kilburn. Thompson's splendid woodwork is to be encountered all over the country, but his life's work was the refitting of Ampleforth, from the choirstalls to the library with its traditional monastic carrels, each monk's chair having a gridiron motif in memory of the abbey's patron St. Laurence, who was martyred on a gridiron.

It was Pentecost when I was last at Ampleforth, and one morning after Pontifical Mass I walked with young Dom Maurus, a Spanish scholar, across the fields to Gilling Castle which had become the prep. school. Refronted by William Wakefield under the influence of Vanbrugh, it retains its Elizabethan panelling and stained glass, its rich ceiling with great plaster pendants like stalactites and a frieze of 'forest work' showing the arms of the holders of the York-shire wappentakes in the year 1585.

The Hansoms and Sir Giles Scott are also represented, along with Thomas Garner, Leonard Stokes, Sir Ninian Comper and other well known architects, at Downside, where the ringing peals of 'great Bede' lead one to an abbey church with the proportions of a cathedral and a concomitant richness in its fittings and furnishings. Long regarded as the aristocrat of English Benedictine monasteries, Downside was often slyly referred to by other monks as 'side'. Yet this superiority was probably deserved in many ways, and not least in scholarship, though one of its savants came under the lash of the formidable Dr. G. G. Coulton in a long and distasteful controversy. Cardinal Gasquet lies now in the abbey church, the white marble effigy of the handsome historian arched over by a rich canopy of Quebec pine and Honduras mahogany. Other monuments include that to Bishop Walmesley the monk-mathematician and scientist, while the body of the beatified Oliver Plunket, the Archbishop of Armagh executed at Tyburn in 1681, rests in a shrine. The most remarkable of the numerous relics is the head of St. Thomas of Hereford, the last holder of a medieval English see to become a canonized saint. This is a startling encounter and it is not only the pagan who may be incredulous for Thomas Cantilupe died in Italy, where his body was boiled to separate the bones from the flesh, the latter being left for burial at Orvieto and the former being brought to Hereford.

Nearer perhaps to the spirit of Subiaco is the group of monas-teries belonging to the Cassinese Congregation. The strangest of them stands above the West Cliff of Ramsgate, overlooking the Regency terraces and Rennie's harbour with its architectural 'fur-nishing' by John Shaw. St. Augustine and his forty companions landed but two miles away, so that naturally this is an abbey dedicated to that intrepid Roman. Yet it might never have existed were it not for Augustus Welby Pugin (the architect of Mount St. Bernard), who in his belief that the lost medieval Gothic age was the only paradise outside Heaven built himself, in 1841, a Gothic

grange on the cliff, where he followed an almost monastic routine
and finally added a church and cloister, all, of course, to his own
designs. A contemporary letter writer callously referred to this as
Pugin's 'Inquisition home'. Yet it is a remarkable house for its time.
A fine open-timbered hall to the full height of the staircase is entered
from a paved courtyard at the back, while the various rooms are rich
in carved stone mantelpieces, panelling, armorial wallpaper embodying the Pugin martlet and the motto *En Avant*, tapestry and
Gothic furniture of his own design.

The church, externally faced with flint, is technically a *tour de
force*, but the architecture is almost unnoticed in the wealth of
colour and decoration, of ornament and furnishing. And in an
alcove of St. Lawrence's Chapel is the effigied cenotaph of Pugin
himself, that medieval man born out of his time. There is a labyrinth
of chapels rich in reliquaries, again to Pugin's design, as are the oak
vestment presses in the sacristy, while the Abbot's Chapel has fragments of stained glass from the Sainte Chapelle in Paris. The
cloister and its adjoining galleries are curious, and one gallery is
filled with monumental Stations of the Cross, Flemish, by de
Bheule, as disturbing as the *pasos* of Spain.

The monastery proper is in a later building on the other side of
the road, so that every time the monks go to church they have to
traverse an underground passage, an odd experience smacking of
recusancy in penal times. The community has long edited *The Book
of Saints*, which is facetiously known as *Who's Who in Heaven*. The
most remarkable monk I knew here was Dom Romanos Rios, who
was always to be found, when the liturgy spared him, in the library
of which he was in charge. He was a Basque from Spanish Navarre
and as a young Benedictine in Spain was sent out to the Spanish
foundation of New Norcia in the depths of the Australian bush. He
later became conventual prior of El Pueyo in Spain, where during
the Civil War he narrowly missed the martyrdom of his fellows.
Dom Romanos was an outspoken monk, and differences of opinion
between himself and his superiors ultimately caused his exile to the
shores of Kent, where he became a prolific writer and Abbot Visitor
of the English Province.

Another abbey of the Cassinese Congregation captured public
imagination when twenty-six years of building by monk-masons
culminated in the consecration of the abbey church in the early

nineteen-thirties. Like Quarr, Buckfast rose beside, virtually on, the
site of a medieval predecessor, and, again like Quarr, its first monks
came from France, this time, in 1882, from Pierre-qui-vire in
Morvan. The community early had a strong German element and
its first abbots were of that nationality. The first of the new line was
Dom Boniface Natter, a native of Würtemberg who had arrived at
Buckfast in his 'teens. He was soon appointed Provincial Visitor, and
on his first official voyage, in the summer of 1906, he arranged to
meet in Barcelona a young Buckfast monk who was then Professor
of Philosophy at the Benedictine College of S. Anselmo in Rome.
Then, accompanied by the young monk, he sailed on the Italian
steamer *Sirio* for a canonical visitation in South America. On the
second day out the ship foundered somewhere near Cartagena, and
three hundred passengers were lost. Among them was the abbot,
Boniface Natter. The younger monk was picked up by a Spanish
cutter and landed in a fishing village where peasants gave him
shelter. Eventually he returned to the valley of the Dart. In what
then passed for a chapter house at Buckfast the bereaved community
met to elect a new abbot. The votes were cast, and the abbot was—
the young shipwrecked professor, Dom Anscar Vonier, then thirty
years of age, who had left his native village in Würtemburg at the
age of thirteen with other boys who were to become monks at
Buckfast.

One remembers across the years the courtly, dignified and
radiant figure of Dom Anscar. He might have been a medieval figure
transported into the twentieth century, but if he resembled the
medieval Dom William Slade of Buckfast he also resembled that
modern Benedictine, Dom Columba Marmion of Maredsous.
Scholar, contemplative, administrator and man of action, he wrote
no fewer than fifteen volumes of theology and philosophy. As a laybrother was once heard to remark, 'Our abbot would 'ammer a
'undred sermons out of the *Amen*'. Even more remarkable was his
audacious decision to rebuild the abbey, virtually beginning with no
resources other than the gift of a sovereign and a cart and horse to
carry stone from a local quarry.

Today the blue and sienna-hued buildings and their crowning
tower rise out of the dappled Devon moorlands. Its style is of that
age when the Norman slowly became Early English, pastiche again,
no doubt, but well done, and resplendent with its series of windows

after the *La Belle Verrière* of Chartres, its great *corona lucis* or candelabra sparkling with scores of candle sconces, and its gleaming enamels from the studio of August Witte, the cathedral goldsmith of Aachen.

Across the years too one remembers a bow scraping a melancholy 'cello in an adjoining cell. And one remembers such things as the parlours of St. Hilarion (the laybrothers' bungalow) and St. Anthony, where, in those days, the honey was extracted and stored, the tonic wine manufactured, linen washed and fruit and vegetables laid out to dry. Those were the days of development and expediency, but today form and order are the hallmarks of Buckfast, and to those external activities have now been added sculpture and stained glass and the revived art of tapestry. Passengers in the drawing-room of the Australia-bound *Iberia* gazing at the threadwork of a festive and idyllic scene of borzois and birds, butterflies and trees, would hardly associate it with Dom Robert of this Devon monastery.

It was not long after the Benedictines of Caldey had moved to Prinknash in Gloucestershire, in 1928, that, as a youth, I first visited the new monastery. Monks were racing up and down ladders repairing roof tiles and masonry, and the entrance hall in which Dom Dunstan—God rest his soul!—gave me tea was stacked with a variety of objects. It was a Heath Robinson chaos, and Heath Robinson himself commemorated it in some delightful water-colours, for his son was a member of the community. It was there that I first found the pattern of the primitive Christian community, and climbing up Cooper's Hill today there is still the same feeling of pleasure and mild excitement, tempered by an awareness of spiritual values, when the Tudor manor house of Cotswold honey-coloured stone comes into view below the crown of Pope's Wood. It is an idyllic setting, and no doubt Dom William Parker, the last abbot of medieval Gloucester, found it so, for he it was who built it as his country seat, though Gloucester's tentacles have spread and the roar of Gloster aircraft is never far away.

In the seventeenth century Prince Rupert made Prinknash his headquarters during his attack on Gloucester in the Civil War, and a contemporary caricature of Charles I with well defined Vandyke beard is scratched on the stone mullion of a window. In the eighteenth and early nineteenth centuries it was the home of the Howell family, who were prosperous Jamaica merchants, and it was Thomas

Bayly Howell who edited at Prinknash the *Complete Collection of State Trials*. The Hon. John Byng records in his famous *Torrington Diaries* a visit to Prinknash, where he received 'a profusion of fine strawberries of the Surinam kind'. And Horace Walpole arriving in 1774 compared the prospect here to Elysium. Richly gabled and mullioned, with old high-pitched roofs and a Tudor arched doorway, the house encloses a forecourt on three sides. On the front is a picturesque high oriel (which cunningly contains a W.C.), on the left is a Victorian wing and on the right is the chapel. The last embodies some sixteenth-century fabric, but the sanctuary is a Victorian addition and its plasterwork might perhaps be called gimcrack. Certainly it is belated Strawberry Hill Gothic, and yet there is a pleasing delicacy about its almost Rococo flourishes.

This is a large community, or it was, for it has now installed colonies at Farnborough and at Pluscarden, a medieval priory in the highlands of Moray. Official meetings of the three priors are referred to by the ribald as the Three Priors Festival. The spiritual and temporal head of his minor dynasty is the abbot of Prinknash, Dom Wilfrid Upson, that holy man, shrewd administrator and staunch friend in need, who is, among other things, an expert cinematographer and perhaps the world's most travelled monk. Dom Wilfrid has had to make many weighty decisions in his time, and the very first of them was when, as a young man, he finally decided, while playing tennis, to become a monk, breaking off abruptly in the middle of the match to write a letter to Caldey.

His community is no less remarkable, since its origin lay in an attempt to restore the Benedictine life under the Anglican aegis. The founder was Dom Aelred Carlyle, who as an ex-medical student of nineteen established in 1893 a brotherhood in the East End of London. For ten years the little group existed precariously, furtively moving about the country, from Yorkshire to the Cotswolds, until in 1903 they managed to secure possession of the Isle of Caldey. Within a short time the community had acquired such influential patrons as Lord Halifax and had begun to raise the splendid buildings to be seen today. The movement was regarded as phenomenal. It was indeed so phenomenal that it could not last, and it soon became clear that their devotional life and liturgical observances would be justified only on a strictly papal basis of authority. Consequently Dom Aelred and almost the whole of his community made their corporate submission to Rome and became fully fledged Benedictines bound by historic rules, constitutions and traditions. Some years later the community moved to Prinknash, and Caldey was purchased by the Cistercian Order.

Meanwhile Dom Aelred, who had now been professed at Maredsous in Belgium, had broken down under the strain of the enormous responsibilities, the anomalies of his position and the debts incurred, and had resigned. He became a missionary in British Columbia, worked among the Indians of the Okanagan, became a parish priest with an immense stretch of the Pacific coast, and finally chaplain of both port and prison at Vancouver. Later he tried his vocation in the *cartuja* of Miraflores in Spain, but found, after all these years, that he was not cut out to be a strictly enclosed and purely contemplative monk. Finally, after an interval of more than thirty years, Dom Aelred, one of the romantic figures of our time, found an eventide home at Prinknash Abbey. Here he spent his last years as a simple monk in the community which he had founded, though the survivors of the Caldey days could be counted on the fingers of one hand. Meeting this slight wiry self-effacing monk, his handsome restful features belying his years, one would little realize that he was once such a controversial figure. He was recently laid to rest in the little hillside burial ground of Prinknash on a wet, grey wintry day, just after the noon angelus had rung out.

Sitting in the parlour after the midday dinner, Father Abbot and his guestmaster would receive the guests, and there would be a rich fund of clerical and non-clerical conversation. I particularly looked forward to seeing a guestmaster of many years, Dom Bede Griffiths, who had the hallmarks of the true hosteller, high vocation, moral integrity, goodwill, infinite patience and tact, with a gentleness of manner at variance perhaps with his lean athletic figure. An old Blue Coat boy and a graduate of Magdalen College, Oxford, he was a natural hermit and before becoming a monk had lived as a solitary in the Cotswolds. He had the sensibility of Vaughan and Traherne and was 'modern' enough to appreciate Virginia Woolf. Later Dom Bede became prior of Farnborough, when I saw less of him, and he has recently gone out to India, with an Indian monk of St. André in Belgium, where, on the edge of a native village in Bangalore, they have established the first strictly contemplative monastery in India.[1]

[1] The Indian venture proved abortive.

At Prinknash I have watched the Middle Ages come to life. I have watched the blending of incense and the weaving of vestments. I have admired the woodcarver of Tyrolean descent whose cunning chisel fashioned the figure on my own desk, and I have seen the potters throw their clay on the wheel. I have seen the monks tramping round and round the silo, treading the silage, as I have seen the dough become bread under their patient hands. I have intruded into the chapter house while they were being tonsured and shaved, and I have followed them as they have carted stone from the quarry to the site of the new abbey. In the dark hours before dawn Brother Simeon bearing a lantern has flung open the door of my cell and called out the traditional greeting '*Benedicamus Domino!*' and replying '*Deo Gratias*' I have tumbled out of my narrow bed to grope my way into the church for the ancient night-office or Vigil, standing with the monks in the hard polished choir stalls as the chant rolled back and forth.

The monks would be back in those stalls a few hours later for Prime, and later for Terce and High Mass. In summer the sun lights up the medieval stained glass with its choir of angels, and the chattering of birds filters through the open windows to relieve the sonorous chant and the swelling organ. Through those windows one looks across to the Malvern Hills of Piers the Plowman. Occasionally the Mass is enlivened by some unexpected incident. The organist manages somehow to weave in a few bars of Sibelius and extemporize upon them. A sleepy acolyte once let go the crozier and it was falling straight for Father Mark's head, but with sudden alacrity the acolyte retrieved it in time.

The liturgical year, like the Mass itself, is a symphony with an ever-recurring motif, variations on a theme. Every day is made to serve the monastery's life and work, from the morning Angelus to the evening Ave bell. There is no day but bears some saint's name, no day that is not consecrated to some special devotion or feast, while the whole of nature, the flowers of the field, the wax of the bee, the ears of corn, salt and incense and wine, even gold and precious stones, as well as simple metals and finely grained wood, are brought into service and invested with a sacramental nature.

At Prinknash, as elsewhere, the liturgical year culminates in the overwhelming ceremonies of Easter. On Good Friday, the crucifix is taken down from the altar and laid on cushions on the chancel steps. Two by two the monks in stockinged feet come forward and, lying prostrate, kiss the cross. This is the medieval rite known as Creeping to the Cross. Then is chanted an ancient eastern litany with responses in Greek and Latin. Now comes the procession to the Place of Repose, returning with the Host, all the monks carrying lighted candles. Black vestments are worn by the celebrant and his assistants. At lunch in the refectory the abbot waits upon his monks, a traditional but still moving gesture. Finally at Compline a relic of the True Cross, encased in a little gold shrine, is carried by the abbot to everyone in turn, each kissing it. (If we are to believe Rohault de Fleury, who at the end of last century wrote a scholarly study of the subject, the Cross remained entire until the seventh century, when, with the encroachment of the Moslems upon Palestine, it was divided and distributed throughout Christendom.) Early next morning, Holy Saturday, the Paschal fire is lighted in the courtyard, and the convent, standing in a circle, forms into a procession and bearing the triple candle reed, lighted from the fire, enters the church. The deacon, in white vestments embroidered with gold and pink eagles, sings the *Exultet*, and the giant Paschal Candle is lighted from the reed. Then follows the first Easter Mass, the heavy purple veils covering all figures and pictures are taken down, and at the *Gloria* the bells ring out and the organ joyfully joins in the singing of the convent. Thus is the Resurrection celebrated, and two by two the monks go forward to receive communion.[1]

When I was last at Prinknash it was the morning of Christmas Day, and I had called on my way to the medieval New Inn at Gloucester, the former hostel for pilgrims to the cathedral-monastery there. Leaving the chapel after Pontifical Mass I entered the courtyard. A monk whom I did not know approached me.

'Do you smoke?' he asked abruptly.

'Too much', I replied, half expecting a gift.

'Good. Give me just two cigarettes. We have a couple of tramps to dinner.'

Pauperum et peregrinorum maxime susceptionum cuia sollicite exhibeatur, quia in ipsis magis Christus suscipitur. 'Let special care be taken in the reception of the poor and of strangers, because in them Christ is more truly welcomed.' Thus the fifty-third chapter of the Rule of St. Benedict.

[1] The revised Order of Holy Week has now superseded some of these ceremonies.

I went on, mounting by the beeches and the oaks. Below me now the monastery lay serene. The waves of the world would beat against its door, but they would not prevail. Driving snow was settling on the wooden crosses on the hillside, where lay so many I once knew, and I thought of Camaldoli and Subiaco and Monte Vergine.

•

INDEX

A

Abelard, Peter, 24
Abingdon, Benedictine Rule at, 18
Acciajuoli, Donato, 104
Acciauoli, Niccola, 98
Acton Burnell, 38
Adalbert, 18
Adhemar, François, 121
Aelred of Rievaulx, 25
Aepli, Kanzler, 133
Aiguebelle Abbey, 54-7, 58, 63
Aix-les-Bains, 91
Albergotti, Chevalier, 34
Alberic, St., 23
Alberti, Leon Battista, 105; *Della famiglia*, 105
Albertoni, Jean, of Turin, 90-1
Albigenses. *See* Catheri
Alfonso XI, King of Spain, 187
Altenburg Abbey, 150
Altomonte, Andreas, 145
Altomonte, Bartolomeo, 145
Altomonte, Martino, 145, 146
Ampleforth Abbey, 38, 212; new church of, 212
Anacletus, St., 24
Andechs monastery, 37
Angele, Seppe, 142-3
Angelico, Fra, 27, 28
Anselm, St., Archbishop of Canterbury, 80
Ansgar, 18
Anthony, St., of Egypt, 15
Anticlericalism, 81, 93
Arllan, 53
Arnold of Brescia, 24
Aragon, Trappists in, 41
Arezzo, 108
Arolla, 136-7
Arsinoë, 16
Asam, Cosmas Damian, 36, 162
Asam, Egid Quiram, 36, 138
Asciano, 107, 111
Assisi, 111, 112-13; Franciscan settlement in, 27; Santa Maria degli Angeli, 111-13; S. Damiano convent, 113; San Francisco, Church of, 113; Carceri, hermitage of, 113; Cathedral, 113, 114-15
Athanasius, St., 16
Augustine, St., of Canterbury, 18
Augustine, St., of Hippo, 25; Rule of, 25-6; Hermits of, *see* Austin Friars
Aula Dei, 204
Austin Friars, 27
Avallon, 85
Avellino, 128
Avignon, 57-8
Avila, 37, 189; Convento de la Santa Teresa, 189; Convento de la Encarnación, 189-90; Santo Tomé monastery, 191-2; San José convent, 191

B

Babel, Johann Baptist, 138
Bacchini, 37
Bacon, Roger, 27
Badia, Franciscan settlement at, 27
Baeda: *Ecclesiastical History of the English People*, 18
Bagnato, Giovanno, 141
Baigent, Francis, 206
Bajet, Buenaventura, 178
Baker, Anselm, 206
Baker, Dom Augustine, 30; *Sancta Sophia*, 30
Banchor, community, 16
Barkworth, Mark, 31
Barlow, Ambrose, 31
Basil, St., 16, 17
Bas-Valais, Trappists in, 41; Convent in, 41
Batalha, Dominican monastery at, 28
Bazzi of Siena. *See* Sodoma
Beaumes-les-Dames Convent, 37
Beauregard, Dom Antoine de, 45
Bec Abbey, 80-1
Bec Hellouin, 80
Bede. *See* Baeda

Behrens, Peter, 145
Belley, 90
Bellot, Dom Paul, 211
Bellinzona, Einsiedeln Benedictine school at, 47
Belmont Abbey, 211
Benedict, St., 16–17, 109–10, 121, 125, 126; and collectivism, 20; Rule of, 17–18; varying interpretations of, 20–1
Benedict Biscop, St., 18, 70
Benedictine Order: early spread of, 18; and the French Revolution, 46; in England, 211
Benediktbeuren Abbey church, 158
Bernard, Dom Marie, 60–1, 64, 71
Bernard, Dom, of Bec, 81, 107
Bernard, St., of Clairvaux, 24–5, 57
Berthon, General, 85
Berwick, Duke of, 31
Besse, Dom, of Ligugé, 76–7; Les moines d'orient avant le concile de Chalcédoine, 76
Beuron: Benedictine Congregation of, 47, 153; village, 152; Abbey, 152–7; St. Maurus Chapel, 154, 156–7; School of Art, 154–6; Lady Chapel, 156
Billi, Dom Ildebrando, 104
Bismarck: Kulturkampf, 47, 153, 160
Bloy, Léon, 135
Bobbio monastery, 16
Bohemia, closing of monastic houses in, 29
Boil, Dom Bernard, 178
Bologna, Fra Antonio de, 110
Bonaventure, Giovanni, 27
Boniface, St., 18
Boquen monastery, 181
Bourbon-Condé, Princess Louise-Adélaide de, 41
Bourg, 87
Bourget, Lac du, 90
Boussac, Marcel, 81–2
Bouvet, Dom Emile, 211
Bovier, Pierre, 136
Brabant, Trappists in, 41
Brangwyn, Sir Frank, 208
Brazilian Congregation, 29
Brémond, Abbé Henri: L'Abbé Tempête, 34
Breuer, Marcel, 211
Brewing, in German monasteries, 37
Brillat-Savarin, 6, 90
Brionne, 79–80

Broadway, monastery at, 39
Bruckmayer, Josef, 171
Bruckner, Anton, 147
Bruges: Val de Grace monastery, 32; Sheen Anglorum monastery, 32; convent of Augustinian Canonesses, 40
Brühl, Schloss, 170
Bruno, St., 21, 31, 94, 99, 202, 203
Brzesc, Palatinate of, 43
Buchau church, 159
Buckfast Abbey, 47, 214–16
Buckingham, Duke of, 39
Buckley, Dom Sigebert, 30
Buisine of Lille, 209
Buonsolazzo College, 106
Burgos, 199–201; Cathedral, 199–200; Las Huelgas nunnery, 200–1
Bursfield Congregation, 29, 31
Bury St. Edmunds, Benedictine Rule at, 19
Butozzi, Dom Albertino, 100
Byng, Hon, John, 217

C

Cabrol, Dom Fernand, 46, 211
Cacciatori, Benoît, 90
Caesarius, St., 70
Caesarius of Heisterbach, 7
Caldey Island, 206–8, 217–18
Camaldolesi, Order of, 20–1; Rule of, 20
Camaldoli: monastery, 100–3; village, 103
Cambrai, Benedictine nuns of, 39
Canisius, Peter, 133
Cannes, 67–8
Canonici, 125
Canterbury, Franciscan settlement at, 27
Caprais, 69
Caracciolo, Dom Raffaele, 123
Cardeña, 204
Carl, Archduke of Bavaria, 42
Carlone, Bartolomeo, 147
Carlone, Carl Antonio, 146, 147
Carlone, Diego Francesco, 139, 144
Carlyle, Dom Aelred, 217–18
Carmel, Mount, 28
Carmelites, Order of, 27, 28; 'calced' and 'discalced' congregations, 28; nunneries, 28; 'deserts' of, 190
Carnot, Pater Maurus, 140
Caronti, Dom Emmanuel, 121, 122

Carpeaux, Jean-Baptiste, 210
Carthusians, Order of, 7, 21–3, 31–2;
exile of, early twentieth century, 47;
monasteries today, 209. *See also*
Charterhouses
Cartusiensis, Dionysius. *See* Ryckel,
Denys de
Casamari Abbey, 122
Casamari, Congregation of, 45
Cassian, 7, 15, 16
Cassinese Congregation, monasteries of,
213–16
Castile, Congregation of, 32
Catalonia, 177
Cathari, the, 27
Catherine, St., of Siena, 28, 106–7
Causer, Sidney, 192
Cavaillon, 66–7
Celestin Lou Tseng-Tsiang, Dom, 208–9
Chabannes, Countess de, 41
Chambéry, 92
Charles-Félix, King of Sardinia and
Count of Savoy, 90
Charterhouses, architectural features of,
22
Chartreuse liqueur, origin of, 92–3
Château-Chalon convent, 37
Chaucer, Geoffrey, 7
Chautard, Dom Jean-Baptiste, 87
Chekhov, on Cannes, 68
Chichester, Carmelite nunnery at, 40
Chiemsee, the, 172
Chimay monastery, 37, 208
Christian, Joseph, of Riedlengen, 158
Chrodegang, Bishop of Metz, 25
Cistercians, Order of, 7, 8, 21, 23–5, 32;
suppressions of, 40 ff.; monasteries in
Britain, 209
Cîteaux Abbey, 21, 23, 86–7; rebuilding
of, 36
Clairvaux, Cistercian monastery at, 25
Clairvaux, Congregation of (Strict
Observance), 32, 45
Cluny, Order of, 24; rebuilding of
monastery, 36
Coelian, monastery on, 18
Coleridge, S. T., 7
Collegeville Abbey, 211
Colonna family, the, 121
Columba, St., 16
Columbanus, St., 16, 18
Colwich, Benedictine nunnery at, 39

Common Observance, Congregation of,
32, 45
Comper, Sir Ninian, 213
Constance, 155
Coppée, François, 48
Cordoba, Fray Luis de, 193–4
Corpo di Cava, monastery of, 131
Cortèse, Gregory, 70
Cotte, Robert de, 36
Coulton, Dr. G. G., 213
Coventry, Benedictine Rule at, 19
Cristóbal, Juan, 199
Croyland monastery, 16
Csorna, Norbertine Order at, 26
Cummings, Richard, 208
Cusa, Nicholaus von, 149
Cuthbert, St., 16
Cuvilliés, François, 166, 169

D

Damian, Cosmas, 139
Damian, Peter, 20 101
Dante, 8
Darlington: Carmelite nunnery at, 40;
Poor Clares at, 40
Death, attitudes to, 8–10
Della, Robbia, Giovanni, 99, 107
Desert Fathers, the, 21
Destailleur, 210
Detry, Père Jules, 92
Diamare, Dom Gregorio, 124
Dickens, Charles, 206
Diesink, Dom Anselm, 144
Diessen Abbey church, 158
Dietmayr, Abbot Berthold, 149
Dieulouard, 38; English Benedictine
monastery at, 31
Disentis Abbey, 140
Dold, Dom Alban, 153
Dollman, 172
Dombes, the, 87–9
Domecq, Dom Pedro de Soto y (Conde de
Puerto Hermoro), 202–3
Dominicans, Order of, 26, 27–8
Donatello, 99
Donaueschingen, 151
Douai Abbey (Flanders), 31, 38
Douai Abbey (Berkshire), 38, 212
Downside Abbey, 38, 212, 213
Dublin, Poor Clares at, 40

Duclair, 76
Dumas, Fernard, 133
Duns Scotus, Johannes, 27
Dunstan, St., 18
Durand, Dom Ursin, 34, 35
Dürer, Albrecht, 206

E

Ealing, Augustinian Canonesses at, 40
Eastern Church, monastic system in, 16
Ebenhausen-Schäftlarn, 169
Eibingen Abbey, 155
Einsiedeln, 36, 138; Our Lady of the
  Hermits, Abbey of, 138-40
Eleanor, Queen, of Spain, 200, 201
Eliot, T. S., 7
El Paular, 204
Ely, Benedictine Rule at, 19
Emmeran, 18
Emmersdorf, 148
Engelberg Abbey, 138, 140
England, Benedictinism in, 18-19
English Congregation, 29, 30
Enichelmeier, Herr, 142
Erdington, Beuron foundation at, 153,
  160-1
Escarré, Dom Aurelius, 178
Espluga de Francoli, 179-80
Estrées, Marshal d', 92
Ethelwold, St., 18
Ettal Abbey, 168-9
Eucalyptine, the preparation of, 117
Eucharius, St., 70
Eugénie, Empress, 210
Eugster, Frater Meinrad, 140
Eustathius, 3
Evesham, Benedictine Rule at, 18
Evolène. 136
Evore, Scala Dei, 22

F

Fano hermitage, 106
Fansaga, Cosimo, 127
Farnborough monastery, 210 217
Farne Islands, 16
Farneta, 47, 48
Faucher, Denis: Annals of Provence, 70
Feichtmayr, Johann Michael, 147, 158

Féraud, Raymond, 70
Ferden, 137
Feuchtmayer, Joseph Anton, 140, 145,
  162
Feuillants, the, 29, 32
Ficino, Marsilio, 105
Finch, Dom Bruno, 32
Fischer, Johann Michael, 36, 158, 164,
  166
Florence, 97; San Marco, 28; Santa
  Maria Novella, 28, 97-8; Santa Croce,
  98
Florentius, Augustinus, 101
Flue, Nicholas von der, 138
Foligno, 115
Fontaine de Vaucluse, 65
Fonte Avallana, 20, 101; hermitage, 106
Fonte Buono. See Camaldoli
Fontevrault, Order of, 25
Fort Augustus monastery, 39, 212
Fossanuova Abbey, 122
Foucauld, Charles de, 55, 82-3
Fourvoirie, 92
Foyatier, 94
France, 190; expulsion of Benedictines
  from, 47; Decree of Secularization in,
  38
Franchi, Don Diego de, 101
Francis, St., of Assisi, 112, 113
Francis II, Emperor of Austria, 42
Franciscans, Order of, 26, 27
Franco, General, military rising under,
  183
Frascati, 106
Frauen-Insel, the, 172, 173-5 ; nunnery,
  175; Abbey church, 175
French Congregation, 46
French Revolution, 38, 39-40
Fribourg, 133-4; University, 133

G

Gall, St., 18
Gallia Christiana, 35
Galluzzo monastery, 98-9
Garner, Thomas, 213
Gasquet, Cardinal, 206, 213
Gaul, monastic life in, 16
Georges, Pierre, 136
Gerbert of Aurillac, 37
Gervase, George, 31

Gesuati, Order of, 36
Gethsemani (Kentucky), 45
Ghirlandaio, Domenico, 105
Giabanni, Dom Anselmo, 100
Gill, Eric, 205
Gilling Castle, 213
Giordano, Luca, 99, 127, 187
Giotto, 98
Giustiniani, Paolo, 105
Glastonbury, Benedictine Rule at, 18
Gloucester, Benedictine Rule at, 19
Goering, Hermann, 78
Gómez, Dom José Anton, 183
Gontard, Dom Gabriel, 77
Gonzalez, Dom Luis Vidaurrazaga, 184
Gordes, 59
Gottweig Abbey, 150
Goya, 204
Graham, Hon. Robert, 34
Granada, Carthusian sacristy at, 36
Grande Chartreuse, the, 20, 21, 47-8, 93-6
Grandi, Guido, 101
Grandmont, Order of, 25
Gray, Thomas, 7
Graziani, Marshal, 98
Greenstock, Dr. David, 198-9
Gregory the Great, St., 17
Gregory XI, Pope, 106
Griffiths, Dom Bede, 218
Gripsholm, Carthusian monastery at, 22
Gröller, Franz, 142-3
Gropius, Walter, 211
Gropper, Gabrielle, 167
Grottaferrata Abbey, 122
Gruyères, 134
Gualbert, John, 20
Guadalupe, 185, 188-9; monastery, 185-8
Guéranger, Dom Prosper, 46; L'Année liturgique, 46
Guglielmo, St., of Vercelli, 129
Guigo, Dom: Consuetudines, 21; Meditationes, 21
Gundulf, Bishop of Rochester, 80
Günther, Franz Ignaz, 169
Gurdon, Dom Edmund, 202
Guthlac, St., 16
Guzman, Dominic, 27

H

Hamburg, Trappists at, 44

Happle, Dom Bernard, 152
Haras-les-Pins, 81
Hautecombe, Abbeye d', 90-1
Hauterive monastery, 181
Hautmar, Dom, 153
Hedley, Dom, 47
Heiligenbronn, convent at, 155
Helyot: Histoire des ordres monastiques, religieux et militaires, 35
Henson, Mgr., 199
Hernández, Gregorio, 196
Herren-Insel, the, 172, 173
Heu, Josef, 212
Hexham, Benedictine Rule at, 18
Hilarion, St., 16
Hilary, St., of Arles, 70
Hildebrandt, Lukas von, 150
Hieronymites, the, origin of, 193
Hoffman, 172
Holmes, Dom Renato, 107
Honfleur, 76
Honoratus, St., 16, 69
Hormisdas, Pope, 17
Houghton, John, 203
Howell, Thomas Bayly, 217
Huber, Hans, 173
Huber, Max, 173
Hugh, St., Bishop of Lincoln, 85
Hurtado, 36
Hussites, the, 29
Huysmans, 76, 77, 83

I

Iltud, St., 70
Inguanez, Dom Maurus, 124
Innocent III, Pope, 27
Iona, monastery on, 16
Ireland, monastic life in, 16
Irmengard, St., shrine of, 175
Isidore of Cremona, 70
Italy: Government policy towards monasteries, 111
Ixard, Michael d', 159

J

Jackson, Richard, 117-20
James II, King, 31, 34
Jansenism, 34, 35

Jarrow, Benedictine Rule at, 18
Jensen, Wilhelm, 175
Jerez, 204
Jerome, St., 193
Jerusalem, Franciscan settlement in, 27
Jesuits, 28
Jocelyn: *Chronicle*, 19
Jodl, General, 175
John, Abbot, of Minden, 29
John, St., of the Cross, 28, 190, 191
John Gualbert, St., of Florence, 101
Josef II, Emperor of Austria, 32, 143, 148
Juan II, King of Spain, 201; tomb, 201–2
Juncosa, Fray Joaquin, 204
Juni, Juan de, 196
Justina, St., of Padua, Congregation of, 29, 143

K

Karl VI, Emperor of Austria, 150
Kaufbeuren, 166
Kempen, Benedictine convent at, 155
Kesselring, Field-Marshal, 102
Kinol-Trap, preparation of, 117
Kippel, 137–8
Kisslegg, 162
Klampfleuthner, Georg, 175
Klosterneuburg monastery, 26, 150
Krammer, Rudolph, 174
Kranich, Dom Timotheus, 154
Kremsmunster Abbey, 36, 143–5
Kuppel, Dom Gerard, 107
Kylemore, Irish Benedictine nuns at, 40

L

La Ferté, Cistercian monastery at, 25
Lamartine, Alphonse, 90
Lambach, 148
Lamspring Abbey, 31, 39
Lancelotti, Secondo: *Historiae Olivetanae*, 109
Landini, Cristoforo, 104, 105
Lanfranc, Archbishop of Canterbury, 80
Lang, Alois, 167
Languedoc, 180
Lanherne, Carmelite nunnery at, 40
Lanspergius, Dom, 23
Lapi, Maurus, 102

La Trappe monastery, 32–4, 40, 82–5
Laurens, Baron du, 55
Lavallaz, Pater Martin du Fay de, 139
Lawrence, D. H., 170, 175
Le Corbusier, 211
Lelesz, Norbertine Order at, 26
Lenz, Dom Desiderius, 155
Le Plantay, 89
Lérins Abbey, 16, 61, 69–75
Les Aubins, 65
Lestrange, Dom Augustine (Louis-Henri de), 40–4, 134
Lesueur, 94
Leutkirch, 162
Lex, Josef, 173–4
Ligugé monastery, 46
Linderhof Schloss, 172
Linz, 145
Lisle, Ambrose Phillips de, 205
Lötschental, 137
Louis XIII, King of France, 32
Louisa Mary (Stuart), Princess, 31
Louvain, 32
Love, Nicholas, 23
Ludwig, Duke of Bavaria, 168
Ludwig I, King of Bavaria, 164, 170
Ludwig II, King of Bavaria, 172
Luengo, Don Antonio, 186
Lugo, Padre Antonio de, 194
Lulworth, Trappists in, 41, 44
Lupus, St., of Troyes, 70
Luxeuil monastery, 16

M

Mabillon, Dom Jean, 34, 35; *Défense des études monastiques*, 34; *Acta Sanctorum*, 34; *De Re Diplomatica*, 34
Maccabe, Dom Sebastian, 98
Madonna del Sasso, Franciscan settlement at, 27
Madrid: Calle San Bernardo, Benedictine priory in, 183–5
Maeterlinck, Maurice, 76
Magnasco, Alessandro, 150
Maier, Dom Vitalis, 165
Maigrauge, nunnery of, 134
Malmesbury, Benedictine Rule at, 18
Marbach, Abbot Heinrich von, 147
Marcet, Dom Antonius, 177
March, Dom, 38

Maréchaux: *Vie de Bernardo Tolomei*, 108
Maredsous Abbey, 155; School of Arts and Crafts, 156
Mares, Frederico, 182
Marie Antoinette, Queen of France, 148
Marie-Christine de Bourbon, 90
Maria-Laach Abbey, 155, 156
Mariotto, Prior, 105
Marmion, Dom Columba, 215
Marseilles, St. Victor monastery, 16, 46
Martell, Charles, 131
Martène, Dom Edmond, 34, 35; *De Antiquis Monachorum Ritibus*, 80
Martin, St., of Tours, 16
Martinez, Dom Rafael Alcocer, 184
Marx, Karl, 20, 174
Mary, proposed Company of, 118
Mary Tudor, Queen of England, 31
Matielli, Lorenzo, 149
Matthews, Dom Edmund, 212
Maubec, Cistercian nunnery of, 53
Maubec, Jerome, 93
Maxime, St., 70
Mayhew, Edward, 30–1
Mazen, Abbot Nicholas de, 29
Meaux, Vicomte de, 55
Mechitar, 37
Medici, Giuliano, 104
Medici, Lorenzo, 104
Melk Abbey, 29, 36, 148–9
Melleraie Abbey, 45
Memmingen, 162
Messkirch, 155
Meximieux, 89, 90
Middle Ages, congregations of, 26–7
Miraflores monastery, 201–4
Mistral, Frédéric, 136
Möhringen, 151–2
Moléon, Sieur de: *Voyages Liturgiques de France*, 35
Molesmes, Benedictine abbey of, 21; dissensions at, 23
Montalegre, 204
Montargis, 37
Mont Collon, 137
Monte Cassino monastery, 17–18, 102, 123–6, 155; rebuilding of, 36
Monte Corona, Congregation of, 105–6
Montélimar, 53
Monte Oliveto, 107–11
Monte Senario, 98

Monte Vergine Abbey, 128–31; The Loreto, 131
Montfaucon, 35
Montgomery, Hugh, 212
Montserrat: village, 179; monastery, 176–89; San Giovanni hermitage, 177; San Juan hermitage, 177; Black Virgin, 177
Moore, Dom Pablo Maria, 202
Moosbrugger, Caspar, 36, 138, 140, 160
Morimond, Cistercian monastery at, 25, 55
Mount Grace, Carthusian monastery at, 22, 31
Mount Melleray monastery, 45, 206
Mount St. Bernard, 45, 205
Muard, Pere Jean-Baptiste, 55
Muin, Claude Honoré de, 36
Munich, 170–1; Nymphenburg Palace, 159, 170; Hofbrauhaus, 170–1
Murten, 133

N

Naples, 127; San Martino monastery, 127
Napoleon, expulsion of Cistercians by, 40 ff.
Napoleonic Wars, 38
Nardo, Fra Giulio di, 129
Natter, Dom Boniface, 215
Neame, Major-General, V.C., 102
Negro, Abbate di, 111
Netherlands, Austrian, 32
Neuschwanstein Castle, 168, 172
Nevill, Dom Paul, 212
New Norcia, 47
Newton Abbot, Augustinian Canonesses at, 40
Nieuport, 32
Nietzsche, 135
Nolle, Dom Lambert, 161–2
Norbert, St., 26
Norbertines, 26
Norman Conquest, and monastic history, 19
Nostradamus: *History of Provence*, 70
Notre-Dame des Dombes, Abbey of, 88
Notre-Dame des Neiges, 55, 83
Nuits St. Georges, 86
Nunraw Castle, monastery in, 206
Nuns, sweets and ices made by, 36–7

O

Oberammergau, 166–8
Ockham, William of, 27
O'Connor, Dom Bede, 139
Olivetans, 80, 107–8
Orcagna, 99
Orcha, Trappist communities at, 42–3
Oswald, St., Archbishop of York, 18
Oswald, St., King of Northumbria, 162
Ottobeuren: town, 162–3; abbey, 36, 163–166; abbey church, 158
Oulton, Benedictine nunnery at, 39
Oxford, Dominican settlement at, 26, 28

P

Pachomius, St., 15–16, 17
Padula, 132
Palencia, Banjamin, 189
Palermo, Santa Catarina Convent, 36
Palomero, Dom Daniel, 184
Pannartz, Arnold, 121
Pannaz, 136
Pantasaph, Franciscan settlement at, 27
Paris: St. Edmond's (outside), 31, 38
Paris, Matthew: Gesta Abbatum, 19
Parker, Dom William, 216
Parkminster Charterhouse, 94, 209–10
Parsons, Robert, 198
Pascal, Blaise, 35
Patrick, St., 16, 70
Patrizi, Patrizio, 108
Paul III, Czar of Russia, 41–2
Paul, the Deacon, 18
Paular, Carthusian sacristy at, 36
Pavia, monastery at, 100
Pedro the Ceremonious, 181
Pépin, Dom Maric, 209
Pereira, Manuel, 202
Pérouges, 89–90
Perret, Auguste, 211
Pershore, Benedictine Rule at, 18
Perugia, 111
Peter, St., of Alcantara, 190
Peter the Venerable, 24
Peterborough, Benedictine Rule at, 19
Petrarch, Provençal house of, 65
Pez, Bernard, 37
Philo: De Vita Contemplativa, 15
Piccolomini, Aeneas Sylvius. See Pius II

Piccolomini, Ambrogio, 108
Pickering, Thomas, 31
Piedmont, Trappists in, 41
Pierre-qui-vire, Benedictine abbey, 47
Pinzutti, Dom Mario, 111
Pitra, Dom (Later Cardinal), 46
Pius II, Pope, 109
Plantin, Christopher, 78
Plunket, Oliver, Archbishop of Armagh, 213
Pluscarden priory, 217
Pobel, 149
Poblet Abbey, 180–3
Podolia, monastery in, 43
Pöllman, Dom Ansgar, 154
Pont Audemer, 76
Pontigny, Cistercian monastery at, 25
Porée, Gilbert de la, 24
Porta Coeli, 204
Port Royal, Convent of, 35
Portugal, Congregation of, 29
Pothier, Dom, 46
Power, James, 44–5
Power, Philip, 31
Pozzi, 139
Prandtauer, Jakob, 36, 143, 144, 146, 149
Preisinger, Anton, 167
Premonstratensians. See Norbertines
Prémontré, 26; the rebuilding of, 36
Princethorpe, Benedictine nunnery at, 39
Prinknash Abbey, 129, 216–21
Pueyo monastery, 177
Pugin, Augustus Welby, 213–14

Q

Quarr Abbey, 47, 210–11
Qualaat Seman, monastery of, 19

R

Ramsey, Benedictine Rule at, 18
Ramsgate, St. Augustine's monastery at, 213–14
Ramos, Dom Toribio, 184, 185
Ramuz, Charles Ferdinand, 136
Rancé, Armand-Jean le Bouthillier de, 32–4, 84, 85; De la Sainteté et des Devoirs de la Vie monastique, 34; Rélations de la Vie et de la Mort de Quelques Religieux de La Trappe, 34

Raoult, Gerard, 79
Ratisbon, St. James's monastery, 39
Rea, Dom Ildephonsus, 125
Reformation, the, 29
Regnier, Henri de, 76
Reselhuber, Dom, 144
Restagno, Senatore, Mayor of Cassino, 123
Reydams tapestries, 144
Ribalto, Francisco, 204
Ribeiro, Manuel, 202
Ribera, Pedro de, 183, 185
Riedlingen, 157
Riehl, Hans, 171
Rios, Dom Romanos, 214
Rinucinni, Alemanno, 104
Ripon, Benedictine Rule at, 18
Risorgimento, the, 111; closures by, 47
Rivera, General Primo de, 193
Rivo Torte, Franciscan settlement at, 27
Robert, St., 21, 23
Roberts, John, 31
Roe, Alban, 31
Rome: early monastic life in, 16; San
    Gregorio monastery, 115; S. Francesca
    Romana monastery, 116; San Paolo
    Fuori le Mura, 116; Piccole Suore
    della Sacra Familia convent, 119
Romuald, St., of Ravenna, 20, 101
Roquebrune, hermitage of, 106
Rosemburg, Count, 34
Rossmark, Pater Bonifatius, 169
Rottam Inn abbey church, 158
Rottenbach, 166
Rupert of Deutz, 18
Ryckel, Denys de, 23, 94

S

Sachseln, 138
Sacro Eremo, the, 103-4, 106
Sacro Speco, monastery of, 16
Sadler, Robert, 30-1
St. André (outside Bruges), monastery of,
    208
St. Albans, Benedictine Rule at, 19
St. Bernard Hospice, 91-2
St. Blasien Abbey, 159
St. Eloi, 89
St. Florian: abbey, 26, 36, 146-7;
    village, 146
St. Gall, Abbey of, 140-1

St. Germain-des-Prés, Abbey of, 34, 35
Saint-Honorat, Ile, 69, 73, 74
St. Hugh's Charterhouse, Sussex, 209
St. Laurent du Pont, 92
Sainte-Marguerite, Ile, 69
St. Maur, Congregation of, 34
St. Maurice, monastery of, 26
St. Maximin, convent of, 28
St. Meinrad, 47
St. Nizier-le-Désert, 88
St. Ottilien, Benedictine Congregation of,
    47
St. Paul-de-Varax, 87
St. Wandrille, Abbey of, 76-9
Sainval, Mademoiselle, 70
Salvi, Dom Laurence, 122
Salzburg, 141; St. Peter's Abbey, 141-2;
    University, 38, 142
Salzillo, 196
Samos monastery, 177
San Bartolomé di Lupiana, 193
San Clodio monastery, 176
San Domenico, Dominican monastery at,
    28
San Estaban, Dominican monastery at,
    28
San Gregorio, 106
San Miniato monastery, 20, 98
San Salvador de Leyre, 204
Sand, George, 40
Sanderi, Antoni: Presbyteri Chorographia
    sacra Brabantiae, 35
Santa Barbara, Franciscan settlement at,
    27
Santamaria, Dom Emilio, 184
Santiponce monastery, 194
Santo Domingo de Silos monastery, 185
Savigny, Order of, 23
Sayre, Olive, 74-5
Schaftlarn: village, 169; monastery, 169
Scheffel, Josef Victor von, 175
Schenck, 37
Schmutzer, Franz, 162
Schmuzer, Joseph, 168
Schneider, Dom Paul, 160-1
Scholastica, St., 126
Schöngau, 166
Schussenried, 159
Schuster, Fritz, 142-3
Schwab, Dom, 144
Schweinheim, Conrad, 121
Schwyz, parish church at, 155

Scot, Maurus, 31
Scott, Sir Giles, 212, 213
Seidl, Martin, 171
Seitenstetten Abbey, 150
Segarra, Dom Ireneo, 178
Segovia, 192, 194–5, 196; El Parral monastery, 192–6
Sénanque: Congregation of, 45; Abbey, 58–65
Serravalle, 100
Sfondratti, Dom Celestin, 38
Sheen Charterhouse, 31
Siena, 106
Signorella, Luca, of Cortona, 109
Síloee, Gil de, 202
Silos, 204
Simeon Stylites, St., 16
Simon Stock, St., 28
Sion, 135
Sitticus, Marcus, Prince-Archbishop of Salzburg, 38, 141–2
Slade, Dom William, 215
Sodoma (Bazzi of Siena), 109
Solesmes, Benedictine Abbey of, 46, 47, 210; St. Cecilia nunnery, 46
Soligny, 81
Sorgue, River, 65
Spain: nineteenth-century closure of monasteries in, 47; civil war in, 183, 193, 194
Spoleto, 115
Stanbrook, Benedictine nunnery at, 39
Staoueli, Abbey of, 63
Stapehill nunnery, 41
Steinhausen; church at, 159–60
Steinhart, Dom Vincent, 162
Stendhal, 96
Stephen Harding, St., 23, 86
Stock, 172
Stokes, Leonard, 213
Strahov, Norbertine Order at, 26
Straub, 168, 169
Strict Observance, Congregation of, 32, 45
Subercaseaux, Dom Pedro, 211
Subiaco: Benedictine Congregation of, 47, 176; monasteries in, 16–17; Santa Scholastica Abbey, 120–2; Cardinal-Abbots of, 121; Sacro Speco, 122
Sublet, 209
Swiss-American Benedictine Congregation, 47

Swithbert, 18
Switzerland, Trappist flight from (1798), 41
Syon Abbey, 39
Syria, monastic life in, 16
Szezureic, Louis, 74

T

Tabennisi, 15
Talleyrand, Charles de, 38, 80
Tamié Abbey, 91
Tarragona, 48
Tassilo III, Duke of Bavaria, 143
Tepl, Norbertine Order at, 26
Teresa, St., of Avila, 28, 190
Terespol, Trappists at, 43–4
Theobald, Archbishop of Canterbury, 80
Theotocopuli, Domenico, 185
Thomas Aquinas, St., 27, 122; Summa Theologica, 27
Thomas, Dominic, 161
Thomas, St., of Hereford, 213
Thompson, Robert, 212
Thumb, Peter, 166
Thun, Lake, 134
Tiron, Order of, 23
Toledo, 185
Tolomei, Bernardo, 107, 108
Torricelli, 139
Trappists, 40–1; houses, in Britain, 205–6
Trasimeno, Lake, 111
Traunkirchen, 142–3
Traversari, Ambrogio, 101, 105
Tre Fontane Abbey, 117–18
Trevi, 115
Trisulti monastery, 100
Troger, Paul, 149
Tubach, church of Franciscan nuns at, 155
Tunstall, Thomas, 31
Tuttlingen, 151, 152

U

Ullathorne, Dom, 47
Unamuno, Miguel de, 204
Upson, Dom Wilfrid, 217
Urban VI, Pope, 107
Urbel, Dom Justo Perez de, 183, 184

V

Vaccaro, Domenicantonio, 131
Valladolid, 196–9; Congregation of, 29;
   College of Santa Cruz, 199; English
   College, 197–9
Valldemosa, Carthusian monastery at, 22
Vallette, Pierre, 136
Vallombrosa, 20, 25, 101
Valsainte, 134–5; Trappists of, 55;
   monastery, 41
Vanvitelli, 36, 131, 132
Vasari, 102
Vauban, Sebastien, 85
Vaucluse, Plateau de, 58
Verona, Fra Giovanni da, 109
Versailleux, 89
Vez, Pater Alexis, 134
Vienna, exiled Trappists in, 42–3
Vignelli, Dom Francesco, 125
Vignola, 112
Villanueva, Dom Antolin Pablos, 184
Villena, Marqués and Marquésa de, 193
Vilvaneyra monastery, 177
Viollet-de-Duc, 73
Volhynia, monasteries in, 43
Vonier, Dom Anscar, 215
Vougeot, 85–6
Voyage Littéraire des deux Benedictins, 35

W

Walcheren, Pierre van der Meer de, 135
Wakefield, William, 213
Waldeck-Rousseau Laws of Association,
   47
Waldensians, the, 27
Walker, Dom Augustine, 39
Walmsley, Bishop Charles, 31, 213
Walpole, Horace, 217

Wearmouth, Benedictine Rule at, 18
Wehnert, Adam, 171
Weingarten: town, 160: abbey, 160–2
Weld, Dom Hugh, 209
Weltenburg, abbey church of, 36
Westmalle monastery, 37
Westminster: monks of, 30; Benedictine
   Rule at, 19
Wez, Benoit de, 36, 158
Wies, 166; church, 159
Wiler, 137
Wilfrid, St., Bishop of York, 18
Wilhering: village, 145; abbey, 145–6
William of St. Thierry, 25
Williams, Dom Thomas, 32
Willibrord, 18
Winchcombe, Benedictine Rule at, 18–19
Winchester, Benedictine Rule at, 19
Witham, 31
Witte, August, 216
Woodchester, Dominican friary at, 28
Woodforde, Julia, 45
Worcester, Benedictine Rule at, 18

Y

Ypres, Irish Benedictines of, 40

Z

Zeiller, Jakob, 168
Zeitter, Wilhelm, 174
Ziegelbauer, 37
Zimmerman, Dominikus, 36, 159, 166
Zimmerman, Johann Baptist, 36, 159, 166
Zuccali, Enrico, 168
Zurbaran, 187, 203
Zurich, Napoleon's victory at, 43
Zwiefalten: abbey, 36, 157–8; village,
   158–9